Alessandro Vinciarelli, Sartajvir Singh, Narayan Vyas and Mona Abdelbaset Sadek Ali (Eds.)
RADAR

Alessandro Vinciarelli, Sartajvir Singh, Narayan Vyas and Mona Abdelbaset Sadek Ali (Eds.)

RADAR

Remote Sensing Data Analysis with Artificial Intelligence

DE GRUYTER

Editors
Prof. Alessandro Vinciarelli
Sir Alwyn Williams Building
18 Lilybank Gardens
Glasgow G12 8QQ, UK
alessandro.vinciarelli@glasgow.ac.uk

Narayan Vyas
I-379 New Bapu Nagar
Near Mayur Sr. Sec. School
Bhilwara 311001, Rajasthan, India
narayanvyas87@gmail.com

Dr. Sartajvir Singh
H. No. 618, Phase 3B1
SAS Nagar, Mohali 160059
Punjab, India
sartajvir.dhillon@gmail.com

Dr. Mona Abdelbaset Sadek Ali
3528 Al Arak Street
Al Zahra Avenue, Al-Hofof
Alahsa 36422, Saudi Arabia
m.ali@kfu.edu.sa

ISBN 978-3-11-157261-1
e-ISBN (PDF) 978-3-11-157297-0
e-ISBN (EPUB) 978-3-11-157320-5

Library of Congress Control Number: 2025936062

Bibliographic information published by the Deutsche Nationalbibliothek
The Deutsche Nationalbibliothek lists this publication in the Deutsche Nationalbibliografie; detailed bibliographic data are available on the internet at http://dnb.dnb.de.

Cover image: DKosig/iStock/Getty Images Plus
Typesetting: Integra Software Services Pvt. Ltd.

www.degruyter.com
Questions about General Product Safety Regulation:
productsafety@degruyterbrill.com

Preface

In modern technologies, incorporating remote sensing with artificial intelligence (AI) plays a significant role in Earth observations. Radio detection and ranging (RADAR) is a one-of-a-kind technology that allows all-weather remote sensing services. With this focus, this book explores the potential applications and advanced algorithms of RADAR-based remote sensing. This book guides researchers, scientists, teachers, and students in monitoring and managing Earth's resources.

This multidisciplinary book explores the recent advancements and applications of AI-driven RADAR-based remote sensing. The introductory chapter comprehensively covers the fundamental principles and science of RADAR-based remote sensing. It also includes the fundamentals of collecting, analyzing, and interpreting remotely sensed images. This chapter is followed by the evolution of RADAR-based remote sensing, that is, synthetic aperture radar (SAR) and scatterometry. It further highlights the potential applications of active and passive microwave remote sensing with the integration of AI. Then, it is followed by various challenges associated with AI-driven RADAR remote sensing.

This book also explores multisource data fusion techniques to enhance image interpretation and to integrate the features of the SAR/scatterometer with the optical dataset for improvement in accuracy. It also involves classification and change detection applications in extracting essential information. Furthermore, deep learning and machine learning approaches expand the applicability range of RADAR-based remote sensing by providing object-level detection and solving complex problems. It also explores the role of the Internet of things (IoT) in remote sensing for real-time data collection and analysis. The book comprises various environmental monitoring sensors for accurate monitoring and prediction analysis.

With the involvement of AI, emerging applications of RADAR-based remote sensing are also discussed, such as crop growth monitoring, weed management, yield estimation, real-time monitoring of soil moisture, classification of crop species, and weather patterns. This book also highlights the monitoring of urban infrastructure and its impact on agricultural land. Moreover, it also covers disaster management via continuous soil moisture monitoring with RADAR-based remote sensing. The book concludes that emerging AI-enabled RADAR applications in real-time scenarios provide the future scope of RADAR remote sensing with AI.

This book is a reference to researchers, scientists, students, and stakeholders to explore the potential of AI-enabled RADAR applications in real-time scenarios. With real-world case studies, it offers insights into mapping different crops, smart irrigation, pest control, and crop yield prediction analysis. Moreover, it delivers comprehensive knowledge of RADAR-based remote sensing in improving precision agricultural practices.

https://doi.org/10.1515/9783111572970-202

Contents

Narayan Vyas*

Integrating Sentinel-1 satellite data with machine learning for land use classification

Abstract: The availability of radio detection and ranging (RADAR) remote sensing data has changed the Earth observation by allowing information to be obtained independently of the weather and environmental conditions. RADAR-based satellites, such as Sentinel-1 and SCATSAT, are beneficial because they can penetrate clouds and work regardless of whether it is night or day, making them indispensable surface mapping sensors. The European Space Agency's (ESA) Sentinel-1 satellite is a RADAR-based Earth observation satellite whose dual-polarization (vertical-vertical and vertical-horizontal) synthetic aperture radar (SAR) provides high temporal resolution with adequate spatial resolution that makes it suitable for monitoring land use and land cover (LULC) changes. The study area in this research is Kota district, situated in the southeastern part of Rajasthan, India, which has a semiarid climate and a mixed area of agriculture, natural vegetation, and waterbodies. Google Earth Engine was used to process and classify Sentinel-1 data collected from February 1, 2024, to February 27, 2024, into several LULC categories, including water, built-up, and land. This study uses random forest, an ensemble machine learning model, for LULC classification. When used to create a land use classification map, it exhibited an overall accuracy of 90.57% and a kappa coefficient of 85.81%, demonstrating near-perfect agreement between the model and actual data.

Keywords: Radio detection and ranging (RADAR), remote sensing, machine learning, Sentinel-1, land use classification

1 Introduction

The Earth observation aims to observe and analyze the movement of the Earth's surface to fight against major global issues such as globalization, urbanization, deforestation, climate change, and resources (unmanned aerial vehicles) [1]. High-resolution

Acknowledgments: The author would like to extend their gratitude to the European Space Agency (ESA) for providing the Sentinel-1 satellite data that formed the foundation of this study. The availability of high-quality RADAR data from Sentinel-1 has been instrumental in conducting this research and achieving meaningful results.

***Corresponding author: Narayan Vyas**, Department of Computer Science and Application, Vivekananda Global University, Jaipur, India, e-mail: narayanvyas87@gmail.com, ORCID: 0000-0003-4225-0764

https://doi.org/10.1515/9783111572970-001

imagery and ground data captured by satellites, especially with advancements in sensor technology, allow researchers to track land cover changes in real time, providing estimates on agricultural productivity, water resource mapping, and assessments of natural disasters [2]. Satellite remote sensing has been rapidly evolving in the era of modern technologies, having transformed access to even the most remote and inaccessible regions of our planet in detail. This information is crucial for policymakers, scientists, and planners who make decisions on the distribution of resources, environmental protection, and disaster management [3]. The Earth observation data has come a long way since the days of optical imagery, and the last few decades have also seen the advent of radio detection and ranging (RADAR)-based sensing that allows users to look down in virtually all weather and day/night conditions. These tools have enhanced the degree of confidence and precision in data recording, allowing comprehensive analysis of surfaces on the Earth [4]. The Earth observation is also crucial to sustainable development because it enables data analysis at scale when combined with geospatial tools and artificial intelligence (AI) [5].

The advent of remote sensing, primarily through RADAR-based satellites such as Sentinel-1 and SCATSAT, has improved surface classification [6]. Optical sensors depend on sunlight and, thus, can be blocked by clouds or darkness [3]. In contrast, RADAR systems use microwave signals that can penetrate cloud cover and obtain data in almost any weather condition. A synthetic aperture radar (SAR) sensor, such as Sentinel-1, emits signals from space that travel to the Earth's surface, and the backscatter is then measured to infer surface properties [7]. SAR-based satellites offer advantages in land classification, as they can discern surface roughness and moisture content. For example, VV (vertical-vertical) and VH (vertical-horizontal) polarizations have been commonly utilized for surface classification; VV experiences higher performance in detecting smoother surfaces such as water, while VH displays a higher response for vegetation and built-up areas [8]. With machine learning (ML) algorithms like random forest (RF), SAR data leads to realistic and highly prescribed land cover class discovery [9]. The method is economical and scalable, making it suitable for larger geographical areas. It provides timely information at an appropriate areal scale for making day-to-day agricultural, planning, and conservation decisions. Due to continuous development in RADAR hardware and global data processing solutions, remote sensing is today one of the central pillars of modern geospatial techniques. Table 1 presents several studies on the RADAR dataset for the Earth observation applications.

The objectives of this study include (a) obtaining satellite data from the RADAR-based satellite Sentinel-1 with the help of the Google Earth Engine (GEE) platform, (b) processing the satellite data to make it suitable for land cover classification, (c) performing land cover classification using the RF algorithm on the GEE platform, and (d) performing accuracy assessment of the thematic maps generated using the RF algorithm and exporting thematic classified maps for visual analysis.

Table 1: Several studies performed using the RADAR dataset.

Characteristics	Methods used	Objectives	Results	Source
Sentinel-1 uses persistent scatterer interferometry (PSI) techniques to monitor ground motion and assess landslide geohazards, while SCATSAT focuses on weather and oceanographic applications, distinguishing their areas of focus	PSI techniques applied to satellite RADAR images	Evaluate landslide geohazards and impacts using PSI data	Identified active deformation areas using PSI data	[10]
Sentinel-1 RADAR satellites can acquire Earth's surface data under any atmospheric conditions, and the paper highlights the advantages of publicly available data and open-source software for effectively using RADAR satellite imagery	Active RADAR systems for Earth's surface data acquisition	Explore Sentinel RADAR satellite system capabilities	Discussed the possibility of using the Sentinel RADAR satellite system	[23]
Sentinel-1, an ESA mission, provides SAR data for ocean research, while SCATSAT, an Indian satellite, focuses on ocean wind vector measurements, complementing Sentinel-1's atmospheric data	SAR-derived surface wind products and validation results	Preliminary studies of Sentinel-1 SAR-derived surface winds	Presented the preliminary studies of SAR-derived surface wind products	[11]
SCATSAT-1, launched by ISRO, is a Ku-band scatterometer satellite used for climate studies and applications like crop yield prediction, while Sentinel-1, part of ESA's Copernicus program, focuses on RADAR imaging for diverse Earth observation tasks	ML-based classification and information fusion	Summarize SCATSAT-1 products and applications globally	Summarized SCATSAT-1's impact on various scientific domains	[12]

Table 1 (continued)

Characteristics	Methods used	Objectives	Results	Source
Sentinel-1 utilizes dual-polarization (VV-VH) data to enhance PSI-based synthetic aperture RADAR (PS-InSAR) analysis, improving ground deformation measurements by increasing the spatial density of measurement points	PS-InSAR method	Evaluate the VH channel's contribution to PS-InSAR analysis	Obtained 186% increase in PS points using the VH channel	[13]
Sentinel-1, using SAR technology, captures high-resolution images for persistent scatterer interferometry (PS-InSAR) to monitor terrain deformations, as demonstrated in a case study in Focșani, Romania	Variation of targets' intensities along SAR acquisitions	Identify persistent scatterer candidates in Focșani, Romania	Two algorithms identified persistent scatterers in Focșani, Romania	[14]
The paper focuses on the Sentinel-1 SAR constellation, which operates in interferometric mode with a wide 250-km swath width, and does not address SCATSAT, which is used for ocean and weather monitoring	CRCD maximum likelihood estimator with spatially varying noise estimates	Extend CRCD to use spatially varying noise estimates	SV-CRCD improved accuracy in flood mapping	[15]
Sentinel-1 is utilized for tropical cyclone assessment as a spaceborne SAR system, while SCATSAT, despite being a RADAR satellite, is not included in this study	Co- and cross-polarized SAR data application	Evaluate tropical cyclones using Sentinel-1 SAR data	SAR co- and cross-polarization improved tropical cyclone wind field estimation	[16]

2 Study area

Kota district, located in the southeastern part of Rajasthan, India, lies at 25.2138°N and 75.8648°E and is known for its semiarid climate and diverse landscape. The region is primarily characterized by agricultural land interspersed with patches of natural vegetation [17]. The Chambal River, which flows through the district, adds to its geographical richness by supporting a variety of ecosystems along its banks [18]. The region's agriculture relies heavily on crops such as wheat, mustard, and soybean, with rice cultivation occurring in irrigated areas. Kota is also known for its horticulture, with papaya, guava, and citrus fruits being prominent. Overall, the district's vegetation is a mix of natural dry forests and cultivated fields, shaped by its climate, topography, and dependence on the Chambal River for irrigation. Figure 1 represents the study area used in this research.

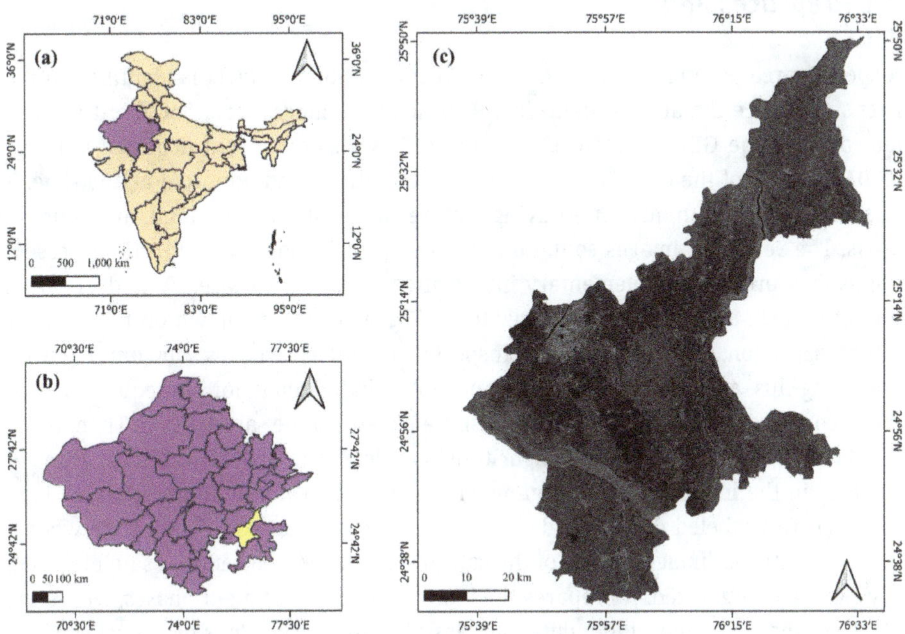

Figure 1: Study area: (a) the map of India, (b) the map of Rajasthan with the study area highlighted, and (c) Sentinel-1 with VV polarization band.

3 Satellite data

The satellite data used for the study in the Kota district was acquired from Sentinel-1, a RADAR-based Earth observation satellite. Sentinel-1 operates using SAR technology, which allows it to capture detailed images of the Earth's surface under all weather conditions, including during cloud cover or at night. The study utilized VV and VH polarization modes, which provide complementary information about surface properties. VV polarization is particularly useful for detecting smooth surfaces such as water, while VH polarization helps identify rougher surfaces like vegetation or built-up areas [19]. The data acquisition period was between February 1, 2024, and February 27, 2024. A median image was generated using the GEE platform to represent RADAR imagery of the study area. During this period, Sentinel-1 captured RADAR imagery that was later processed to classify the region into water, built-up areas, and land. Figure 2 represents the study area along with VH and VV polarization images.

4 Methodology

4.1 Preprocessing

A specific area of interest on the map, the region of interest (ROI), is identified in the first stage. Once the area is identified, RADAR-based images from Sentinel-1 are collected using the GEE platform [20]. Sentinel-1 is a satellite that acquires detailed RADAR images of the Earth's surface under all weather conditions and at any time. It is, therefore, truly unique for studying features like water bodies, land, and built-up areas. The Sentinel-1 images containing the two polarizations, VV and VH, are essential as they provide complementary information about the surface. VV and VH are a mix of vertical and horizontal polarizations. These layers are shown on the map for visual inspection, with the data to be inspected and interpreted, as shown in Figure 2. Following this, each layer is exported and stored individually for subsequent assessment, comparable to setting aside two disparate views of the same region. Then, training data is generated for the RF algorithm, so it learns to identify different types of surfaces in the images. Various regions are marked as water, built-up areas, or land to do so. This labeled data provides a reference so the computer can relate what it sees in the RADAR images to one of the categories. This phase keeps the satellite imagery clean and organized. It prepares the images for the subsequent phases, where the ML algorithm will analyze the data and classify different portions of the selected region. The detailed flowchart for the preprocessing steps performed in this research is given in Figure 3.

4.2 Classification

Analysis and classification of the preprocessed Sentinel-1 satellite images to extract useful information from the ROI are performed in this stage. It consists of training, testing an ML model, and visualizing the results. The pipeline begins to be computed over RADAR images that were previously prepared by reducing them to only the VV

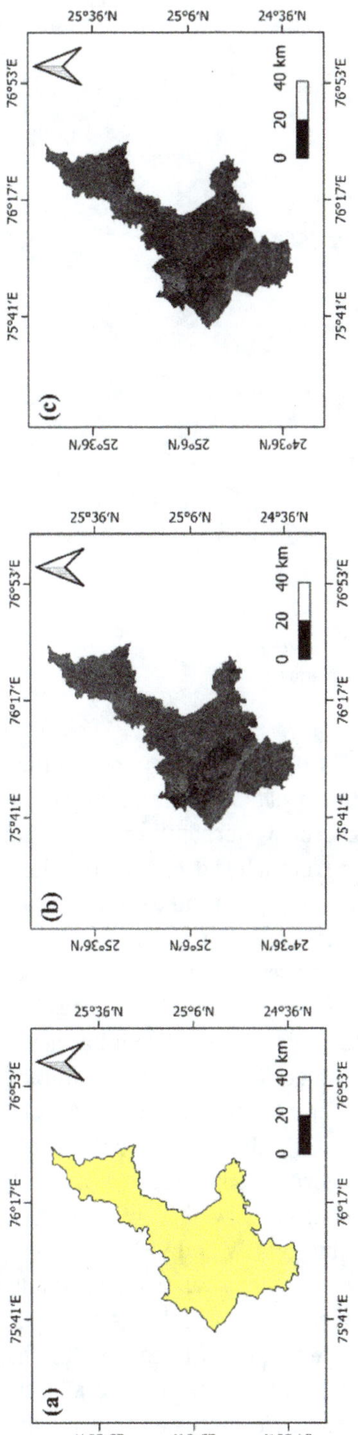

Figure 2: Study area: (a) the boundary of the study area, (b) the Sentinel-1 VH polarization band of the study area, and (c) the Sentinel-1 VV polarization band of the study area.

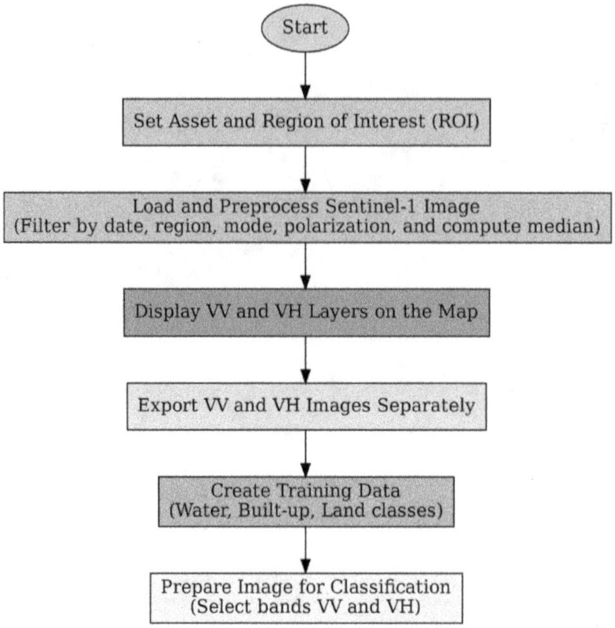

Figure 3: Steps to preprocess the Sentinel-1 dataset using the GEE platform.

and VH layers. These layers have surface properties of the region. Samples are then taken from these images using previously built training data. The training data includes labeled samples of different surface types, including water, built-up areas, and land. This sampling process involves extracting data from labeled regions that help shape the ML model using the GEE platform [21]. After sampling the data, it is separated into two groups: training and testing groups. The training set is to train the model to learn the patterns in the data, while the testing set is only to test how well the model has learned. Here, 80% of the data is used for training and 20% for testing. This ensures the model is trained on diverse examples and tested on data it has never encountered, verifying the model's accuracy. The RF algorithm consists of building multiple decision trees, each based on the input data for predictions, which was used in this research to generate thematic classified maps [22]. All the trees' outputs are combined to create the final prediction, making the algorithm powerful and robust. It allows the model to learn how to classify the types of surfaces (water, built-up areas, and land) from the two polarizations of the Sentinel-1 images (VV and VH).

Once the model is trained, it is utilized to classify the entire satellite image. It falls under semantic segmentation, which means the model predicts a label (e.g., water, built-up, or land) for each spatial location in the image it learned from training the model. The model's performance on the testing set was evaluated using several accuracy measures on the GEE platform. It consists of creating a confusion matrix with the number of areas correctly and incorrectly classified. From this, key metrics are derived, such as overall accuracy (OA), which indicates whether the model is correct; the kappa coefficient (KC), which is a statistical measure of agreement; and producer's accuracy (PA) and consumer's accuracy (CA), which are measures of reliability. Overall classification can be applied to ordinal, nominal, categorical, or continuous variables. The classification is done, the performance is assessed, and the results are visualized. Different land categories are assigned distinct colors; for instance, water areas are represented in blue, built-up areas in yellow, and land in green. This allows for the visualization of the region's spatial allocation of surface types. Following this, the classified image is displayed on a map, which is examined and exported as a file for further analysis. The final product is useful in many applications, such as urban planning, water resource management, and environmental monitoring. This process enables systematically accurate satellite data analysis, providing valuable information about the area of interest.

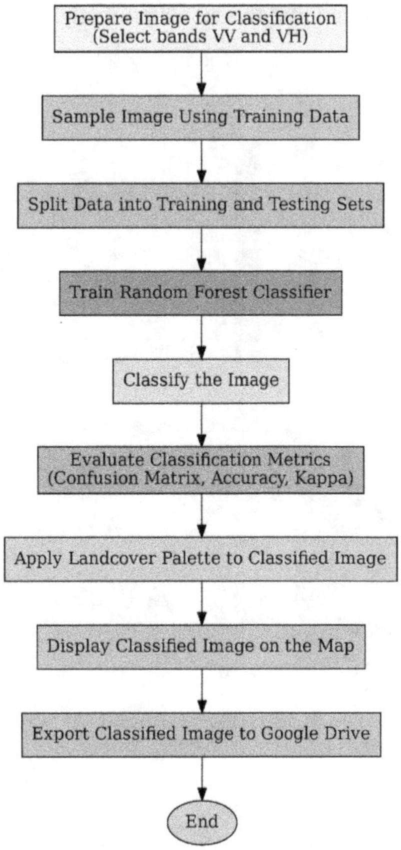

Figure 4: Methodology for generating thematically classified maps.

5 Results

The confusion matrix is a tool used to evaluate how well a classification model performs by comparing its predictions to the actual classes. It is like a table that shows the number of times the model correctly or incorrectly labeled different categories. For example, suppose the model is trying to classify areas as water, built-up, or land. In such case, the confusion matrix will show how many areas were correctly labeled as each category and how many were mislabeled as something else. This helps understand where the model is doing well and where it might be making errors. The confusion matrix of the RF classifier, as shown in Figure 4, reveals how accurately the model classified the different land types. PA measures how often the model correctly identifies a particular class out of all the actual instances of that class. For water, the PA is 85.71%, meaning the model correctly identified 85.71% of all the actual water areas, but it missed 14.29%, which were mislabeled as something else. Built-up areas have a PA of 90.00%, meaning 90% of the actual built-up areas were labeled correctly, with 10% missed. The PA is 100.00% for land, indicating that the model perfectly identified all actual land areas without missing any.

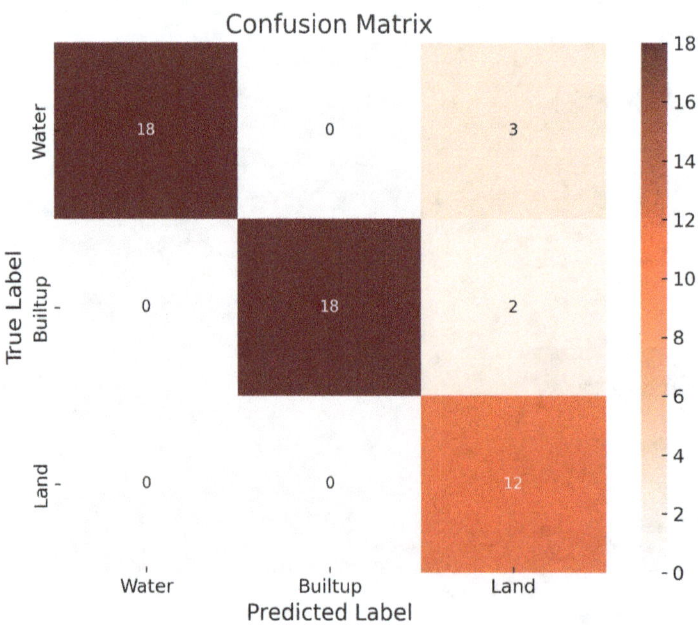

Figure 5: Confusion matrix of classified outcomes.

CA, on the other hand, measures how reliable the model's predictions are for each class. If the model labels an area as water, the CA indicates how likely that area is water. For water and built-up areas, the CA is 100.00%, meaning every area labeled as water or built-up by the model was indeed correct. The CA drops to 70.59% for land, meaning only 70.59% of the areas labeled as land were actually land, while 29.41% were misclassified as land incorrectly. Omission error (OE) indicates how many actual areas of a class were missed by the model. The OE is 14.29% for water, meaning the model missed 14.29% of actual water areas. For built-up areas, the OE is 10.00%, and for land, the OE is 0.00%, meaning the model did not miss any actual land areas. On the other hand, commission error (CE) indicates how many areas were falsely labeled as a particular class. For water and built-up areas, the CE is 0.00%, meaning no other classes were incorrectly labeled as water or built-up. For land, the CE is 29.41%, meaning 29.41% of the areas labeled as land were something else.

Looking at the overall performance, the model's OA is 90.57%, meaning the model correctly classified about 9 out of 10 areas. This is a strong indicator of the model's overall reliability. Additionally, the KC is 85.81%, which measures how much better the model performed than random guessing. A KC of 85.81% indicates a very good level of agreement between the model's predictions and the actual data. In simpler terms, the model performed very well in identifying built-up and water areas, with perfect CA and no CE for these categories. It struggled slightly with land, incorrectly misclassifying 29.41% of the areas as land. Despite this, the OA and KC obtained using the RF algorithm show that the model is robust and reliable for most classifications. These results highlight the model's strengths in handling built-up and water classifications and suggest the potential for more accurate improvement in distinguishing land areas. The detailed results obtained using the RF classifier in the study area are shown in Table 2, while Figure 6 represents the thematic map generated using the RF classifier. A graphical representation of the classification results is shown in Figure 7.

6 Conclusion

The present study showed that RADAR satellite data, such as Sentinel-1, could be effectively used for land cover classification in semiarid regions like the Kota district of Rajasthan when integrated with ML classifiers. The VV and VH polarizations of Sentinel-1 blend information with upper layers of land cover, revealing water, built-up land, and land use. This was particularly useful since RADAR data can be collected regardless of weather or time of day, which is key for reliably and consistently analyzing this data type. In addition, using an ensemble classifier such as RF further emphasized the effectiveness of ML in remote sensing. The model performed quite robustly, achieving an OA of 90.57% and a KC of 85.81%. The classification was relatively good, particularly for water and built-up areas, where the classification was perfectly reliable. On the other hand, for land types, 29.41% of the regions were misclassified, indicating a difficulty in dealing with land having complex land cover types. In conclusion, this study further underpins the application of Sentinel-1 RADAR data and ML

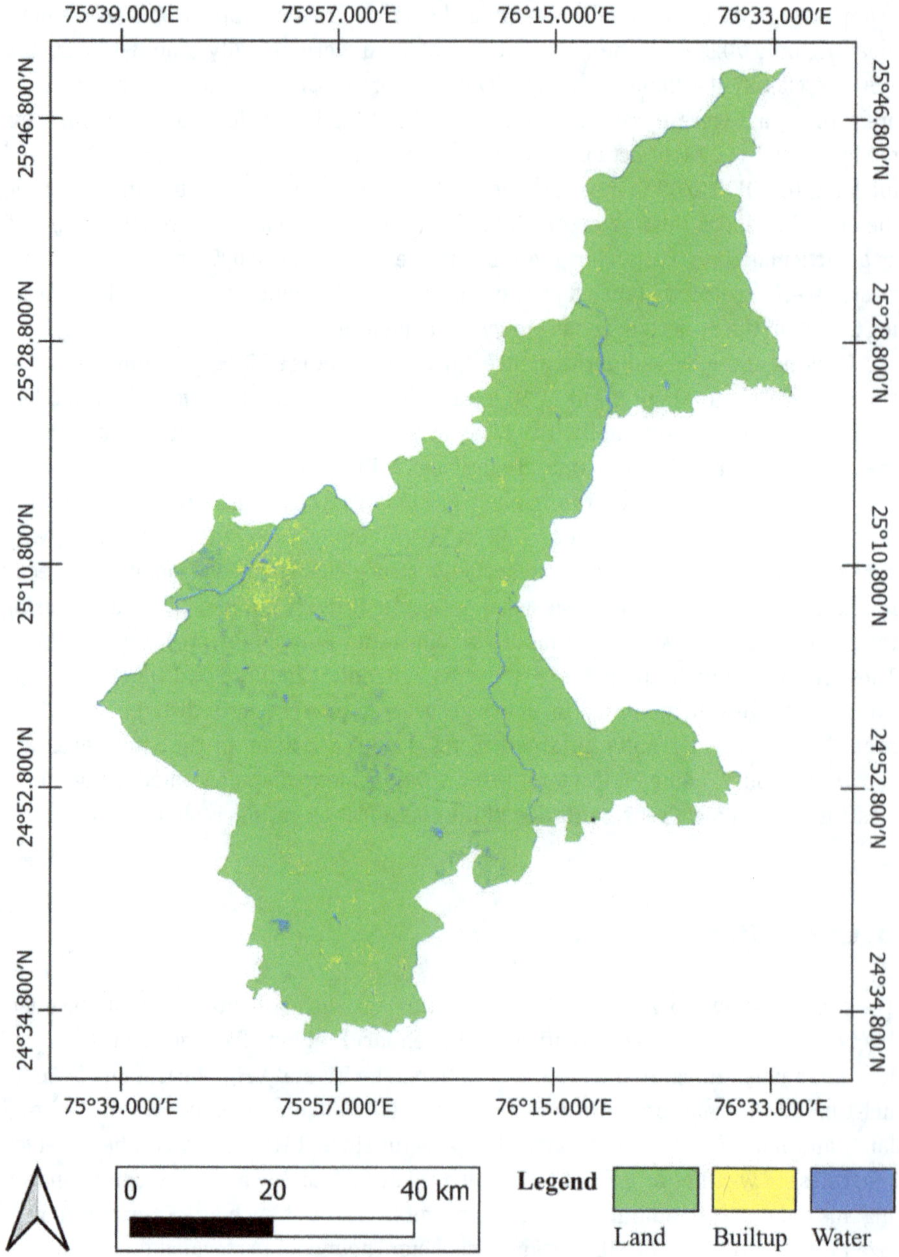

Figure 6: Thematically classified outcome generated using the RF classifier.

Table 2: Accuracy measures.

Class	PA	CA	OE	CE
Water	85.71%	100.00%	14.29%	0.00%
Built-up	90.00%	100.00%	10.00%	0.00%
Land	100.00%	70.59%	0.00%	29.41%
				OA = 90.57%, KC = 85.81%

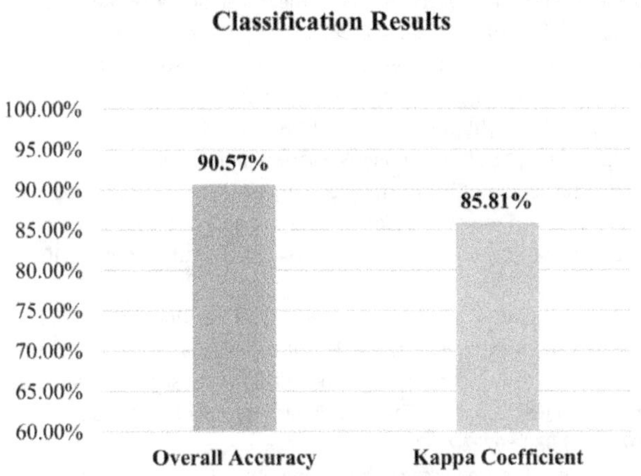

Figure 7: Graphical representation of the accuracy measures.

algorithms in geospatial analysis. Insights from the findings can help in resource management, urban planning, and environmental monitoring of similar regions. Future work can include other data sources, such as optical satellite images or multitemporal data, to improve classification quality even further. The current approach also illustrates how increasingly remote sensing and data-driven methods are forcing us to look at Earth's dynamic surface landscapes with new perspectives.

References

[1] Yin, J., Dong, J., Hamm, N.A.S., Li, Z., Wang, J., Xing, H., Fu, P. 2021. Integrating remote sensing and geospatial big data for urban land use mapping: A review. International Journal of Applied Earth Observation and Geoinformation, 103, 102514, https://doi.org/10.1016/j.jag.2021.102514

[2] Abijith, D., Saravanan, S. 2021. Assessment of land use and land cover change detection and prediction using remote sensing and CA Markov in the northern coastal districts of Tamil Nadu, India. https://doi.org/10.21203/rs.3.rs-576976/v1

[3] Beamish, A., Raynolds, M.K., Epstein, H., Frost, G.V., Macander, M.J., Bergstedt, H., Bartsch, A., Kruse, S., Miles, V., Tanis, C.M., Heim, B., Fuchs, M., Chabrillat, S., Shevtsova, I., Verdonen, M., Wagner, J. 2020. Recent trends and remaining challenges for optical remote sensing of Arctic tundra

vegetation: A review and outlook. Remote Sensing of Environment, 246, 111872, https://doi.org/10.1016/j.rse.2020.111872

[4] Wilkinson, R., Mleczko, M.M., Brewin, R.J.W., Gaston, K.J., Mueller, M., Shutler, J.D., Yan, X., Anderson, K. 2024. Environmental impacts of earth observation data in the constellation and cloud computing era. Science of the Total Environment, 909, 168584, https://doi.org/10.1016/j.scitotenv.2023.168584

[5] Andries, A., Morse, S., Murphy, R.J., Lynch, J., Woolliams, E.R. 2022. Using data from earth observation to support sustainable development indicators: An analysis of the literature and challenges for the future. Sustainability, 14, 1191, https://doi.org/10.3390/su14031191

[6] Kaur, R., Tiwari, R.K., Maini, R. 2024. Detection of soil moisture variations with fusion-based change detection algorithm for MODIS and SCATSAT-1 datasets. Journal of the Indian Society of Remote Sensing, 52, 2575–2592, https://doi.org/10.1007/s12524-024-01967-2

[7] Cheng, G., Ding, H., Yang, J., Cheng, Y. 2023. Crop type classification with combined spectral, texture, and radar features of time-series Sentinel-1 and Sentinel-2 data. International Journal of Remote Sensing, 44, 1215–1237, https://doi.org/10.1080/01431161.2023.2176723

[8] Abbasi, M., Shah-Hosseini, R., Aghdami-Nia, M. 2023. Sentinel-1 polarization comparison for flood segmentation using deep learning. Proceedings, 87, 14, https://doi.org/10.3390/IECG2022-14069

[9] Belgiu, M., Drăguţ, L. 2016. Random forest in remote sensing: A review of applications and future directions. ISPRS Journal of Photogrammetry and Remote Sensing, 114, 24–31, https://doi.org/10.1016/j.isprsjprs.2016.01.011

[10] Bianchini, S., Solari, L., Barra, A., Monserrat, O., Crosetto, M., Catani, F. 2021. Sentinel-1 PSI data for the evaluation of landslide geohazard and impact. In: Guzzetti, F., Mihalić Arbanas, S., Reichenbach, P., Sassa, K., Bobrowsky, P.T., Takara, K. (Eds.) Understanding and Reducing Landslide Disaster Risk: Volume 2 From Mapping to Hazard and Risk Zonation, Cham: Springer International Publishing, 447–455. https://doi.org/10.1007/978-3-030-60227-7_52

[11] Li, X. 2017. Application sentinel-1 SAR data for ocean research and operation. In: 2017 Progress in Electromagnetics Research Symposium – Fall (PIERS – FALL). Presented at the 2017 Progress in Electromagnetics Research Symposium – Fall (PIERS – FALL), 2098–2101. https://doi.org/10.1109/PIERS-FALL.2017.8293484

[12] Singh, S., Sood, V., Tiwari, R.K., Kaur, R., Sharma, A. 2024. Endeavours of Scatterometer Satellite (SCATSAT-1) in earth exploration: An overview of products, applications and emerging trends. Physics and Chemistry of the Earth, Parts A/B/C, 134, 103601, https://doi.org/10.1016/j.pce.2024.103601

[13] Shamshiri, R., Nahavandchi, H., Motagh, M. 2018. Persistent scatterer analysis using dual-polarization Sentinel-1 data: Contribution from VH channel. IEEE Journal of Selected Topics in Applied Earth Observations and Remote Sensing, 11, 3105–3112, https://doi.org/10.1109/JSTARS.2018.2848111

[14] Dănişor, C., Popescu, A., Datcu, M. 2016. Persistent scatterers detection on synthetic aperture radar images acquired by Sentinel-1 satellite. In: Advanced Topics in Optoelectronics, Microelectronics, and Nanotechnologies VIII. Presented at the Advanced Topics in Optoelectronics, Microelectronics, and Nanotechnologies, vol. VIII, SPIE, 269–275. https://doi.org/10.1117/12.2243284

[15] Martin, J.C., Dobbs, K., Koehler, F.W. 2018. Sentinel-1 spatially varying maximum-likelihood coherent change detection. In: 2018 IEEE Radar Conference (RadarConf18). Presented at the 2018 IEEE Radar Conference (RadarConf18), 1234–1238. https://doi.org/10.1109/RADAR.2018.8378739

[16] Zhu, L., Geng, X., Xie, T., Hu, L., Yan, X.-H. 2021. Comparison of the application of co- and cross-polarized sentinel-1 synthetic aperture radar data to tropical cyclone evaluation. Remote Sensing Letters, 12, 229–238, https://doi.org/10.1080/2150704X.2020.1843734

[17] Rajasthan Budget Analysis 2022–23 [WWW Document], n.d. PRS Legislative Research. URL https://prsindia.org/budgets/states/rajasthan-budget-analysis-2022-23 (accessed 12.29.24).

[18] Singh, S., Meraj, G., Kumar, P., Singh, S.K., Kanga, S., Johnson, B.A., Prajapat, D.K., Debnath, J., Sahariah, D. 2023. Decoding Chambal River shoreline transformations: A comprehensive analysis using remote sensing, GIS, and DSAS. Water, 15, 1793, https://doi.org/10.3390/w15091793

[19] Mandal, D., Vaka, D.S., Bhogapurapu, N.R., Vanama, V.S.K., Kumar, V., Rao, Y.S., Bhattacharya, A., 2019. Sentinel-1 SLC preprocessing workflow for polarimetric applications: a generic practice for generating dual-pol covariance matrix elements in SNAP S-1 toolbox. https://doi.org/10.20944/preprints201911.0393.v1

[20] Kumar, L., Mutanga, O. 2018. Google Earth Engine applications since inception: Usage, trends, and potential. Remote Sensing, 10, 1509, https://doi.org/10.3390/rs10101509

[21] Pech-May, F., Aquino-Santos, R., Rios-Toledo, G., Posadas-Durán, J.P.F. 2022. Mapping of land cover with optical images, supervised algorithms, and Google Earth Engine. Sensors, 22, 4729, https://doi.org/10.3390/s22134729

[22] Albert, G., Ammar, S. 2021. Application of random forest classification and remotely sensed data in geological mapping on the Jebel Meloussi area (Tunisia). Arabian Journal of Geosciences, 14, 2240, https://doi.org/10.1007/s12517-021-08509-x

[23] Vujasinović, M. and Skorup, D. (2021) "POSSIBILITY OF USING SENTINEL RADAR SATELLITE IMAGES," Contemporary Theory and Practice in Construction. University of Banja Luka, Faculty of Architecture, Civil Engineering and Geodesy. https://doi:10.7251/stp2215267v.

Amit Sharma*, Sarita Naruka, and Gowri Choudhary

A systematic review of deep learning techniques in microwave remote sensing: challenges, applications, and future directions

Abstract: Microwave remote sensing has emerged as a vital tool for Earth observation due to its ability to operate in all-weather and day-or-night conditions, which are significant limitations of optical sensors. This chapter systematically reviews deep learning (DL) techniques for microwave remote sensing to enhance data interpretation and application accuracy. The chapter highlights the effectiveness of Siamese networks and autoencoders in change detection applications. Challenges such as the scarcity of labeled data, computational costs, and model interpretability are discussed, along with potential solutions such as transfer learning and federated learning. The review also emphasizes the role of synthetic aperture radar (SAR) data in capturing spatial and temporal features. By exploring the strengths and limitations of these methods, the chapter provides insights into the future scope of DL applications in microwave remote sensing, aiming to effectively support environmental monitoring, disaster management, and sustainable development initiatives.

Keywords: Microwave remote sensing, deep learning, disaster management, environmental monitoring, autoencoders, Siamese networks

1 Introduction

Microwave remote sensing is an important technique that utilizes electromagnetic waves from the microwave region to obtain information on the surface and atmosphere of the Earth. In contrast to optical remote sensing, which has severe limitations imposed by atmospheric conditions, namely clouds and daylight availability,

*Corresponding author: Amit Sharma, Department of Computer Science and Application, Vivekananda Global University, Jaipur, Rajasthan, India, e-mail: dr.amittech@gmail.com, ORCID: 0000-0001-9825-3978
Sarita Naruka, Department of Computer Science and Engineering, Rajasthan Technical University, Kota, India, e-mail: narukasarita24@gmail.com, ORCID: 0009-0004-5335-6286
Gowri Choudhary, Department of Computer Science and Engineering, Rajasthan Technical University, Kota, India, e-mail: rgk.choudhary@gmail.com, ORCID: 0000-0001-5582-8372

https://doi.org/10.1515/9783111572970-002

microwave remote sensing is all-weather, day-or-night conditions. Microwave sensors have the added ability to penetrate clouds, vegetation, and some soil layers, meaning that in many situations where an optical sensor cannot function, a microwave sensor can [1]. Microwave remote sensing can be either active or passive. Active systems, including synthetic aperture radar (SAR), send microwave signals to the ground and retrieve the backscattered signals for information. SAR has been used for land cover classification, urban mapping, and agricultural classification [2]. It is also useful in disaster management, including monitoring floods and assessing the damage caused by earthquakes [3]. In contrast, passive microwave sensors detect emitted microwave radiation passively and are extensively used to retrieve sea ice concentration, snow cover, soil moisture, and atmospheric water vapor content. Researchers need these sensors to cope with climate change and preserve limited resources on this planet efficiently. Additionally, the capacity to access data independent of solar illumination and atmospheric attributes makes microwave remote sensing vital for various applications, from agricultural monitoring to military surveillance. With the increasing demand for timely, accurate, and reliable geospatial information, microwave remote sensing is becoming increasingly ubiquitous in the current toolbox of remote sensing technologies [4].

Another key mission is SCATSAT-1, an Indian satellite designed to continue the flow of ocean wind vector data from a scatterometer [5]. The Ku-band scatterometer is used for weather forecasting, cyclone prediction, and ocean surface wind vector measurements (SCATSAT-1). Moreover, other missions with L-band SAR, such as Japan's ALOS-2 (Advanced Land Observing Satellite), have contributed significant value to forest monitoring and several geological applications. This significant microwave frequency and sensor diversity across the missions demonstrates their ability to address various environmental parameters and represents a key group of sensors for climate studies, disaster management, and sustainable development [6]. Figure 1 highlights various microwave remote sensing-based satellite missions.

Machine learning (ML) techniques are frequently used in microwave remote sensing to improve data interpretation. Microwave data is often high-dimensional and noisy, making it difficult to achieve accurate and efficient results with traditional methods [7]. ML techniques, mainly supervised learning methods such as support vector machines (SVMs), random forest (RF), and artificial neural networks (ANNs), have been widely used and have achieved outstanding results in some specific tasks, including land cover classification, soil moisture estimation, and target detection. Specifically, SVM is well-suited for capturing nonlinear relationships in SAR data, making it practical for urban and agricultural classification. For instance, RF algorithms also use ensemble learning to achieve more robust classification by combining predictions from several decision trees, which correspond remarkably well to the speckle noise intrinsic to SAR images [8]. Table 1 shows recent research trends in microwave remote sensing utilizing deep learning (DL)-based algorithms.

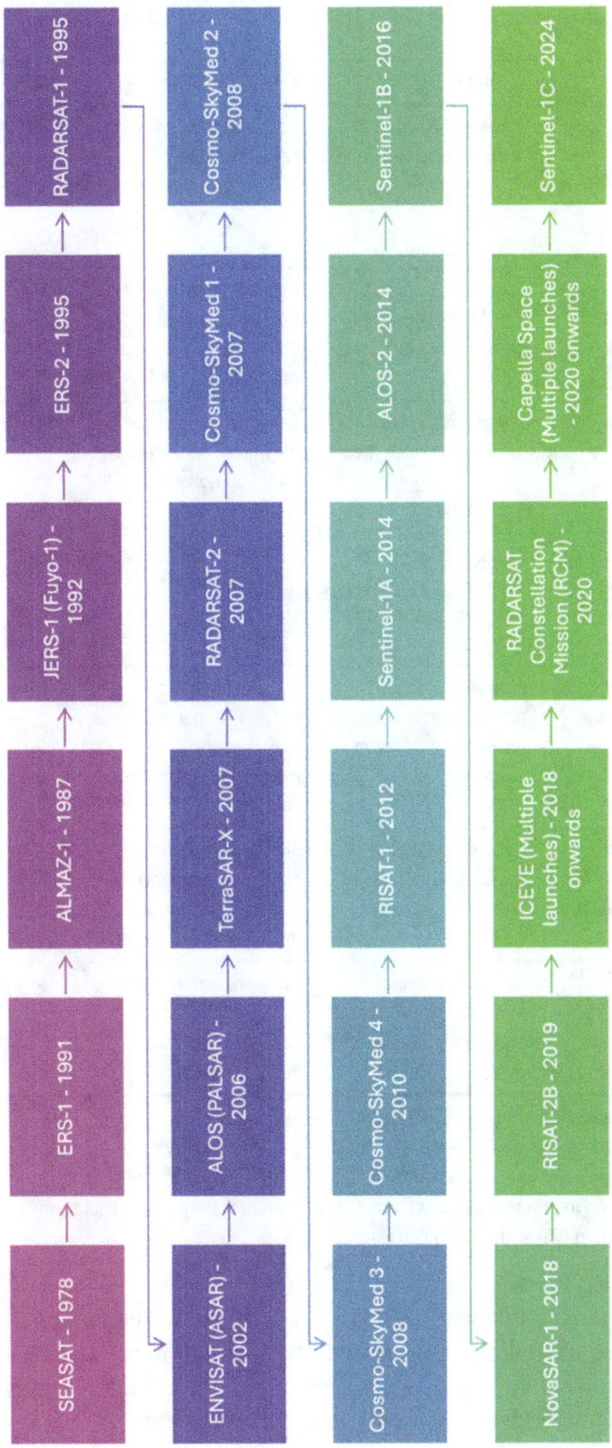

Figure 1: Key missions based on microwave remote sensing-based satellites.

Table 1: Recent research on microwave remote sensing with DL-based algorithms for change detection.

Algorithm	Methodology	Application	Limitations	Source
CAE[1], Commonality AE[2], Segmentation Algorithms	Extracts features, learns standard features, and generates segmentation maps	Change detection in optical and SAR[3] images	Relies on unchanged regions; limited generalization	[9]
FCN[4] & Siamese Autoencoder	It uses an SN[5] to extract features and detect changes	Change detection in UAV[6] aerial images for crop monitoring	Relies on UAV image quality; may face challenges in large-scale applications	[10]
SN, U-Net[7]	Uses dense connections for feature retention and a cross-entropy loss function	Change detection in VHR[8] satellite images	Sensitive to edge details; may face challenges in handling noisy data	[11]
Deep Siamese Semantic Segmentation Network	Treats change detection as a binary semantic segmentation task	Change detection in remote sensing images, focusing on land cover changes	Limited by the availability of annotated data; computational cost	[12]
GAS-Net[9]	Utilizes GAM[10] for context learning and FAM[11] for feature aggregation	Change detection in remote sensing images for urban expansion and deforestation	Sensitive to class imbalance; performance may degrade with increasing class complexity	[13]
CNN[12] based Framework with Mask R-CNN	Uses a building extraction network for binary change detection	Detecting building changes in VHR aerial imagery	Sensitive to parallax errors; performance depends on accurate instance segmentation	[14]
Bi-SRNet[13]	Merges temporal features in a deep CD[14] unit using attention mechanisms	Semantic change detection in HR[15] remote sensing images	Complexity may lead to higher computational costs and limited interpretability	[15]

Commonality autoencoder (CAE[1]), autoencoder (AE[2]), SAR (synthetic aperture radar[3]), fully convolutional network (FCN[4]), Siamese network (SN[5]), unmanned aerial vehicle (UAV[6]), U-shaped network (UNet[7]), very high resolution (VHR[8]), global-aware Siamese network (GAS-Net[9]), global attention module (GAM[10]), feature attention module (FAM[11]), convolutional neural network (CNN[12]), bidirectional super-resolution network (Bi-SRNet[13]), change detection (CD[14]), and high resolution (HR[15]).

Furthermore, generative adversarial networks (GANs) have also been used for super-resolution of SAR images, speckle noise reduction, and apparent SAR image recovery [16]. DL models have a distinct advantage over traditional ML techniques, such as SVM and RFs, when working with high-dimensional and correlated data. DL models can automatically learn complex patterns and correlations in the data. The capacity of DL to integrate spatial, spectral, and temporal information harmoniously gives it a pronounced advantage over traditional microwave remote sensing data exploitation approaches, providing new perspectives on results in this discipline [17]. Land use land cover (LULC) classification is a significant application of microwave remote sensing and provides crucial information for environmental monitoring, resource management, and urban planning. SAR, a microwave sensor, can penetrate clouds and works independently of solar illumination; thus, it has been considered a key tool for LULC mapping, especially for regions with frequent cloud cover [18].

SAR can broadly discriminate among land cover types based on its sensitivity to surface roughness, moisture content, and structural characteristics typical of forests, urban areas, water bodies, and agricultural fields. High spatial resolution images and ground object classification are generally inseparable problems in remote sensing, and stepwise distinction is an effective method to reduce the complexity of classification by integrating derived information from images or environmental resources into the ground object classification model. Alternatively, in PolSAR data, the double-bounce and volume scattering characteristics observed have been used to enhance the discrimination between urban and vegetated regions [19]. DL has recently advanced unprecedentedly in improving LULC classification task accuracy using microwave data. In recent years, convolutional neural networks (CNNs) have been widely utilized in extracting spatial features directly from SAR images and have gained notably higher accuracy based on far-level feature extraction compared to traditional ML. CNNs enable the differentiation between spectrally similar but structurally different land cover types by capturing high-level multiscale contextual and topological information [20]. In addition, recurrent neural networks (RNNs), especially long short-term memory (LSTM) networks, have been applied for temporal SAR data analysis to detect land cover changes over time in urban growth and forest loss. Due to the scarcity of labeled SAR datasets, transfer learning has proven practical, allowing pretrained models to be fine-tuned for specific LULC tasks. Such developments highlight the ability of DL to overcome the restrictions of traditional methods, thus enabling LULC classification from microwave remote sensing to be both more precise and operationally viable [21]. Table 2 summarizes recent DL algorithms for LULC in remote sensing.

One of the key advantages of microwave remote sensing is its application in change detection, which aims to detect and quantify changes in land surface features by comparing the images taken over time. Accurate change detection is essential in several applications, such as environmental monitoring, disaster assessment, urban expansion analysis, and resource management. SAR and microwave sensors have unique advantages for change detection, including their ability to penetrate clouds and operate in all-weather, day-and-night conditions [29]. The coherent characteristics of SAR data allow for the identification of very slight changes in surface roughness, moisture, and structural properties, making it suitable for different applications. Deforestation detection, flood extent mapping, and urban growth detection methods,

Table 2: Recent research on microwave remote sensing with DL-based algorithms for LULC.

Algorithm	Methodology	Application	Limitations	Source
CNN[1]	Fixed CNN architecture, cross-validation, and comprehensive feature extraction	LULC[2] classification using radar and hyperspectral images	Limited to fixed CNN architecture and lacks exploration of different architectures	[22]
CNN and CapsNet[3]	CNN for feature extraction and CapsNet for classification	Scene classification in remote sensing images	High computational cost and limited to three benchmark datasets	[23]
UNet[4] and convolutional LSTM[5]	Spatial-temporal segmentation and post-classification refinement	Multitemporal LULC classification using VHR[6] satellite data	High intraclass variance and computationally intensive	[24]
Deep-LSTM and autoencoder	Feature extraction with AE[7] and band selection with deep-LSTM	LULC classification using hyperspectral images	Limited training samples and time-consuming process	[25]
CGAN[8]	CGAN to synthesize multispectral Sentinel-2 images	LULC classification and synthetic image generation	Limited to Sentinel-2 data and challenges in capturing spectral variance	[26]
RF[9], DNN[10], and SVM[11]	PCC[12] using RF and DNN for LULC change detection	LULC change detection using multitemporal LANDSAT[13] images	Limited to bitemporal images and lacks the complexity of DL-based approaches	[27]
Deep CNN, RF, SVM, and KNN	Semantic segmentation of PolSAR[16] data and pre-trained on ImageNet	Urban area mapping and LULC classification for high-resolution SAR[17] data	Limited labeled datasets for SAR and potential misclassification in complex urban environments	[28]

Convolutional neural network (CNN[1]), land use land cover (LULC[2]), capsule network (CapsNet[3]), U-Net convolutional network (UNet[4]), long short-term memory (LSTM[5]), very high resolution (VHR[6]), autoencoder (AE[7]), conditional generative adversarial network (CGAN[8]), random forest (RF[9]), deep neural network (DNN[10]), support vector machine (SVM[11]), post-classification comparison (PCC[12]), land satellite (LANDSAT[13]), K-nearest neighbors (KNN[14]), polarimetric SAR (PolSAR[16]), and synthetic aperture radar (SAR[17]).

such as differential SAR interferometry, are frequently used to identify subcentimeter movements in surface height associated with landslides, earthquakes, and subsidence.

However, with the growing attention to DL, its automatic feature extraction and classification abilities have greatly facilitated advances in change detection. More specifically, CNNs have successfully extracted spatial features from multitemporal SAR data, with the ability to detect changes in built-up areas and vegetation cover accurately [30]. Additionally, RNNs, particularly LSTM networks, have enabled the analysis of temporal sequences, significantly improving the monitoring of gradual land use changes and climate-related events. The application of GANs has also been investigated because it can enhance change detection and generate high-resolution SAR images, which can then reduce the effects of noise. DL methods involve an inherent automatic feature extraction property that outperforms classical ML techniques in terms of accuracy and scalability by eliminating the need for handcrafted features, thus being a powerful solution for change detection in microwave remote sensing [31].

2 Key applications of microwave remote sensing

Microwave remote sensing is widely used in various applications, such as LULC classification, flood detection, urban mapping, and soil moisture estimation. Figure 2 highlights eight essential applications of microwave remote sensing, including land cover classification, flood monitoring, soil moisture estimation, and earthquake damage assessment, using DL methods.

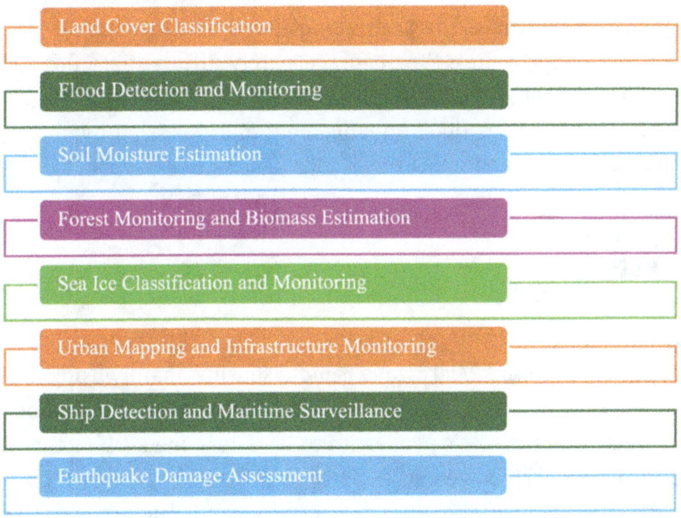

Figure 2: Key applications of microwave remote sensing with DL techniques.

2.1 Land cover classification

Microwave remote sensing has a wide range of applications, among which land cover classification is the most popular. Land cover maps play an important role in environmental monitoring, urban planning, and resource management. Because of their capability to look through the clouds and their sensitivity to surface roughness and dielectric properties, SAR data are widely implemented for this purpose [32]. DL algorithms, especially CNNs, have better classification performance in recent years due to their automatic hierarchical spatial feature extraction capabilities from SAR images. Using the backscatter signatures and textural patterns, the CNN can effectively classify the pixels within a given satellite image into different urban, agricultural, forest, or water body classes. Although fine-tuning pretrained models has consistently provided higher accuracy in classifying land cover types, it remains a challenge due to the scarcity of labeled SAR datasets, making transfer learning a practical solution [33].

2.2 Flood detection and monitoring

Microwave remote sensing is an effective flood detection and monitoring technique under all weather conditions. SAR sensors can be a timely and reliable source of information under many adverse conditions since they are sensitive to surface water, and the extent of inundation areas can be determined from the differences in the intensity of backscattering. Variants like CNNs and other new classification models (e.g., U-Net architectures) have also improved the accuracy of flood extent mapping [34]. Using semantic segmentation approaches, they can accurately differentiate flooded areas from nonflooded ones. Moreover, experimental results ascertain RNN integration to analyze time-series SAR data for flood advancement and recession dynamics, which is significant in responding to and managing floods [35].

2.3 Soil moisture estimation

Soil moisture estimation is a key parameter in agricultural management, drought monitoring, and hydrological modeling. Microwave remote sensing, mainly using passive sensors (i.e., radiometers) and active sensors (i.e., SAR), can penetrate soil, allowing moisture variations related to dielectric properties to be determined. DL methods, including CNNs and LSTM networks, have successfully retrieved soil moisture from SAR time-series data [36]. These models efficiently learn spatial and temporal patterns linked to soil dielectric characteristics, improving precision compared to commonly employed empirical models.

2.4 Forest monitoring and biomass estimation

Monitoring forests and estimating biomass are essential for carbon stock assessments and deforestation control. SAR sensors operating in the L-band and P-band, which are capable of penetrating forest canopies, remain essential data sources for biomass estimation. In contrast to pixel-based analysis, DL approaches such as CNNs or 3D CNNs have been applied to derive structure maps and estimate the above-ground biomass from SAR images by utilizing the spatial and volumetric characteristics of SAR images [37]. Unlike conventional backscatter-based models that primarily rely on the backscatter reflection mechanism, these methods consider the complex scattering mechanisms of forest canopies and outperform traditional methods. Also, with autoencoders, supervised learning of hierarchical features has become possible, increasing accuracy in retrieving forest parameters [38].

2.5 Sea ice classification and monitoring

The classification and monitoring of sea ice is an essential issue, as it not only relates to the impacts of climate change but also ensures safe navigation for maritime operations. C-band SAR is popular because it can discriminate between several ice types through their backscatter intensity and texture. Assessment of sea ice types, including multi-year ice, first-year ice, and open water, has outperformed conventional methods via DL models, especially CNNs and capsule networks [39]. Compared to traditional threshold-based methods, these models better capture spatial dependencies and textural variations in SAR data. The advent of RNNs has enhanced the ability to monitor temporal variability in ice dynamics, which is essential for climate studies.

2.6 Urban mapping and infrastructure monitoring

Urban mapping and infrastructure monitoring applications exploit the high resolution of SAR sensors to identify built infrastructure, such as buildings and roads, and to measure structural deformations. ML approaches, such as mask R-CNN and FCNs, have been applied to SAR data for building footprint extraction and damage assessment. These methods excel at pixel-level classification and can accurately identify urban features. The improved penetration, encoding of spatial hierarchies, and rotational invariance in urban structures have also become prominent factors for using capsule networks, primarily to indicate their effectiveness in monitoring building damages and urban subsidence in post-disaster environments [40].

2.7 Ship detection and maritime surveillance

Ship detection and maritime surveillance enable coastal security, anti-piracy, fisheries management, and more. SAR sensors are appropriate because they can identify metallic objects on the water's surface. Various DL architectures, such as You Only Look Once (YOLO) and faster R-CNN, have been extensively applied to SAR images, functioning in real-time and accurately detecting vessels, their types, and their locations

[41]. They use bounding box regression and object classification-based models to detect ships under complicated sea conditions. Transfer learning has been adopted to improve detection, as it allows pretrained architectures to be adapted to SAR data to mitigate the challenges of insufficient labeled datasets.

2.8 Earthquake damage assessment

Microwave remote sensing has proven to be an essential tool for disaster response and recovery planning for earthquake damage assessment. Because of its ability to detect surface displacements and damage to structures, SAR is an instrumental tool to be used immediately after an earthquake. ML methods with interferometric SAR (InSAR), for instance, have proven notably effective for detecting damaged buildings, landslides, and surface ruptures, highlighting their potential usage for extracting features from output data or prior studies on possible features for use cases following a natural disaster. CNNs can use such detailed spatial features that would be able to differentiate between intact and damaged structures at a computational level using SAR coherence and backscatter data [42]. Furthermore, including LSTM networks allows for temporal analysis of SAR data to evaluate changing damage or recovery trends, which is valuable information that can be provided to the emergency response team.

3 Future scope

Microwave remote sensing is a mature field that has generated massive amounts of data from satellites over the four decades since its inception; however, combining microwave remote sensing with DL methods provides the potential for significant future advancements in environmental monitoring, disaster management, and climate studies. SAR data analysis can benefit from transformer architectures and attention mechanisms to extract spatial and temporal features more efficiently than conventional CNNs and RNNs, which is one of the critical growth areas [24]. In addition, with the rise of multimodal DL, researchers can consolidate microwave remote sensing data with optical and LiDAR datasets for applications such as urban mapping and forest monitoring [43]. Finally, improving computational efficiency via model pruning, quantization, edge computing, and so on is necessary for real-time high-resolution SAR data processing from satellites. With the growth of satellite constellations, unsupervised and semisupervised learning will play a much more significant role in addressing the lack of labeled data for DL models [44].

4 Conclusion

The rise of DL has been a driving factor for new ways of processing Earth observation data. DL models, such as CNNs, RNNs, and GANs, have made it possible to automatically learn the underlying spatial and temporal patterns in SAR and scatterometer observations, achieving high performance in land cover classification, flood detection, soil moisture retrieval, and urban mapping applications. They have also reduced some of the limitations of traditional ML approaches, which primarily rely on manual feature engineering. DL has successfully characterized the complex interrelation between backscatter and dielectric properties, facilitating higher classification accuracy. Yet, there are still some challenges with DL in microwave remote sensing that need to be addressed. The relatively higher computational requirements of DL approaches can prove to be cumbersome, particularly as the amount of labeled SAR datasets is limited, which restricts scalability and the potential for real-time implementations. Advances in federated learning, transfer learning, and models that unify conventional ML and DL could help resolve some of these issues.

References

[1] Vreugdenhil, M., Greimeister-Pfeil, I., Preimesberger, W., Camici, S., Dorigo, W., Enenkel, M., Van der Schalie, R., Steele-Dunne, S., Wagner, W. 2022. Microwave remote sensing for agricultural drought monitoring: Recent developments and challenges. Frontiers in Water, 4, https://doi.org/10.3389/frwa.2022.1045451

[2] Vyas, N., Sethi, G.K., Singh, S. 2024. Comparative analysis of different classifiers on fusion of sentinel datasets for agriculture land. In: 2024 4th International Conference on Technological Advancements in Computational Sciences (ICTACS). Presented at the 2024 4th International Conference on Technological Advancements in Computational Sciences (ICTACS), 1173–1177. https://doi.org/10.1109/ICTACS62700.2024.10840995

[3] Dong, J., Crow, W.T., Tobin, K.J., Cosh, M.H., Bosch, D.D., Starks, P.J., Seyfried, M., Collins, C.H. 2020. Comparison of microwave remote sensing and land surface modeling for surface soil moisture climatology estimation. Remote Sensing of Environment, 242, 111756. https://doi.org/10.1016/j.rse.2020.111756

[4] Gao, H., Nie, N., Zhang, W., Chen, H. 2020. Monitoring the spatial distribution and changes in permafrost with passive microwave remote sensing. ISPRS Journal of Photogrammetry and Remote Sensing, 170, 142–155. https://doi.org/10.1016/j.isprsjprs.2020.10.011

[5] Brisco, B., Mahdianpari, M., Mohammadimanesh, F. 2020. Hybrid compact polarimetric SAR for Environmental monitoring with the RADARSAT constellation mission. Remote Sensing, 12, 3283. https://doi.org/10.3390/rs12203283

[6] Misra, T., Chakraborty, P., Lad, C., Gupta, P., Rao, J., Upadhyay, G., Kumar, S.V., Kumar, B.S., Gangele, S., Sinha, S., Tolani, H., Vithani, V.K., Raman, B.S., Rao, C.V.N., Dave, D.B., Jyoti, R., Desai, N.M. 2019. SCATSAT-1 scatterometer: An improved successor of OSCAT. Current Science, 117, 941–949.

[7] Bhowmick, S.A., Cotton, J., Fore, A., Kumar, R., Payan, C., Rodríguez, E., Sharma, A., Stiles, B., Stoffelen, A., Verhoef, A. 2019. An assessment of the performance of ISRO's SCATSAT-1 scatterometer. Current Science, 117, 959–972.

[8] Koyama, C.N., Shimada, M., Ohki, M., Tadono, T. 2023. From ALOS-2 to ALOS-4: Japan's pioneering L-band SARs for global vegetation monitoring, state-of-the-art and future perspectives. Sensors, Systems, and Next-Generation Satellites XXVII. Presented at the Sensors, Systems, and Next-Generation Satellites XXVII, SPIE, 103–110. https://doi.org/10.1117/12.2680110
[9] Wu, Y., Li, J., Yuan, Y., Qin, A.K., Miao, Q.-G., Gong, M.-G. 2022. Commonality autoencoder: Learning common features for change detection from heterogeneous images. IEEE Transactions on Neural Networks and Learning Systems, 33, 4257–4270. https://doi.org/10.1109/TNNLS.2021.3056238
[10] Mesquita, D.B., Santos, R.F.D., Macharet, D.G., Campos, M.F.M., Nascimento, E.R. 2020. Fully convolutional Siamese autoencoder for change detection in UAV aerial images. IEEE Geoscience and Remote Sensing Letters, 17, 1455–1459. https://doi.org/10.1109/LGRS.2019.2945906
[11] Fang, S., Li, K., Shao, J., Li, Z. 2022. SNUNet-CD: A densely connected Siamese network for change detection of VHR Images. IEEE Geoscience and Remote Sensing Letters, 19, 1–5. https://doi.org/10.1109/LGRS.2021.3056416
[12] Yang, L., Chen, Y., Song, S., Li, F., Huang, G. 2021. Deep Siamese networks based change detection with remote sensing images. Remote Sensing, 13, 3394. https://doi.org/10.3390/rs13173394
[13] Zhang, R., Zhang, H., Ning, X., Huang, X., Wang, J., Cui, W. 2023. Global-aware Siamese network for change detection on remote sensing images. ISPRS Journal of Photogrammetry and Remote Sensing, 199, 61–72. https://doi.org/10.1016/j.isprsjprs.2023.04.001
[14] Ji, S., Shen, Y., Lu, M., Zhang, Y. 2019. Building instance change detection from large-scale aerial images using convolutional neural networks and simulated samples. Remote Sensing, 11, 1343. https://doi.org/10.3390/rs11111343
[15] Ding, L., Guo, H., Liu, S., Mou, L., Zhang, J., Bruzzone, L. 2022. Bi-temporal semantic reasoning for the semantic change detection in HR remote sensing images. IEEE Transactions on Geoscience and Remote Sensing, 60, 1–14. https://doi.org/10.1109/TGRS.2022.3154390
[16] Kong, Y., Liu, S. 2024. DMSC-GAN: A c-GAN-Based framework for super-resolution reconstruction of SAR images. Remote Sensing, 16, 50. https://doi.org/10.3390/rs16010050
[17] Mohamed, E.S., Naqishbandi, T.A., Bukhari, S.A.C., Rauf, I., Sawrikar, V., Hussain, A. 2023. A hybrid mental health prediction model using support vector machine, multilayer perceptron, and random forest algorithms. Healthcare Analytics, 3, 100185. https://doi.org/10.1016/j.health.2023.100185
[18] Chachondhia, P., Shakya, A., Kumar, G. 2021. Performance evaluation of machine learning algorithms using optical and microwave data for LULC classification. Remote Sensing Applications: Society and Environment, 23, 100599. https://doi.org/10.1016/j.rsase.2021.100599
[19] Zhang, X., Xu, J., Chen, Y., Xu, K., Wang, D. 2021. Coastal wetland classification with GF-3 Polarimetric SAR imagery by using object-oriented random forest algorithm. Sensors, 21, 3395. https://doi.org/10.3390/s21103395
[20] Hu, W., Li, Y., Zhang, W., Chen, S., Lv, X., Ligthart, L. 2019. Spatial resolution enhancement of satellite microwave radiometer data with deep residual convolutional neural network. Remote Sensing, 11, 771. https://doi.org/10.3390/rs11070771
[21] Habi, H.V., Messer, H. 2021. Recurrent neural network for rain estimation using commercial microwave links. IEEE Transactions on Geoscience and Remote Sensing, 59, 3672–3681. https://doi.org/10.1109/TGRS.2020.3010305
[22] Carranza-García, M., García-Gutiérrez, J., Riquelme, J.C. 2019. A framework for evaluating land use and land cover classification using convolutional neural networks. Remote Sensing, 11, 274. https://doi.org/10.3390/rs11030274
[23] Zhang, W., Tang, P., Zhao, L. 2019. Remote sensing image scene classification using CNN-CapsNet. Remote Sensing, 11, 494. https://doi.org/10.3390/rs11050494
[24] Zhu, Y., Geiß, C., So, E., Jin, Y. 2021. Multitemporal relearning with convolutional LSTM models for land use classification. IEEE Journal of Selected Topics in Applied Earth Observations and Remote Sensing, 14, 3251–3265. https://doi.org/10.1109/JSTARS.2021.3055784

[25] Tejasree, G., Agilandeeswari, L. 2024. Land use/land cover (LULC) classification using deep-LSTM for hyperspectral images. Egyptian Journal of Remote Sensing and Space Science, 27, 52–68. https://doi.org/10.1016/j.ejrs.2024.01.004

[26] Dedring, T., Rienow, A. 2024. Synthesis and evaluation of seamless, large-scale, multispectral satellite images using generative adversarial networks on land use and land cover and Sentinel-2 data. GIScience & Remote Sensing, 61, 2364460. https://doi.org/10.1080/15481603.2024.2364460

[27] Tahraoui, A., Kheddam, R. 2024. LULC change detection using combined machine and deep learning classifiers. In: 2024 IEEE 7th International Conference on Advanced Technologies, Signal and Image Processing (ATSIP). Presented at the 2024 IEEE 7th International Conference on Advanced Technologies, Signal and Image Processing (ATSIP), 403–408. https://doi.org/10.1109/ATSIP62566.2024.10638952

[28] Garg, R., Kumar, A., Bansal, N., Prateek, M., Kumar, S. 2021. Semantic segmentation of PolSAR image data using advanced deep learning model. Scientific Reports, 11, 15365. https://doi.org/10.1038/s41598-021-94422-y

[29] Tavakoli, N., Siami-Namini, S., Adl Khanghah, M., Mirza Soltani, F., Siami Namin, A. 2020. An autoencoder-based deep learning approach for clustering time series data. SN Applied Sciences, 2, 937. https://doi.org/10.1007/s42452-020-2584-8

[30] Ye, P. 2022. Remote sensing approaches for meteorological disaster monitoring: Recent achievements and new challenges. International Journal of Environmental Research and Public Health, 19, 3701. https://doi.org/10.3390/ijerph19063701

[31] Wu, P., Su, Y., Duan, S., Li, X., Yang, H., Zeng, C., Ma, X., Wu, Y., Shen, H. 2022. A two-step deep learning framework for mapping gapless all-weather land surface temperature using thermal infrared and passive microwave data. Remote Sensing of Environment, 277, 113070. https://doi.org/10.1016/j.rse.2022.113070

[32] Ma, Z., Mei, G., Xu, N. 2024. Generative deep learning for data generation in natural hazard analysis: Motivations, advances, challenges, and opportunities. Artificial Intelligence Review, 57, 160. https://doi.org/10.1007/s10462-024-10764-9

[33] Ouma, Y.O., Cheruyot, R., Wachera, A.N. 2022. Rainfall and runoff time-series trend analysis using LSTM recurrent neural network and wavelet neural network with satellite-based meteorological data: Case study of Nzoia hydrologic basin. Complex & Intelligent Systems, 8, 213–236. https://doi.org/10.1007/s40747-021-00365-2

[34] Ghosh, D., Cabrera, J. 2022. Enriched random forest for high dimensional genomic data. IEEE/ACM Transactions on Computational Biology and Bioinformatics, 19, 2817–2828. https://doi.org/10.1109/TCBB.2021.3089417

[35] Agrawal, S., Khairnar, G.B. 2019. A comparative assessment of remote sensing imaging techniques: Optical, Sar and Lidar. International Archives of the Photogrammetry, Remote Sensing and Spatial Information Sciences, XLII-5-W3, 1–6. https://doi.org/10.5194/isprs-archives-XLII-5-W3-1-2019

[36] Zhang, S., Fu, H., Zhu, J., Han, W., Hu, J. 2022. A General Implementation of the Neumann volume scattering model for PolSAR data. IEEE Geoscience and Remote Sensing Letters, 19, 1–5. https://doi.org/10.1109/LGRS.2022.3204594

[37] Nawaz, A., Jie, C., Yang, W., Yong-Chen, P., Can, S. 2024. SAR image interpretation using CNN and contrastive learning. In: IGARSS 2024 – 2024 IEEE International Geoscience and Remote Sensing Symposium. Presented at the IGARSS 2024 – 2024 IEEE International Geoscience and Remote Sensing Symposium, 11284–11287. https://doi.org/10.1109/IGARSS53475.2024.10641473

[38] Navacchi, C., Reuß, F., Wagner, W. 2025. Using a neural network to model the incidence angle dependency of backscatter to produce seamless, analysis-ready backscatter composites over land. Remote Sensing, 17, 361. https://doi.org/10.3390/rs17030361

[39] Mastro, P., Masiello, G., Serio, C., Pepe, A. 2022. Change detection techniques with synthetic aperture radar images: Experiments with random forests and Sentinel-1 observations. Remote Sensing, 14, 3323. https://doi.org/10.3390/rs14143323

[40] Yan, J., Liu, J., Liang, D., Wang, Y., Li, J., Wang, L. 2023. Semantic segmentation of land cover in Urban areas by fusing multisource satellite image time series. IEEE Transactions on Geoscience and Remote Sensing, 61, 1–15. https://doi.org/10.1109/TGRS.2023.3329709

[41] Canty, M.J. 2019. Image analysis, classification and change detection in remote sensing: With algorithms for Python, 4th ed., Boca Raton: CRC Press, https://doi.org/10.1201/9780429464348

[42] Koukiou, G. 2024. SAR features and techniques for Urban planning – A review. Remote Sensing, 16, 1923. https://doi.org/10.3390/rs16111923

[43] Saidi, S., Idbraim, S., Karmoude, Y., Masse, A., Arbelo, M. 2024. Deep-learning for change detection using multi-modal fusion of remote sensing images: A review. Remote Sensing, 16, 3852. https://doi.org/10.3390/rs16203852

[44] Yuan, Q., Shen, H., Li, T., Li, Z., Li, S., Jiang, Y., Xu, H., Tan, W., Yang, Q., Wang, J., Gao, J., Zhang, L. 2020. Deep learning in environmental remote sensing: Achievements and challenges. Remote Sensing of Environment, 241, 111716. https://doi.org/10.1016/j.rse.2020.111716

Yash Mahajan*, Ajay Pal Singh, Inderjeet Singh, Suvigya Yadav, Aaryan Aneja, and Mohd. Vaqui

Fundamentals of active and passive microwave remote sensing: principles and applications

Abstract: Microwave remote sensing is widely utilized across various disciplines for Earth observation. This chapter explores both the fundamental principles and practical applications of microwave remote sensing, with a focus on the distinctions between active and passive approaches. Active microwave remote sensing, particularly radar systems, provides high-resolution, independent data that is essential for applications such as disaster monitoring, environmental mapping, and infrastructure assessment. However, its significance is comparatively lower in studies related to atmospheric analysis, oceanography, and climate monitoring, where passive microwave remote sensing is more relevant. Additionally, this chapter discusses key concepts, including the interaction of microwave radiation with the Earth's surface, and highlights the growing role of artificial intelligence in enhancing data analysis and interpretation. Furthermore, it examines the integration of microwave remote sensing with contemporary applications, particularly in addressing environmental challenges, societal issues, and technological advancements.

Keywords: Microwave remote sensing, active sensing, passive sensing, radar systems, synthetic aperture radar, radiometers, Earth observation, environmental monitoring, artificial intelligence, data analysis, climate monitoring, disaster management

***Corresponding author: Yash Mahajan**, Department of Computer Science and Engineering, Chandigarh University, Mohali, Punjab, India, e-mail: gyash724@gmail.com, ORCID: 0009-0000-2530-0366
Ajay Pal Singh, Department of Computer Science and Engineering, Chandigarh University, Mohali, India, e-mail: apsingh3289@gmail.com
Inderjeet Singh, Department of Computer Science and Engineering, Chandigarh University, Mohali, India, e-mail: er.inderjeetsingh1989@gmail.com
Suvigya Yadav, Department of Computer Science and Engineering, Chandigarh University, Mohali, India, e-mail: suvigyayadav2003@gmail.com
Aaryan Aneja, Department of Computer Science and Engineering, Chandigarh University, Mohali, India, e-mail: aryananeja41@gmail.com
Mohd. Vaqui, Department of Computer Science and Engineering, Chandigarh University, Mohali, India, e-mail: mohdvaqui002@gmail.com

https://doi.org/10.1515/9783111572970-003

1 Introduction

1.1 Overview of remote sensing

Remote sensing is the acquisition of information about an object or phenomenon without making direct physical contact with it. This process involves obtaining data from a distance through satellite or airborne sensors to detect and measure the reflected or emitted electromagnetic radiation coming from objects on Earth's surface. Important applications of remote sensing include environmental monitoring, Earth sciences, and the planning and management of urban spaces, disasters, and resources [1].

1.2 Importance of microwave remote sensing in modern applications

Microwave remote sensing has played a paramount role in the modern world in terms of penetration through clouds, vegetation, and certain soil media. This is an advantage, especially in applications where continuous data acquisition is required, such as climate monitoring, agriculture, disaster management, and military surveillance. Active microwave sensing, primarily radar systems, generates its energy source for illumination. Satellites such as Sentinel-1 are prominently used for agricultural classification [2]. Passive microwave sensing detects natural microwave radiation emitted by the Earth's surface. It is widely used in meteorology and climatology for variables such as moisture content within the atmosphere, surface sea temperature, and soil moisture content [3].

1.3 Active versus passive remote sensing: key distinctions

The applications and limitations of microwave remote sensing depend on the differences in active and passive sensing definitions. In active remote sensing, a signal is sent toward a target, and the return signal is then sensed. Examples include radar systems, such as synthetic aperture radar (SAR). These systems can measure the distance, speed, and composition of objects [4]. Active remote sensing is being used generously in terrain mapping, monitoring infrastructure, and environmental changes, such as detecting deforestation and glacier movements.

Passive systems are not energy emitters but only collectors of radiating energy, as they emanate from the Earth and rely on material properties and surface temperatures. Passive microwave sensors, including radiometers, are widely used to measure humidity, sea surface temperature, and ice coverage, as well as atmospheric and oceanographic variables. These measurements are quite vital for understanding climate trends, water cycling, and also natural calamities such as floods and droughts. Active sensors are used when the data resolution has to be high, and the data has to be independent of natural light. If measurements of naturally occurring radiation over a vast area are needed, then passive sensors are preferred.

In summary, both active and passive microwave remote sensing are essential in today's data collection efforts, each suited for different aspects of Earth observation. Active systems such as radar provide detailed high-resolution images for structural and environmental monitoring, while passive systems facilitate scientists to monitor natural emissions critical for the study of atmospheric and oceanic phenomena [5].

2 Theoretical foundations of microwave remote sensing

Microwave remote sensing is performed using microwaves from the electromagnetic spectrum within the frequency band used to observe and analyze physical and environmental phenomena on the Earth's surface. This section discusses some of the theoretical underpinnings that make microwave remote sensing a versatile and powerful tool in scientific and practical applications. Understanding the nature of microwave radiation, its interaction with the Earth's surface, and its properties of polarization and scattering forms the basis on which this technology can be designed for effective application [6].

2.1 Electromagnetic spectrum and microwave bands

The electromagnetic spectrum is a broad range of waves with different wavelengths and frequencies, spanning from the short wavelengths of gamma rays to the long wavelengths of radio waves. Different parts of the spectrum are used for various observation purposes in remote sensing. Each region of the spectrum offers unique advantages by making measurements of the relevant physical properties of the observed phenomena.

The frequency range is from 300 MHz to 300 GHz, while the wavelength spans from 1 mm to 1 m. This portion of the electromagnetic spectrum is most useful for remote sensing operations due to its good penetration through clouds and, to an appreciable extent, through vegetation and soil. The microwave band is further divided into three bands, namely L-band, X-band, and C-band, with specific benefits in remote sensing applications. X-band (8–12 GHz) and C-band (4–8 GHz) frequencies are commonly applied in radar remote sensing for higher-resolution imaging in SAR systems. With regard to these higher frequency bands, much detailed information about the surface can be obtained and is useful for applications such as urban infrastructure mapping, disaster management, and environmental monitoring.

Each microwave band interacts with the Earth's surface uniquely, depending on its wavelength and frequency, which determines the kind of information it can obtain. For instance, shorter wavelengths, or higher frequencies, are more sensitive to surface roughness as well as vegetation structure and are much less able to penetrate dense forest canopies or the ground to acquire information about subsurface properties [7]. However, longer wavelengths, or lower frequencies, penetrate deeper into the densest forest canopies or the ground, providing access to subsurface properties. Because of such differences, choosing the appropriate microwave band is a crucial decision in designing remote sensing missions.

2.2 Interaction of microwave radiation with the Earth's surface

Interaction of microwave radiation with the Earth's surface involves a set of extremely complex physical principles that define the reflection, absorption, and scattering of incoming microwave radiation depending on various parameters such as surface roughness, moisture content, or dielectric characteristics of the materials involved. Such an interaction forms the basis for the interpretation of data collected through remote sensing [8]. The dielectric constant of the material plays a significant role in this as well. The dielectric constant is essentially a measure of how strongly a substance can store electrical energy in an electric field, which influences the extent of the microwave radiation that is reflected into the sensor and absorbed.

Another factor in how microwave interaction affects a surface is its roughness. If a surface is relatively smooth compared to the wavelength of incoming microwave radiation, it will reflect most of that energy in a specular or mirror-like fashion. This effectively returns very strong, focused signals to the sensor. If the surface is relatively rough, on the other hand, it will scatter the energy in many directions, returning much weaker signals. Surface roughness is mostly evaluated in terms of the wavelength of the incident radiation, so the same surface will exhibit different responses to various wavelengths (or microwave bands), depending on the scale of its roughness. In the man-made environment, the interaction of microwaves with urban developments is also very important. Buildings and other infrastructure elements can reflect microwave radiation in complex ways through the material composition, geometry, and orientation of those buildings. This characteristic is quite significantly exploited in SAR applications, where detailed structural features of an urban landscape can be analyzed with a great deal of precision. Since microwaves can penetrate some materials, such as vegetation or thin walls, it is also possible to view features that cannot be seen because they are hidden or subsurface [9].

2.3 Scattering, reflection, and absorption mechanisms

There is scattering, reflection, and absorption of microwave radiation on the Earth's surface. These mechanisms are essential in explaining how remote sensing data is collected and interpreted. Scattering occurs when the incoming microwave radiation encounters a rough surface, meaning energy spreads in multiple directions. The degree of scattering depends on how rough the surface is compared to the wavelength of the incident radiation. In such a case, it becomes very minimal when the surface is smooth relative to the wavelength, and most of the energy is coherently reflected to the sensor. When the surface is rough compared to the wavelength, the energy scatters in all directions, which thus weakens the signal coming back to the sensor. Scattering also relies on the distribution, shape, and size of the items placed on the surface; these items can include, for example, vegetation, rocks, and buildings.

Active microwave remote sensing, particularly by radar, sends microwave pulses toward the target, after which it records the energy reflected by the target. This reflected signal carries information regarding the distance to the target and surface characteristics. The strength and timing of this reflected signal are indications of the distance and nature of the surface. If the surface is rough compared with the wavelength, it causes a diffuse reflection, where the returned signal is weak and dispersed in many directions. Specular reflection on a smooth surface leads to a strong, confined return signal [10].

This depends on the dielectric properties of the material; however, among other materials, water is one of the strongest absorbers of microwave energy. By re-emitting the absorbed energy in the form of thermal radiation, this can then be detected using radiometers. The absorbed energy can then be translated into physical properties such as moisture content or temperature. Mechanisms of scattering, reflection, and absorption determine microwave radiation's interaction with different surfaces. These are critical processes, and knowledge about their nature forms the foundation for interpreting remotely sensed data, from which meaningful information regarding Earth's surface can be teased out.

2.4 Polarization in microwave remote sensing

Polarization refers to how the electric field component of electromagnetic radiation is oriented. In microwave remote sensing, polarization also strongly influences how microwaves interact with surfaces and how they are received by sensors. The vast majority of microwave sensors can transmit and receive microwaves in both horizontally and vertically polarized states; therefore, it is possible to acquire additional information about the surfaces being monitored [11]. Microwave radiation can be polarized in various ways. It has two primary polarization states called horizontal polarization (H-pol) and vertical polarization (V-pol). In H-pol, the electric field is parallel to the Earth's surface, while in V-pol, it is perpendicular to the Earth's surface. Transmitting and receiving microwave radiation in different polarization states by a remote sensing system can retrieve more information about the properties of the surface.

Dual-polarization systems send microwaves in one polarization state and receive them in both horizontal and vertical polarizations. Quad-polarization systems can transmit and receive in both horizontal and vertical polarizations, providing even more complete information. These types of systems enable the measurement of cross-polarized returns; for example, transmitting horizontally and receiving vertically, which provides additional insights into surface roughness, vegetation structure, and other physical characteristics. Polarization is very useful in differentiating various types of surfaces and materials. In vegetation studies, the difference between horizontally and vertically polarized returns is useful for assessing the structure and density of the vegetation canopy.

3 Active microwave remote sensing

The development of active microwave remote sensing systems plays an essential role in modern Earth observation as it exploits microwave signal transmission and reception for surface property and phenomenon analysis based on a wide range of applications. Unlike the naturally emitted radiation on which passive systems rely, active microwave sensors, mainly radar systems, emit microwave pulses and record the energy returned to the sensor. They are especially useful because they can function independently of light and weather; therefore, data gathering can be done uninterruptedly under clouds and during nights.

3.1 Principles of radar systems

Radar systems, the foundational technology of active microwave remote sensing, operate by sending microwave pulses toward a target and measuring the time it takes for the returning reflected signal, or "echo," to reach the sensor. The basic principle of radar relies on the fact that microwave radiation penetrates through atmospheric particles, such as clouds, and interacts with objects on the Earth's surface. The transmitter generates a microwave pulse, which is directed toward the target. The receiver collects the reflected signal, which is then analyzed by the processor for meaningful information [12].

There are essentially two classes of radar systems used within active microwave remote sensing: the RAR and the SAR. Both have different characteristics as well as applications, though SAR has become more dominant because it offers higher resolution and versatility. Figure 1 shows how AI-based data processing can be integrated with microwave remote sensing workflows. The flowchart illustrates how AI makes signal processing more sophisticated by identifying patterns in real time as well as making predictive analytics.

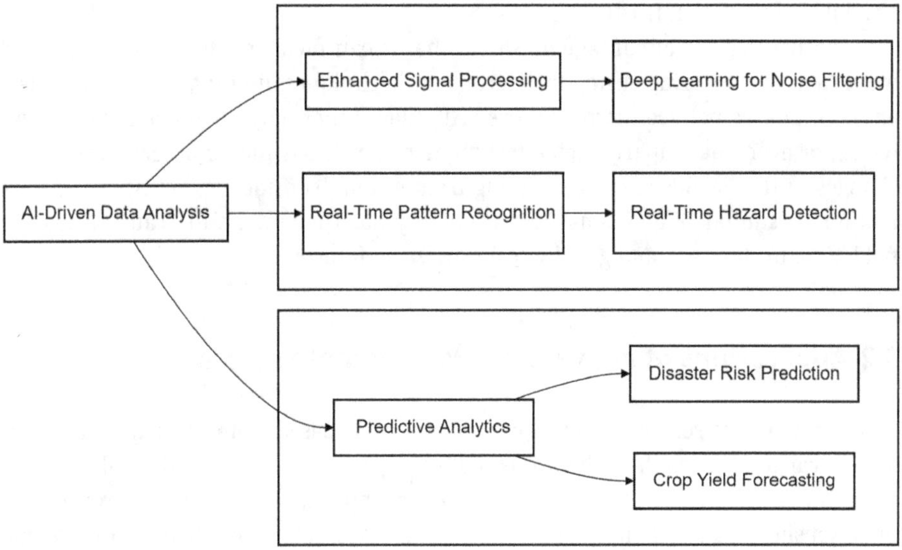

Figure 1: AI-driven data analysis for decision-making.

Real aperture radar (RAR) uses a physical antenna to receive the returned microwave signals. The resolutions of RAR are antenna size-dependent and on the wavelength of the transmitted signal. Generally, a larger antenna size gives more resolutions because the antenna discriminates better for finer details on the Earth's surface. However, there are some practical constraints regarding the size of the antenna that can be deployed for airborne or spaceborne applications [13]. RAR systems are primarily used for real-time data acquisition over large areas, for example, ship navigation, weather monitoring, and air traffic control. Such systems tend to be relatively simple in their design and operation but relatively low in resolution. The limitation of the wavelength for spaceborne systems is especially true, where it is unrealistic to deploy antennas large enough to provide the desired resolution for detailed surface mapping [14].

SAR avoids resolution limitations imposed by RAR by using advanced signal processing techniques to simulate a much larger antenna or "synthetic aperture." SAR achieves this effect by moving the radar platform; for example, a low-flying aircraft or satellite over a long flight path and recording signals reflected from the viewing scene over time. These signals are then combined to simulate the performance of a large antenna, offering very much higher resolution than could be achieved with a

RAR of equivalent size. The resolution of SAR is independent of the altitude of the platform, which makes it possible to achieve relatively high-resolution imaging from space, where it is infeasible to deploy large antennas. Under adverse weather conditions or nighttime, SAR systems can yield images of the Earth's surface with a very high degree of detail. This makes SAR a highly useful tool in applications requiring consistent, high-resolution data, such as environmental monitoring, disaster response, or analysis of urban infrastructure [15].

Another critical advantage of SAR is that it can measure the deformation and movement of the surface using interferometric techniques. InSAR analyzes the differences in phases between two or more SAR images that may have been taken days, weeks, or even years apart. Such a technique makes it possible to observe very small changes in the Earth's surface resulting from ground subsidence, landslides, glacier motion, or similar phenomena. This capability has fundamentally transformed the field of natural hazard and geophysical process monitoring.

3.2 Applications of active microwave remote sensing

Active microwave remote sensing, particularly radar-based systems, is applied across a wide range of disciplines due to its ability to provide high-resolution, all-weather data. In this section, we explore some of the key applications of active microwave remote sensing in surface monitoring, disaster management, and urban planning. One of the most essential methods for remote monitoring of the Earth's surface, and more specifically those linked to agriculture, forestry, and hydrology, is active microwave sensing [16].

Radar in agriculture is used to monitor soil moisture, health, and crop growth patterns. Being sensitive to moisture content, microwave radiation means that radar data can provide some valuable information about the availability of water for crops, thus helping in irrigation management and saving water resources. SAR is particularly useful in this context since it can penetrate cloud cover and provide consistent data throughout the growing season. In the forestry sector, radar systems are employed for mapping forest cover, biomass assessment, and deforestation tracking. SAR systems are particularly relevant in tropical zones, where heavy cloud cover consistently impedes the optical view from space. Radar data allows for the observation of fine-scale changes in the structure of forests related to losses and degradation, which is important for monitoring deforestation processes as well as the health of forests.

Remote sensing by radar is used in monitoring hydrology, including water bodies, river dynamics, and flood events. The extent of flooding can even be detected by changes in surface water levels in SAR systems, even under cloudy and rainy conditions. The ability of soil to feel moisture, together with the sensitivity of radar to surface roughness, is exploited in the ongoing monitoring of soil moisture, which is critical for understanding drought conditions or managing water resources. The ability of radar to penetrate vegetation and detect subsurface water movement is also valuable for hydrological studies [17]. Active microwave remote sensing is an essential part of the disaster management platform, as it provides quick and accurate information concerning natural hazards, even in the most inhospitable environmental conditions. Radar systems, especially SAR, are extensively applied in monitoring and in response to a wide variety of disasters, such as floods, landslides, and earthquakes.

One of the most common applications of radar remote sensing in disaster management is flood monitoring. Radar systems can penetrate clouds and rain, thus allowing real-time data on flood extent and water levels during and after floods. SAR features prominently in areas prone to flooding since it can continuously monitor flood dynamics and supply high-resolution images of affected areas. This information is very important for emergency response teams and the government in their efforts to control flood risks and minimize the effects on affected communities [18]. Active microwave technology can further be implemented to monitor landslides through detection. Here, the InSAR technique is used to identify ground deformation as well as slope instability that can lead to landslides. Several SAR images taken at different times are compared, enabling InSAR to easily detect areas of slow ground movement prone to sudden landslides. This early detection capability makes it possible to deploy mitigation measures, such as evacuation or engineering interventions, which can reduce risks to human lives and property.

Another critical application of radar systems is the monitoring and assessment of damage following an earthquake. InSAR can be used to measure ground displacement, especially that caused by seismic activity. Precise maps of the effects can thus be produced. The information obtained is useful both for determining the extent of damage to infrastructure and for understanding the geophysical processes that led to the earthquake. InSAR data are also applied to monitor fault lines and identify areas that may experience future seismic activity. In urban regions, active microwave remote sensing monitors infrastructure and evaluates land use for planning development initiatives in towns. Therefore, it is quite useful in places with high population density, where information about buildings, roads, and other features of the infrastructure is of key use in effective planning and management [19].

SAR systems are widely applied in urban infrastructure surveillance as they capture changes in the structure with the stability of buildings, bridges, and other infrastructures. InSAR technology is highly beneficial for monitoring ground subsidence and deformation that might seriously affect the safety and integrity of urban infrastructures. For example, SAR data may indicate zones of subsidence due to underground construction or natural processes, such as groundwater extraction, which may damage buildings and roads. Another application of radar remote sensing is land-use classification and the monitoring of urban growth. SAR systems are powerful at high resolution, and they can be used for mapping the accuracy of land-use/cover patterns along with the detection of changes in urban development. This information is critical to urban planners and policymakers responsible for city growth management and sustainable development.

In summary, active microwave remote sensing, notably by systems based on radar, SAR, and RAR, is highly important in a broad range of applications, from surface monitoring in agriculture and forestry to disaster management and urban planning. Its all-weather capability and high resolution make it a highly important tool in many fields, thereby contributing to more informed decisions and to understanding and managing natural and human-made environments [20].

4 Passive microwave remote sensing

In contrast to the active version, passive microwave remote sensing does not involve the transmission of microwave pulses toward a target but is instead based on the detection of natural microwave radiation emitted by the Earth's surface and atmosphere. This type of remote sensing enhances knowledge of the thermal and radiative properties of the Earth's surface and atmosphere, and its results can be applied to an extremely broad range of scientific and practical applications. Passive systems measure natural emissions over a microwave frequency range, allowing for the monitoring of critical environmental parameters such as temperature, humidity, soil moisture, and snow cover. The remaining chapter outlines the underlying principles of passive microwave sensing and explores several of its most important applications in atmospheric monitoring, oceanography, and cryospheric studies.

4.1 Principles of passive systems

The core principle of passive microwave remote sensing is the fact that microwave radiation naturally emitted from Earth's surface and atmosphere can be detected and measured. The amount and characteristics of this emitted radiation provide a means of ascertaining valuable information concerning the physical properties of the object or surface from which it originates. The naturally occurring radiation from which these measurements are derived is formed based on the measurements collected by passive microwave sensors.

4.1.1 Blackbody radiation and brightness temperature

Radiative emission by a physical blackbody is the basis of passive microwave remote sensing. A physical blackbody is an idealized body that absorbs all incident electromagnetic radiation and re-emits it according to predictable statistics across a range of wavelengths. The radiation from a blackbody varies with temperature; the hotter the object, the more it emits at shorter wavelengths. Planck's law is used to describe the relationship between the temperature of an object and the radiation it emits. It quantifies spectral radiance as a function of temperature and wavelength. In general, no natural object is a perfect blackbody. Still, many surfaces on the Earth, such as oceans, vegetation, and snow, behave similarly to blackbodies in the microwave region of the electromagnetic spectrum. This allows scientists to estimate the temperature and emissivity (the efficiency with which an object emits radiation) of these surfaces from the intensity of the radiation measured by passive microwave sensors [21].

In passive microwave remote sensing, the brightness temperature of the Earth's surface is often described in terms of the emitted radiation. Brightness temperature is defined as the measured radiative temperature of a scene by an observing sensor, and the value of which is proportional to the physical temperature of the radiating object and its emissivity. Brightness temperature is important because it allows remote sensing systems to approximate physical properties, such as soil moisture, sea surface temperature, and atmospheric humidity, by measuring the intensity of the emitted microwave radiation.

The brightness temperature sensed by a passive microwave sensor depends on the surface's material properties, the atmosphere's temperature gradient, and the sensor's viewing angle. For example, in oceanography, it can be sea surface temperature from the measured brightness temperature of the ocean surface, and in meteorology, it involves the derivation of the brightness temperature of the atmosphere in relation to the amount of water vapor within the atmosphere, cloud cover, and atmospheric temperature profiles. Due to its ability to measure these properties noninvasively and continuously, passive microwave remote sensing can be particularly useful in environmental monitoring and climate research [22]. Figure 2 illustrates the upcoming satellite missions and global monitoring programs, such as the NISAR Mission and the Sentinel-1 Program. These missions are expected to provide crucial data for monitoring global surface deformation, ecosystems, and environmental changes.

4.1.2 Passive microwave sensors: radiometers

The radiometer is perhaps the simplest remote sensor used in passive microwave remote sensing. It is highly sensitive, detecting the natural microwave radiation emitted from the Earth's surface and atmosphere. Based on the principle of finding the intensity of incoming microwave radiation, which is selected within specific frequency bands corresponding to various microwave wavelengths, a particular radiometer is chosen to achieve the best possible detection of properties in a surface or atmosphere. Radiometers are typically transported on satellites or aircraft so that continuous large-scale observations of the Earth's surface and atmosphere become possible. A radiometer essentially consists of an antenna that collects incoming radiation and a re-

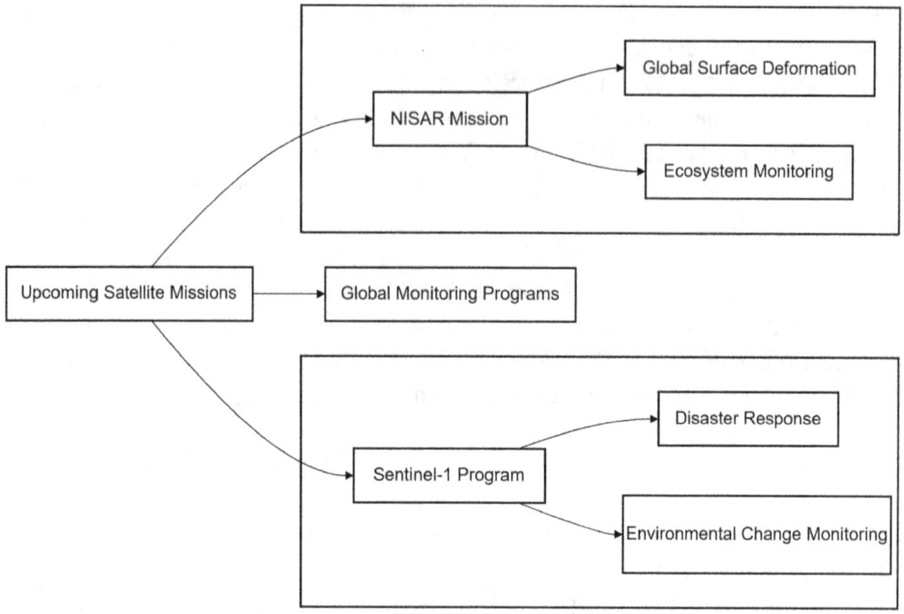

Figure 2: Upcoming satellite missions and global monitoring programs.

ceiver that converts electromagnetic energy into electrical signals. These signals are then processed to yield brightness temperature, which can then be used to infer the physical properties of the surface or atmosphere under observation. One of the main benefits of using passive microwave radiometers is their ability to operate in almost any environmental condition. Unlike optical sensors, which are affected by cloud cover or interference from atmospheric layers, the signal intensity may penetrate clouds and provide correct measurement even under adverse weather conditions. Such a capability is highly important in precipitation measurements, sea surface temperature monitoring, and analysis of snow cover, for such applications require data that should be quite accurate in terms of acquisition.

This means that passive microwave sensors can be used during both day and nighttime conditions and, therefore, offer continuous observations over Earth's surfaces. In that sense, such sensors are appropriate for long-term monitoring of environments as well as studying seasonal and interannual changes in important environmental parameters. This is accomplished by passive microwave radiometers, which are well-known from various Earth-observing missions, such as NASA's Soil Moisture Active Passive satellite and the AMSR series.

4.2 Applications of passive microwave remote sensing

Passive microwave remote sensing has a wide range of applications, spanning various domains such as atmospheric monitoring, oceanography, and the study of cryospheric environments like snow and ice. These applications leverage the unique ability of passive microwave sensors to detect naturally emitted radiation and provide critical information about the Earth's physical and environmental processes. The following section highlights some of the most important applications of passive microwave remote sensing.

4.2.1 Atmospheric monitoring: precipitation, temperature, and humidity profiling

One of the most significant uses of passive microwave remote sensing involves atmospheric monitoring, particularly in terms of precipitation and temperature profiles, as well as atmospheric humidity. This is because passive microwave radiometers are sensitive to the naturally emitted microwave radiation originating from water vapor and liquid water in the atmosphere, as well as from ice particles, thus making them very useful for atmospheric weather pattern observations and changes.

The microwave emission from hydrometeors in the form of raindrops, snowflakes, and others that constitute rainfall is very useful in determining the intensity of rainfall and its distribution. The scattering and absorption of radiation by hydrometeors make it possible to assess and detect storm systems through radiometers that are tuned to particular microwave frequencies. For instance, the GPM mission satellites employ passive microwave sensors to provide global rainfall data. These sensors are helpful in weather forecasting, flood prediction, and climate studies.

Besides precipitation, passive microwave sensors also have a variety of applications in measuring atmospheric temperature profiles and humidity. Based on the brightness temperature at a range of microwave frequencies, radiometers can monitor how the temperature and water vapor content at different altitudes change. Information of such type could be highly important for studying the vertical structure of the atmosphere and for monitoring weather phenomena like tropical cyclones, heat waves, and cold fronts. At the same time, atmospheric humidity is peculiarly one of the first drivers of weather patterns and plays a central role in the global water cycle. Passive microwave data, therefore, becomes instrumental in improving weather models and tracing the effects of climate change on the dynamics of the atmosphere. In conclusion, passive microwave remote sensing is a powerful tool for observing and monitoring a wide range of environmental processes, from atmospheric dynamics to oceanography and cryospheric changes. The ability of passive systems to detect naturally emitted radiation, even under adverse weather conditions, makes them indispensable for long-term environmental monitoring and climate research. Passive microwave sensors provide further advancements in this field by measuring critical parameters, including precipitation, temperature, humidity, sea surface temperature, salinity, snow depth, and concentration of ice.

5 Data analysis in microwave remote sensing

Data analysis is the most important step in remote sensing, where raw microwave data is converted into meaningful information for use. In microwave remote sensing, data complexity, in addition to the peculiar characteristics of microwave radiation, necessitates specific techniques for preprocessing, feature extraction, and interpretation. We will start this section by presenting the fundamental steps carried out in the microwave remote sensing data analysis pipeline. In the preprocessing step, it is necessary to remove noise, calibrate and georeference the data, and correct for terrain. Feature extraction methods include texture analysis, classification techniques, and object-based image analysis (OBIA), which is fundamental for detecting and characterizing surface features. Finally, we will address the integration of AI and ML into the discipline with an overview of how these advanced techniques alter the way microwave data is analyzed and interpreted.

5.1 Preprocessing of microwave data

Microwave remote sensing data, particularly from active systems like radar, typically require extensive preprocessing before they can be effectively analyzed. Raw data from radar systems often contain noise and distortions that must be corrected to ensure accurate interpretation. Preprocessing involves a range of steps, including noise reduction, calibration, georeferencing, and terrain correction, which are crucial for producing reliable and meaningful datasets.

5.1.1 Noise reduction and calibration techniques

Noise is one of the major problems in microwave remote sensing, and it originates from various aspects, including the sensor itself, environmental conditions, or even the interaction between microwave radiation and the Earth's surface. Speckle noise is one such problem identified in radar imagery. It is a form of granular random noise introduced due to the coherent nature of radar signals. The interference of multiple scattered signals causes this noise. Speckle noise obscures much-needed information in the data, reducing the information gathered from the images. Noise removal is one of the preprocessing pipeline tasks. Speckle filtering techniques are applied to lower the noise level with the good preservation of the important features of the image. Various filters, such as the Lee filter, Frost filter, and Gamma MAP filter, are often applied to reduce speckles in radar images. These filters apply statistical models in smoothing out noises without severely degrading the image resolution; however, one must be cautious not to allow extreme smoothing, which may cause a loss of critical spatial details.

It calibrates measured backscatter values to correct variations in sensor performance and reflect the true intensity of the microwave signals returned from the surface. The data comparison step is necessary if data from different sensors or acquisition times need to be compared because it ensures measured values are consistent. Geometric calibration corrects distortions in the spatial positioning of the data. These distortions can occur due to factors such as motion on the part of the sensor, Earth's curvature, or topographic variations. Microwave sensors, whether airborne or satellite, may also change their orientation or altitude when data is collected, thus causing misalignment between the recorded data and the true geographic location of the observed features. Geometric calibration aligns the data to a standard coordinate system so that features in a radar image can be accurately mapped to their real-world locations.

5.1.2 Georeferencing and terrain correction

Once the radar data have been denoised and calibrated, they need to be georeferenced, which aligns the data with geographic coordinates. Georeferencing is the process of transforming the raw pixel matrix of the radar image into a spatially consistent map by assigning geographic coordinates to each pixel, and this is very important for fusing the radar data with other sources of geospatial data, such as satellite imagery, GIS data, or even ground-based measurements. This georeferencing ensures that features within the radar data can be correctly overlaid and compared with other datasets, facilitating richer analysis. Traditionally, georeferencing of data generally relies on using ground control points' visible features whose geographical coordinates are known. The matchups of these GCPs in the radar image with the corresponding locations on the ground are then translated into spatial rectifications of the radar data to a given coordinate system. This transformation is often performed using affine, polynomial, or spline interpolation methods that account for the degree of distortion in the data.

Corrections for terrain also play an important role in radar remote sensing; this is critical in systems like SAR, as these changes can introduce large distortions in the radar signal. Terrain corrections address how the topography of the Earth's surface influences the nature of a radar signal, which can lead to imaging effects such as foreshortening, layover, or shadowing. These distortions occur because radar systems measure the range of a target rather than its vertical height; hence, distortions in steep terrain occur in some ways. The operation of terrain correction algorithms with DEM is possible because it allows adjustments to the radar data to remove these distortions and provide a closer representation of the Earth's surface.

5.2 Feature extraction techniques

Feature extraction is the procedure for identifying and characterizing specific surface features or patterns within the radar data. It is a critical step in the data analysis pipeline, providing vital information on different land covers, surface roughness, vegetation, the architecture of urban structures, and many other environmental features. In microwave remote sensing, advanced feature extraction techniques often depend on texture analysis, classification methods, and OBIA. Texture analysis can be an effective tool in the feature extraction of microwave remote sensing, given that radar data is often dominated by complex textural patterns characteristic of the physical properties of the observed surface. Textures refer to spatial arrangements of pixel intensities in an image, which provide information about surface roughness, vegetation density, and other structural properties.

There are several methods for texture analysis, but the most popular one is the gray-level co-occurrence matrix (GLCM). GLCM measures the frequency of pixel intensity pairs at a given distance and direction to obtain an estimate of spatial relations between pixels. Metrics for texture consist of contrast, correlation, energy, and homogeneity derived from the GLCM. These metrics measure various textural characteristics of a radar image. They can also distinguish between different surface types, such as forests, agricultural fields, or urban areas, to name but a few. Once the textural features are extracted, classification techniques are employed to categorize the radar data into several distinct land cover classes or surface types. Classification methods can be broadly divided into two categories: supervised and unsupervised approaches. Supervised classification involves using a user's known examples of different land cover types; the classification algorithm is then guided based on the training data. Common supervised classification algorithms include support vector machines, random forests, and neural networks.

In contrast to supervised classification, unsupervised classification does not use training data. Instead, it uses clustering algorithms to group pixels in the image into particular classes based on their spectral or textural properties. K-means clustering is one of the most common unsupervised algorithms, where data are partitioned into a specified number of clusters based on the similarity of the pixels. This classification is applied mostly when ground truth data are unavailable or during exploratory analyses to look for unknown patterns in the data. Artificial intelligence (AI) has revolutionized the field of remote sensing, and its integration into microwave data analysis has opened up new possibilities for automated feature extraction, pattern recognition, and decision-making. AI techniques, particularly those based on machine learning (ML) and deep learning (DL), have proven highly effective in handling the complex, high-dimensional datasets generated by microwave sensors.

In microwave remote sensing, AI techniques have recently been widely applied to improve signal processing and recognition tasks. Unlike traditional methods of signal processing, which are, in reality, effective and often based on a predefined model and assumptions about the data, the AI-based method allows the pattern to learn directly from the data and flexibly consider and adapt to the type of analysis applied.

DL algorithms, particularly convolutional neural networks (CNNs), have shown specific promise in performing tasks that involve radar signal processing. In this manner, CNNs are structured to learn automatically from spatial hierarchies of features; thus, they are quite suited for complex spatial patterns in radar imagery, for which a large amount of training data may allow the network to be configured with minimal interference from human operators to recognize patterns of buildings, roads, or vegetation. This capability is very useful for applications where very fast and accurate feature extraction is required, such as in post-disaster response or tracking of urban areas. Figure 3 presents a graphical representation of trends in sensor technology, which is rapidly advancing. The diagram categorizes these advances into the following streams: high-resolution, lightweight sensors and SAR constellations, as well as advances driven by AI, such as noise reduction algorithms and ML for data interpretation. This symbiosis is going to work together toward improving the capability of microwave remote sensing systems to collect data with greater precision, accuracy, and efficiency.

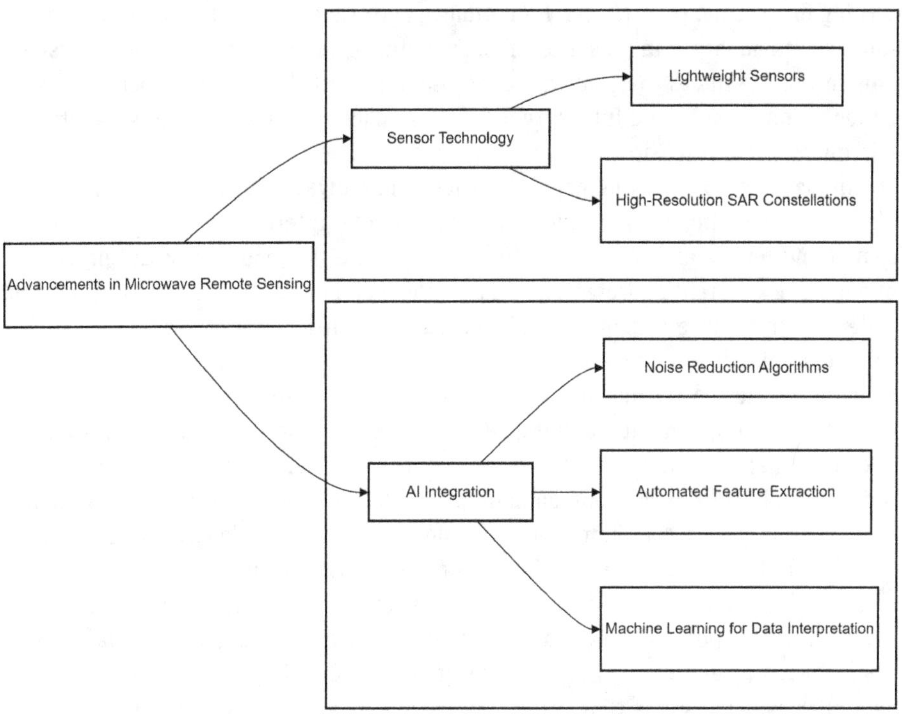

Figure 3: Advancements in sensor technology and AI integration.

AI techniques are also used to enhance pattern recognition from radar data. For instance, time-series analysis using recurrent neural networks and long short-term memory has been used to identify temporal patterns such as surface deformations, vegetation growth, or changing water levels. These methods can monitor dynamic processes such as subsidence and glacier flow where traditional static analysis falls short.

6 Challenges, limitations, and future trends in microwave remote sensing

Microwave remote sensing is both active and passive. It represents a powerful Earth observation tool with unique capabilities essential to several environmental and geophysical applications. Indeed, like any technology, it is not problem-free; atmospheric and environmental interference, among other factors, represents a challenge, as do spatial or even temporal resolution constraints and some unavailability of data concerning processing. Despite such limitations, microwave remote sensing is developing rapidly with advances in sensor technology, AI integration, and new satellite missions. This section discusses the challenges and limitations of the discipline before moving on to the innovations and future trends that are likely to shape the next generation of microwave remote sensing systems.

In Figure 4, some of the major obstacles in microwave remote sensing have been identified, including atmospheric and environmental interference, the limitations of spatial and temporal resolutions, and problems with the availability and processing of data. The different subcategories enable how detailed factors like absorption from water vapor, surface roughness, and constraints during data processing escalate the complexity in the analysis and interpretation of microwave data. This flowchart describes how these problems interplay, and it is clear why special algorithms and models need to be implemented to mitigate their effects. Without a doubt, interference is one of the major challenges encountered in microwave remote sensing, encompassing both atmospheric and environmental interference. Microwave radiation is less dependent on atmospheric conditions than radiation of shorter wavelengths, such as visible or infrared. However, some constituents of the atmosphere interact with microwave radiation, and those interactions can be quite strong in certain frequency ranges. In clouds, water vapor, oxygen, and liquid water absorb and scatter microwave radiation, which may attenuate or distort the signal. The effect is highly significant for passive microwave systems that detect the Earth's or atmospheric emitted radiation. Higher humidity environments often degrade the measurement quality, especially for lower-frequency microwave bands. This makes acquiring reliable surface properties, such as soil moisture or sea surface temperature, more challenging.

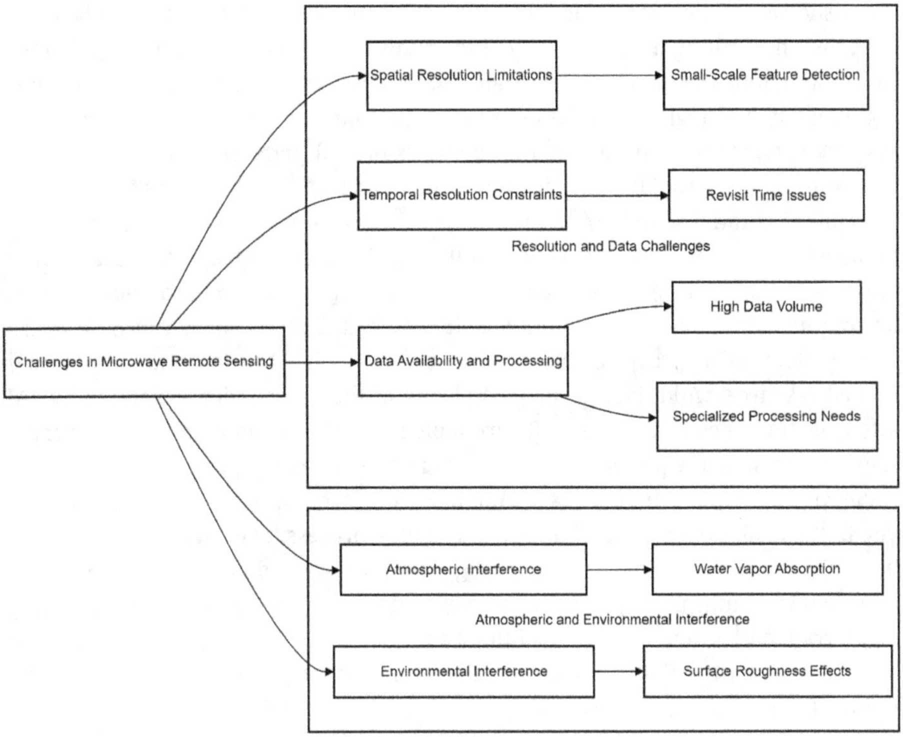

Figure 4: Overview of challenges in microwave remote sensing.

Surface roughness, vegetation, and urban infrastructure are other environmental factors that may also complicate the interpretation of microwave data. For instance, increased scattering effects caused by surface roughness may obscure the underlying characteristics of the surface being measured. Buildings and other structures in urban areas make it difficult to obtain a clear signal reflection, while also introducing distortions that make it difficult to retrieve precise data. These types of interference have resulted in developing rather complex algorithms and models. Still, they often cannot fully correct the issues, especially when interference from two or more different factors occurs simultaneously, such as in heterogeneous landscapes. Spatial and temporal resolution limitations are another significant challenge in microwave remote sensing. Microwave sensors, especially radar systems, can obtain high spatial and temporal resolution images but usually require large antennas or sophisticated signal processing techniques like SAR. The constraints of size and weight imposed by the satellite platform become problematic for spaceborne systems, especially when the antennas required for many applications cannot be made large enough to attain the desired resolutions. For instance, the resolution of radar imagery in environmental monitoring may not be high enough to capture information on small-scale features, such as the presence of individual trees or minor deformations in the land surface, thereby limiting the granularity of the analysis. Another limitation is the temporal resolution or the data collection rate. While microwave systems can operate during both day and night and in all weather conditions, the revisit time of spaceborne systems is typically restricted by the satellite's orbital path. This can result in data gaps, especially for rapidly changing phenomena such as floods or landslides.

Other limitations, aside from these physical constraints, include problems related to the availability and processing of data that might restrict the effective usage of microwave remote sensing. This means that huge storage capacity and computing power are required to handle the voluminous data output from radar and passive microwave systems. This proves a challenge to some organizations, especially those with limited resources. Additionally, the complexity of the information generated by SAR also calls for special skills and software tools for analysis. Many microwave remote sensing datasets are public and can be retrieved through space agencies such as NASA and the ESA. Although vast in number, they are not particularly user-friendly due to their inherent scale and the advanced data processing techniques that need to be applied to them. Moreover, processing raw microwave data into useful information involves multiple steps, including calibration, noise reduction, georeferencing, and terrain correction. If any one of these steps is performed incorrectly, it might introduce errors; thus, the verification of the final products to be accurate and reliable is quite time-consuming and costly.

Even with these challenges, prospects for microwave remote sensing appear bright; in many ways, new sensor technologies and AI integration will likely overcome many of the limitations of microwave remote sensing. This includes innovation, for example, in developing more compact, lightweight radar and passive microwave sensors that would enable a much greater spread of platforms, such as small satellites or unmanned aerial vehicles. These developments will improve spatial and temporal resolutions. More frequent data acquisition with better spatial resolution over the bandwidth available should alleviate both the spatial and temporal resolution limiting factors. Thus, small satellite constellations hosting SAR sensors will eventually replace some current SAR platforms and provide near-continuous global coverage at higher resolutions. This will permit more timely and detailed monitoring of environmental phenomena like deforestation, glacier retreat, and urban expansion, which are often critical for decision-makers and researchers.

As shown in Figure 5, future microwave remote sensing will be described in terms of developments in sensor technologies and AI. The next flowchart describes key developments concerning resolution capability, coverage frequency, and AI integration for analysis and decision-making. These improvements will greatly enhance microwave remote sensing's precision, efficiency, and applicability to various environmental and geophysical applications.

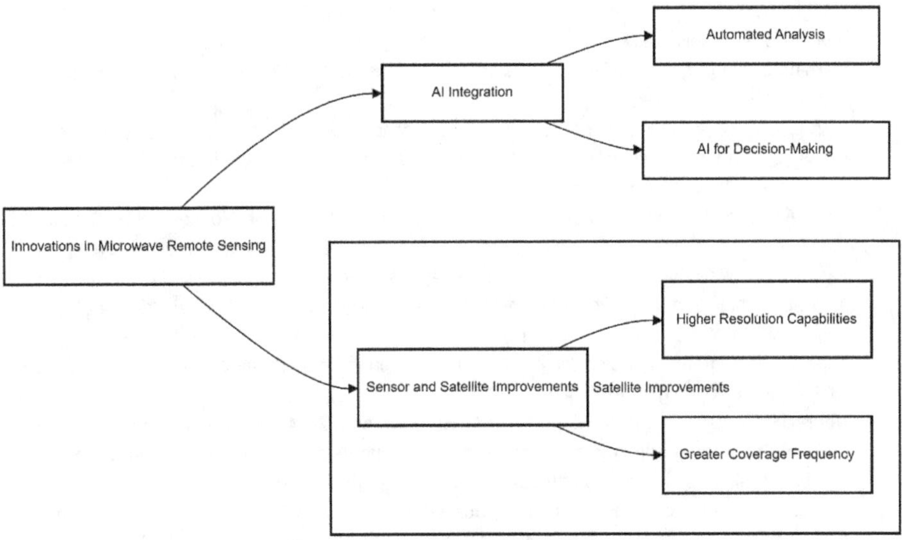

Figure 5: Innovations and future outlook.

7 Conclusion

These innovations include overcoming problems such as atmospheric interference, spatial resolution, and processing constraints. These advancements will ensure more accurate and efficient Earth observations through microwave remote sensing. This will generate precious data for environmental management, disaster response, and scientific research. As AI-driven data analysis continues to improve, the near future promises to be a powerful era for understanding and managing the complex dynamics of Earth's systems through microwave remote sensing.

References

[1] Han, W., Zhang, X., Wang, Y., Wang, L., Huang, X., Li, J., Wang, S., Chen, W., Li, X., Feng, R., Fan, R., Zhang, X., Wang, Y. 2023. A survey of machine learning and deep learning in remote sensing of the geological environment: Challenges, advances, and opportunities. ISPRS Journal of Photogrammetry and Remote Sensing, 202, 87–113. https://doi.org/10.1016/j.isprsjprs.2023.05.032

[2] Vyas, N., Sethi, G.K., Singh, S. 2024. Comparative analysis of different classifiers on fusion of sentinel datasets for agriculture land. In: 2024 4th International Conference on Technological Advancements in Computational Sciences (ICTACS). 2024 4th International Conference on Technological Advancements in Computational Sciences (ICTACS), IEEE, doi: 10.1109/ictacs62700.2024.10840995

[3] Dubey, A.K., Kumar, P., Chembolu, V., Dutta, S., Singh, R.P., Rajawat, A.S. 2021. Flood modelling of a large transboundary river using WRF-Hydro and microwave remote sensing. Journal of Hydrology (Amsterdam), 598, 126391. https://doi.org/10.1016/j.jhydrol.2021.126391

[4] Sedighi, A., Hamzeh, S., Alavipanah, S.K., Naseri, A.A., Atkinson, P.M. 2024. Ensembles of multiple models for soil moisture retrieval from remote sensing data over agricultural areas: A deep learning-based framework. Remote Sensing Applications, 35, 101243. https://doi.org/10.1016/j.rsase.2024.101243

[5] Li, Z.-L., Leng, P., Zhou, C., Chen, K.-S., Zhou, F.-C., Shang, G.-F. 2021. Soil moisture retrieval from remote sensing measurements: Current knowledge and directions for the future. Earth-Science Reviews, 218, 103673. https://doi.org/10.1016/j.earscirev.2021.103673

[6] Mladenova, I.E., Jackson, T.J., Njoku, E., Bindlish, R., Chan, S., Cosh, M.H., Holmes, T.R.H., De Jeu, R.A.M., Jones, L., Kimball, J., Paloscia, S., Santi, E. 2014. Remote monitoring of soil moisture using passive microwave-based techniques – theoretical basis and overview of selected algorithms for AMSR-E. Remote Sensing of Environment, 144, 197–213. https://doi.org/10.1016/j.rse.2014.01.013

[7] Lubczynski, M.W., Leblanc, M., Batelaan, O. 2024. Remote sensing and hydrogeophysics give a new impetus to integrated hydrological models: A review. Journal of Hydrology (Amsterdam), 633, 130901. https://doi.org/10.1016/j.jhydrol.2024.130901

[8] Nouraki, A., Golabi, M., Albaji, M., Naseri, A.A., Homayouni, S. 2024. Enhanced root zone soil moisture monitoring using multitemporal remote sensing data and machine learning techniques. Remote Sensing Applications, 36, 101354. https://doi.org/10.1016/j.rsase.2024.101354

[9] Castellanos, P., Colarco, P., Espinosa, W.R., Guzewich, S.D., Levy, R.C., Miller, R.L., Chin, M., Kahn, R.A., Kemppinen, O., Moosmüller, H., Nowottnick, E.P., Rocha-Lima, A., Smith, M.D., Yorks, J.E., Yu, H. 2024. Mineral dust optical properties for remote sensing and global modelling: A review. Remote Sensing of Environment, 303, 113982. https://doi.org/10.1016/j.rse.2023.113982

[10] Gupta, D.K., Prashar, S., Singh, S., Srivastava, P.K., Prasad, R. 2022. Introduction to RADAR remote sensing. In: Radar Remote Sensing, Elsevier, 3–27. https://doi.org/10.1016/B978-0-12-823457-0.00018-5

[11] Bizzi, S., Bozzolan, E., Marra, F., Cavalli, M. 2025. Quantifying earth surface processes via remote sensing technologies. In: Climate and Anthropogenic Impacts on Earth Surface Processes in the Anthropocene, Elsevier, 105–119. https://doi.org/10.1016/B978-0-443-13215-5.00010-3

[12] Mahanta, D.K., Bhoi, T.K., Komal, J., Samal, I., Mastinu, A. 2024. Spatial, spectral and temporal insights: Harnessing high-resolution satellite remote sensing and artificial intelligence for early monitoring of wood boring pests in forests. Plant Stress, 11, 100381. https://doi.org/10.1016/j.stress.2024.100381

[13] Luo, L., Wang, X., Guo, H. 2024. Transitioning from remote sensing archaeology to space archaeology: Towards a paradigm shift. Remote Sens Environ, 308, 114200. https://doi.org/10.1016/j.rse.2024.114200

[14] Kautz, M., Feurer, J., Adler, P. 2024. Early detection of bark beetle (Ips typographus) infestations by remote sensing – A critical review of recent research. Forest Ecology and Management, 556, 121595. https://doi.org/10.1016/j.foreco.2023.121595

[15] Merkouriadi, I., Ruiz, J.J. 2024. Monitoring snow by combining physical snow models and microwave remote sensing techniques. In: Geographical Information Science, Elsevier, 29–50. https://doi.org/10.1016/B978-0-443-13605-4.00001-1

[16] Yang, S., Huang, Q., Yu, M. 2024. Advancements in remote sensing for active fire detection: A review of datasets and methods. Science of the Total Environment, 943, 173273. https://doi.org/10.1016/j.scitotenv.2024.173273

[17] He, J., Zhang, S., Cui, X., Feng, W. 2024. Remote sensing for shallow bathymetry: A systematic review. Earth-Science Reviews, 104957. https://doi.org/10.1016/j.earscirev.2024.104957

[18] Ma, Y., Huang, X.-D., Yang, X.-L., Li, Y.-X., Wang, Y.-L., Liang, T.-G. 2023. Mapping snow depth distribution from 1980 to 2020 on the Tibetan plateau using multi-source remote sensing data and downscaling techniques. ISPRS Journal of Photogrammetry and Remote Sensing, 205, 246–262. https://doi.org/10.1016/j.isprsjprs.2023.10.012

[19] Cao, J., Luo, Y., Zhang, X., Fan, L., Tao, J., Nam, W.-H., Sur, C., He, Y., Gulakhmadov, A., Niyogi, D. 2024. Assessing the responsiveness of multiple microwave remote sensing vegetation optical depth indices to drought on crops in Midwest US. International Journal of Applied Earth Observation and Geoinformation, 132, 104072. https://doi.org/10.1016/j.jag.2024.104072

[20] Knyazkov, D. 2022. Simulation of microwave remote sensing of the Ocean. IFAC-PapersOnLine, 55, 19–24. https://doi.org/10.1016/j.ifacol.2022.09.066

[21] Yang, C., Li, Q., Hu, Z., Chen, J., Shi, T., Ding, K., Wu, G. 2019. Spatiotemporal evolution of urban agglomerations in four major bay areas of US, China and Japan from 1987 to 2017: Evidence from remote sensing images. Science of the Total Environment, 671, 232–247. https://doi.org/10.1016/j.scitotenv.2019.03.154

[22] Cao, W., Zhou, W., Yu, W., Wu, T. 2024. Combined effects of urban forests on land surface temperature and PM2.5 pollution in the winter and summer. Sustainable Cities and Society, 104, 105309. https://doi.org/10.1016/j.scs.2024.105309

Nitin Arora*, Sakshi, Kuldeep Kumar, and Abdullah Alzahrani

Comprehensive overview of active and passive microwave remote sensing satellite sensors

Abstract: With technological advancements, microwave remote sensing has become indispensable for environmental monitoring and resource management. Real-time microwave remote sensing involves the use of radar and entails the transmission of signals to obtain highly accurate information on environmental parameters such as precipitation, soil moisture, plant structure, and terrain features for accurate management. On the other hand, active microwave remote sensing requires emitted energy that bounces back and is sensed by the system. In contrast, passive microwave remote sensing is based on natural microwave emissions from the Earth's surfaces, which is very useful for measuring soil moisture and atmospheric conditions and is free from any interference from emitted signals. This chapter explains the technical prospects, working procedures, and comparatively better features of both approaches to highlight their importance in agricultural research supervision, resource management, and most importantly, sustainability. Readers will be able to learn and understand from real cases, applications, and real-world examples that demonstrate how these technologies work and can be applied to improve crop yields, optimize water use, and manage the effects of climate change.

Keywords: Microwave remote sensing, radar technology, terrain mapping, active remote sensing, passive remote sensing, resource management, sustainability

1 Introduction

Due to advancements in science and technology, there have been major changes in the quality of navigation and data analysis. Of the many fields that have been impacted by these advancements, remote sensing has greatly benefited, especially remote sensing by microwaves, which has proven to be very fundamental in obtaining significant environmental information [1]. This technology utilizes microwave signals

***Corresponding author: Nitin Arora**, Department of Computer Science and Engineering, Chandigarh University, Mohali, Punjab, India, e-mail: nitinarorask@gmail.com
Sakshi, Department of Computer Science and Engineering, Chandigarh University, Mohali, India, e-mail: sakshikauhsal329@gmail.com
Kuldeep Kumar, Department of Computer Science and Engineering, Chandigarh University, Mohali, India, e-mail: kuldeep8437@gmail.com
Abdullah Alzahrani, Oakland University, Rochester, MI, USA, e-mail: alzahrani2@oakland.edu

https://doi.org/10.1515/9783111572970-004

to make measurements and provide additional information about precipitation, soil moisture, plant structures, underlying surfaces, and more.

Microwave remote sensing can be broadly categorized into two types: active and passive. While active microwave remote sensing uses a microwave signal transmitted to the Earth's surface and reflected to be captured by the remote sensing system, passive microwave remote sensing solely depends on the emitted microwave energy from the Earth's surface. It is especially effective in monitoring the dynamics of atmospheric conditions and the degree of soil moisture without interference with emitted signals. Thus, the accuracy and timeliness of acquiring such data through these techniques are effective for agricultural management, resource assessment, and the improvement of sustainability. This chapter discusses the essential principles and real-world applications of active and passive microwave remote sensing. With a focus on practicality, the book provides examples of how these technologies can increase yields, reduce water usage, and support mitigation and adaptation to tackle climate change. By pointing out the strengths and weaknesses of one approach over the other, readers will benefit from understanding the significance of microwave remote sensing in promoting crop research and resource utilization.

2 Active microwave remote sensing

Active microwave remote sensing is an approach that involves the use of radar equipment to transmit microwaves to the Earth's surface and then evaluate the echoed signal. Active remote sensing systems emit their own signal, unlike passive remote sensing, which relies on naturally emitted or reflected energy; they are, therefore, unaffected by the seasonality of light.

2.1 Principle of RADAR

Radar, an acronym for radio detection and ranging, is an electronic system that employs radio waves to determine objects' ranges, angles, or velocities. The basic concept of radar is to emit a pulse of radio frequency (RF) energy and compute the time taken by the echo to reach the source after reflecting off an object (Figure 1) [2]. This time is combined with the speed of the radio waves, which is the speed of light, to calculate the distance to the object.

Here is a detailed breakdown of the principles of radar:

1. **Transmission:** A radar system involves the emission of short-wave front radio signals, usually at microwave frequencies. These waves are capable of penetrating

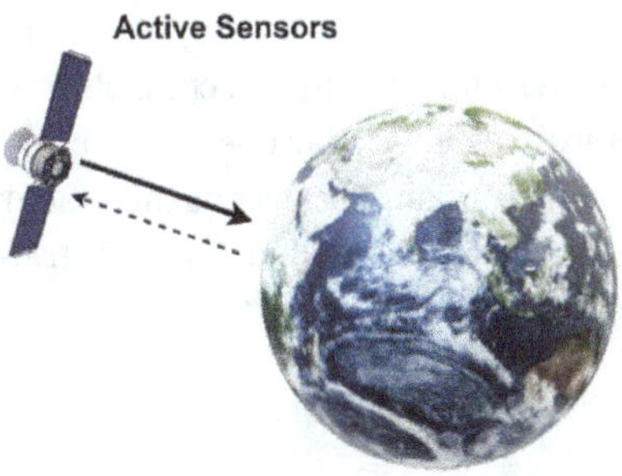

Figure 1: Illustration of a radar system, demonstrating the fundamental process of active microwave remote sensing.

through the atmosphere, clouds, rain, and other forms of weather, which makes radar appropriately suited for uses such as weather monitoring and aircraft control.

2. **Reflection:** When radio waves are directed at an object, they bounce off in every direction in which they are emitted. Regarding most of these waves, they are reflected back to the radar system involved. They, therefore, vary with the size, shape, and type of material the object is made from.
3. **Reception:** The receiver of this radar records all the reflected waves sent from the target that form the echo. Powerful techniques enhance and quantify such feeble reflections of signals.
4. **Time measurement:** The time interval that encompasses the start of the pulse emission to the rise of the echo is defined. The distance is calculated using formula (**1**). They also used the formula to determine the distance between two points of interest as follows:

$$\text{Distance} = \frac{\text{speed of light} \times \text{time delay}}{2} \tag{1}$$

   The use of division by 2 here allows for the distance that the radio waves must travel to produce the echo.
5. **Doppler effect:** If an object is moving relative to the source of the waves, there will be a variation in the signals reflected and transmitted between the two objects, known as the Doppler effect:

$$\Delta f = \frac{2v}{\lambda} \tag{2}$$

   This frequency shift helps determine the object's velocity, where Δf is the frequency shift, v is the relative velocity, and λ is the wavelength of the transmitted waves (**2**).
6. **Data interpretation:** A radar system processes the received signals and forms a picture of the scene or a representation of an object, commonly referred to as radar pictures or plots. The information provided includes reference details on the coordinates of objects and their movement, while dynamics within the given radar configuration scope are indicated [3].

Remote sensing using active microwave technology, which utilizes radar systems, has the advantage of being effective in monitoring the environment and detecting objects. By using microwave signals for transmitting and receiving, the radar does not require external light, yet it can measure distance, speed, and motion. Because of this, radar has found extensive use in several areas, such as weather identification, airport traffic control, and topographic information gathering.

2.2 RADAR equation

The given radar equation represents the received power of a signal, P_r, in a radar system. It is employed in determining the power of the signal that is transmitted through the radar system, reflected from a target, and received (refer to Figure 2) [4–6]. The equation is:

$$P_r = \frac{(4\pi)^3 R^4 K_a n_R d R_e K T_0 \gamma \delta_R}{P_t G_t G_r \lambda^2 A_z t_i} \tag{3}$$

An extended but less frequently used form of the radar equation considers additional terms, such as the Earth's surface, but does not account for receiver sensitivity and atmospheric absorption:

$$R = K_a \cdot \sqrt[4]{\frac{P_s \cdot G^2 \cdot \lambda^2 \cdot A_z \cdot t_i}{K \cdot T_0 \cdot n_R \cdot (4\pi)^3 \cdot d}} \cdot \sin\left(\frac{2\pi \cdot h_m \cdot \sin\gamma}{\lambda}\right) \cdot e^{-0.115\delta_R \cdot Re} \tag{4}$$

where (R) is the distance to the target, (K_a) is the loss factor, (P_s) is the transmitted power, (G) is the antenna gain, (λ) is the wavelength, (A_z) is the effective reflection surface, (t_i) is the pulse length, (K) is Boltzmann's constant, (T_0) is the absolute temperature (in kelvin), (n_R) is the noise figure of the receiver, (d) is the clarity factor of the display, (h_m) is the height of the reflecting surface, (γ) is the reflected beam angle, (δ_R) is the break-even factor, and (R_e) is the distance of the absorbing medium.

Explanation of additional terms: (K_a) is the loss factor, considering all system losses; (λ) is the wavelength of the transmitted signal; (A_z) is the effective reflection surface area; (t_i) is the pulse length, indicating the duration of the transmitted pulse; (K) is the Boltzmann's constant, a physical constant that relates temperature and energy; (T_0) is the absolute temperature in kelvin; (n_R) is the noise figure of the receiver, representing how much noise the receiver adds to the signal; (d) is the clarity factor of the display, related to how clearly the received signal can be displayed and interpreted; (γ) is the reflected beam angle, which affects how the signal is scattered upon reflection; (δ_R) is the break-even factor, determining the balance point where the received signal is strong enough to be useful against the background noise; and (R_e) is the distance of the absorbing medium.

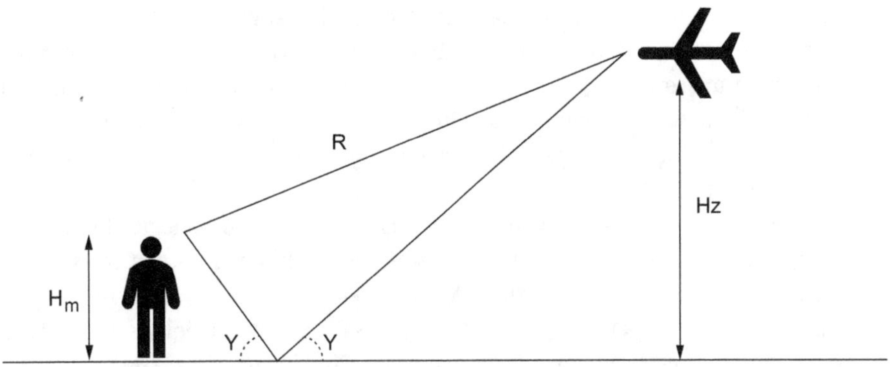

Figure 2: Detour of ground reflections.

Note: This extended radar equation provides a more comprehensive model by incorporating various practical factors that affect radar signal propagation and reception.

2.3 Applications of active microwave sensing

1. **Topographic mapping:** This is most commonly used in generating accurate digital elevation models of the Earth's surface, which involve the measurement of the phase shift of SAR images obtained from the two-imagery angle. These models are crucial in blending urban planning and development, infrastructural planning, and calamity management, as they contain important information on altitude that is useful in construction and developmental planning [7].
2. **Surface deformation monitoring:** Ground deformities due to tectonic activities can be measured using interferometric SAR techniques, and the technique is extensively used in seismology. This includes the evaluation of the changes in the Earth's surface after an earthquake with the aim of reconstructing the earthquake process or even predicting possible future earthquakes. Furthermore, radar data is useful in identifying the slope's motion and the landslide's initial phases 9 + 6, which can be useful in risk estimation and establishing an initial warning system [8]. In areas with volcanic activities, active microwave sensors capture crucial changes in the structures of volcanoes, such as the inflation and deflation of magma chambers, which are critical for eruption monitoring purposes.
3. **Vegetation and biomass assessment:** In forestry, SAR data can supplement vegetation cover to provide details such as the heights of trees, which are important in the mensuration of the forest, the number of trees, and biomass, which are crucial for the management of forests and the estimation of carbon stock. This is paramount in carrying capacity research on the distribution of species in ecosys-

tems [9]. Radar also assists in analyzing temporal changes in deforestation and forest degradation, factors that contribute to conservation and policy formulation. Active microwave sensors provide descriptions of the growth, health, and biomass of crops in agriculture, enabling farmers to adopt precision agriculture [10–12]. This includes crop evaluation, determination of potential crop yield, and regulation of water for crops.

4. **Oceanography:** Active microwave sensing is employed in oceanography to measure the sea surface height and wavelengths. Radar altimeter data of the sea surface height is used to support the work on ocean circulation, sea level fluctuations, and climatic variation. Chen et al. [13] said it was crucial for identifying ocean currents and predicting the threat of flooding in specific coastal regions. It is also important to mention that SAR systems can be applied to define the heights and direction of waves, which are necessary for ship navigation, coastal region management, and meteorological processes. Scatterometers are similar to radar instruments, but they are capable of measuring the backscatter from the ocean due to wind speed and direction. They are needed for meteorological research, climate investigations, and storm chasing, including hurricanes and cyclones.

3 Passive microwave remote sensing

3.1 Principle of passive microwave remote sensing

Passive microwave remote sensing is a process whereby microwaves emitted by the surface and atmosphere of the Earth are detected. Whereas active microwave remote sensing employs transmitting its own signal, passive systems merely receive and record the microwave energy emitted by objects [14]. Microwave radiation emitted by an object depends on the temperature of the object as well as the emissivity rating of the object. Emissivity is one of the key parameters that determine the ability of an object to radiate in comparison with a black body at the same temperature. Due to emissivity and temperature differences between different surfaces, passive microwave sensors can effectively identify different materials or states, including soil moisture, sea ice concentration, and atmospheric vapor.

Figure 3 represents the basic characteristics of passive microwave remote sensing. In this process, the Sun acts as the sole source of emitted RF energy, which is then reflected by the Earth's surface and captured by the passive sensor onboard the satellite. The collected data undergo advanced image processing through radiometric correction and spatial interpolation to accurately convert the raw RF signals into meaningful images. This ensures a precise representation of Earth's surface features, and the final image is produced accordingly. Radiometric correction is the correction of sensor data in response to deviations in sensitivity attributes related to the sensor sys-

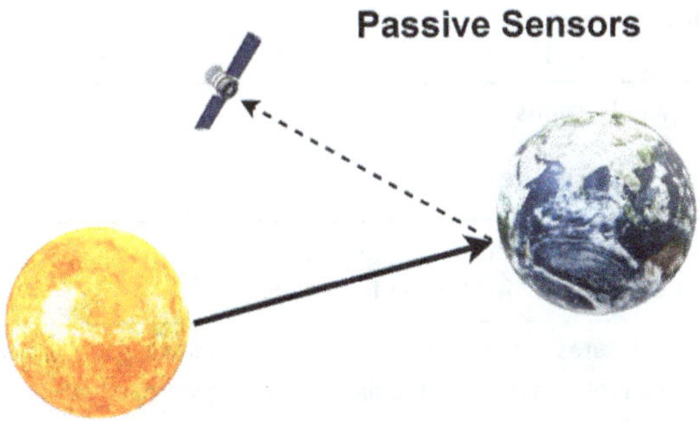

Figure 3: Illustration of a radar system demonstrating the fundamental process of passive microwave remote sensing.

tem and environmental factors within which the system operates. This process ensures that the intensity measurements obtained in one captured image reflect the real radiance of the Earth's surface, thereby providing accurate results and greater uniformity. Similarly, spatial interpolation is a process of increasing the accuracy of an image by infilling values at sample points that have not been measured. This method enhances the spatial resolution intensity of the image, thus yielding a more qualified and detailed description of the surface texture.

3.2 Types of radiometers

In passive remote sensing, the major function of a radiometer is to act as a receiver of the emitted or reflected energy from the Earth's surface or from the atmosphere [15–17]. Some of the common radiometers employed in passive remote sensing are listed in Table 1.

Table 1 shows three types of radiometers, each of which has a different purpose depending on the wavelength or frequency range. Microwave radiometers are used to measure the radiation coming from the surface of the Earth and atmosphere; hence, they are utilized in the study of precipitation phenomena and the temperature of the Earth's surface. Thermal infrared radiometers are at the heart of temperature change detection and the estimation of the gaseous content of the atmosphere. They are particularly important in analyzing heat and other related atmospheric phenomena. VNIR radiometers operate in the visible and near-infrared wavelengths and are mainly used in ecological and agricultural research. Their capacity to quantify the reflection of sunlight helps in the analysis of vegetation conditions and changes in land cover. These two radiometers can be used together to form a complete system for measuring environmental processes and helping climate science, agriculture, and environmental management by providing information based on different radiation spectra and surface characteristics.

Table 1: Different types of radiometers and their applications.

Radiometer type	Frequency range/ wavelength	Applications
Microwave radiometers	1–100 GHz	Measures Earth's surface temperature, precipitation, and conditions of land/water formations.
Infrared radiometers	3–14 μm	Measures thermal infrared emissions, which are useful for surface temperature readings, detecting warm objects, and analyzing gases in the air.
Visible and near-infrared (VNIR) radiometers	0.4–1.4 μm	Measures reflected sunlight, which is used to analyze vegetation vigor, land utilization, and surface reflective characteristics.

3.3 Applications of passive microwave remote sensing

Passive microwave remote sensors are employed for tracking the status of moisture in the topsoil layer, sea surface temperature, snow and ice, and vegetation water content, which are very critical in decision-making for agricultural practices, hydrological analysis, and climate change investigations [18]. They also help in atmospheric research by determining profiles of water vapor, cloud liquid water, and temperature, which are essential in meteorology and climate modeling. Additionally, these sensors are used in applications such as ocean salinity, land surface temperature, sea ice concentration, and precipitation estimation, thereby playing a crucial role in environmental monitoring and disaster management [19, 20].

4 Comparative analysis of active and passive microwave remote sensing

Microwave remote sensing plays a crucial role in Earth observation, and it is basically divided into two categories: active and passive remote sensing. Active microwave remote sensing is defined as the transmission of signals and the reception of backscattered signals, which include surface roughness and high-resolution movements. This capability makes it particularly suitable for uses such as the creation of topographic maps, studies of surface changes, and studies of plant cover density. On the other hand, passive microwave remote sensing involves the identification of emissions in the microwave frequency domain and is well-suited to measuring the state of the atmosphere and the hydrological cycle. This type of work is significantly useful for climate, hydrological, and environmental research [21, 22].

Table 2 highlights the key differences and applications of active and passive microwave remote sensing:

Table 2: Differences between active and passive remote sensing.

Aspect	Active microwave remote sensing	Passive microwave remote sensing
Principle	Emission and detection of backscattered signals	Detection of naturally emitted microwave radiation
Types of sensors	Synthetic aperture radar (SAR) and scatterometers	Radiometers
Control	Control over a signal's frequency, polarization, and timing	Depends on the frequency and intensity of natural emissions
Topographic mapping	High-resolution surface mapping using interferometric SAR	Not applicable
Surface deformation	Monitoring earthquakes, landslides, and volcanic activity	Not applicable
Vegetation analysis	Assessing vegetation structure and biomass	Estimating crop conditions and moisture content.
Oceanography	Measuring sea surface height, wave patterns, and wind speed	Observing sea surface temperatures and oil spills
Climate studies	Limited to indirect applications	Monitoring atmospheric parameters such as temperature and humidity
Hydrology	Not directly applicable	Measuring soil moisture, snow cover, and ice extent
Environmental monitoring	Limited to surface characteristics	Observing changes in sea surface temperature and environmental anomalies

Although passive and active microwave remote sensing techniques are very different from one another, they are both important due to their particular abilities and disadvantages. This makes active systems suitable for obtaining well-defined surface data required in topographic mapping, measuring surface deformation, and surveying vegetation cover. Passive systems should be employed to monitor the condition of the atmosphere as well as the hydrosphere. More importantly, they hold significant value in climatology trends, hydrology, and other environmental studies.

5 Image processing in remote sensing

Image processing involves several steps that take place in a given sequence, one after another, to ultimately produce the desired result (refer to Figure 4). The steps are explained in detail below:

Step 1. **Data collection:** This process begins when the electromagnetic radiation emitted by the Earth's surface is received as signals by the sensors on the satellite. Radiometers on the satellite just measure the emitted or reflected radiation at other bands of wavelengths. This raw data serves as the source for subsequent data processing.

Step 2. **Data collection: Preprocessing: Radiometric correction** assists in addressing issues with parameters influenced by the atmosphere and obtaining real radiance values, as the sensitivity of the sensor may be altered. Also timely, geometric correction alters the orientation of spatial data to conform to a map or coordinate system in order to reduce distortion caused by satellite movement, the Earth curvature, and actual terrain [23].

Step 3. **Data collection: Image construction:** Cubic interpolation in the spatial dimension helps increase the image's resolution because it interpolates any missing areas or coordinates with an estimated value. **Filtering** then removes all the noise and other unwanted features obtained during data acquisition, enhancing the quality and precision of the images.

Step 4. **Data collection: Data calibration:** The process of **conversion to radiance** standardizes raw digital numbers and quantitatively transforms these numbers back into true radiance values. Normalization, in its simplest form, is used to scale the values of various sensors at different time points to the same range.

Step 5. **Data collection: Image generation:** In **image formation**, the data acquired in various bands are fused in such a manner as to produce an integrated picture of the Earth's surface. There are also additional tools that assist in the above visual analysis, and they are visualization tools that include the contrast control and color vision to bring out certain aspects to aid in the analysis.

Step 6. **Data collection: Analysis and interpretation:** Feature extraction considers tiny areas of the image for features like vegetation cover or water bodies. This is then followed by **classification**, where the pixels are grouped into different land cover types or other suitable classes, with the final output being a thematic map suitable for uses such as decision-making on land use, among other uses.

Step 7. **Data collection: Output:** The last one generates the image, which is then stored along with the computational process and classification as a final product. This is also useful for some purposes, ensuring that the data feeding into the analysis is sufficient for the task [24–26].

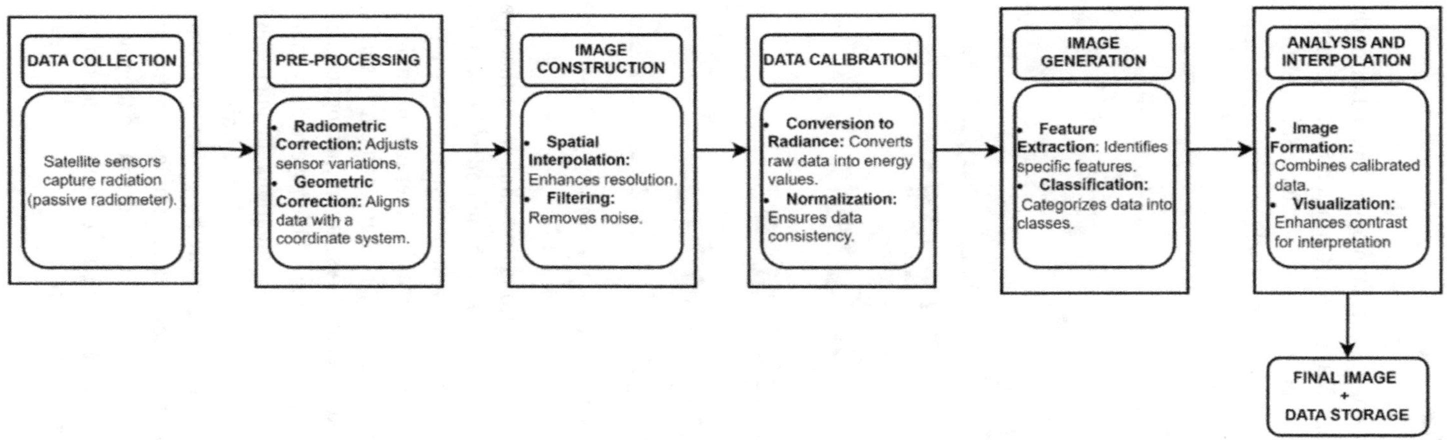

Figure 4: A flowchart showing the key steps in passive remote sensing image processing, from data collection to final image generation and analysis.

6 Challenges and limitations

Every system has its own flaws, and the ever-changing technology discussed throughout the chapter also has its own shortcomings. Many shortcomings have been eradicated with the change of era, but still there is room for improvement. Some of these fields requiring research and development are mentioned below:

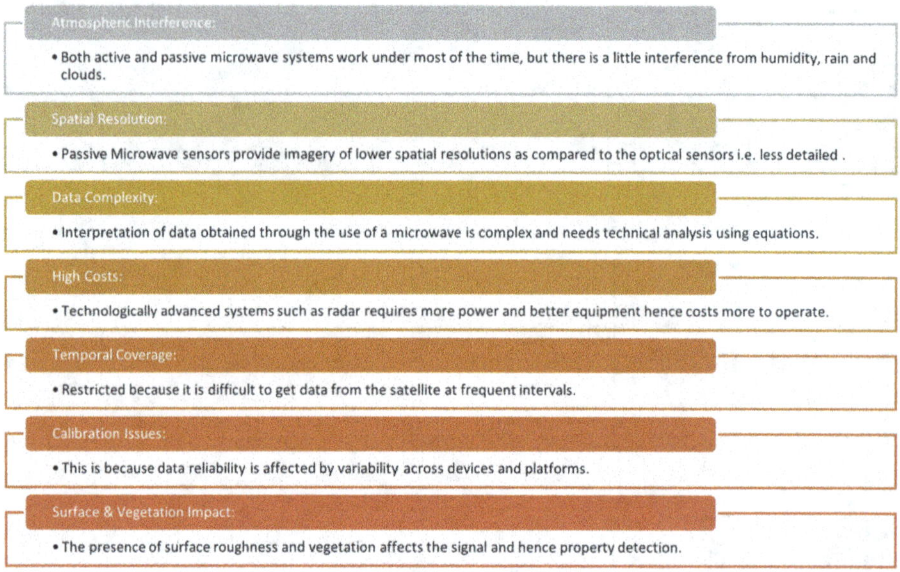

Figure 5: Limitations and challenges in active and passive microwave remote sensing.

Figure 5 also provides an overview of several limitations and challenges that are characteristic of microwave remote sensing systems. One of the major issues is atmospheric interference, which is less pronounced in active and passive microwave systems than humidity, rain, or cloud cover. However, it is still vulnerable to environmental conditions, thereby affecting the data quality. Another problem is spatial resolution; passive microwave systems have lower spatial resolution than optical sensors, which result in reduced image quality [27]. Furthermore, microwave data analysis is not easy and needs expertise and involves the use of equations for microwave data analysis. This can be a drawback for those who are not specifically trained in the field. Another challenge is the high operating costs, especially for active microwave systems such as radar. These systems require more power and complex instruments, and are therefore expensive to operate and maintain [28]. Moreover, due to the revisit times of satellites, temporal coverage is often limited, making it difficult to get continuous data, especially for real-time monitoring of certain areas.

Another major issue is calibration because different microwave systems from different manufacturers yield different results. When "uniformity" has to be met across devices, let alone ones that cannot share a common platform, the veracity of the data is potentially at risk. Another limitation of microwave remote sensing systems is the large amount of data produced, particularly when large areas are being imaged with relatively coarse resolution. The roughness of the surface and the vegetation can make it even worse by adding noise that interferes with the detailed physical features of the surface in question. Of the two, vegetation poses a major challenge to the correct interpretation of surface properties since it interferes with the correct reading of the surface [29]. All these problems make microwave remote sensing a difficult task in accurately measuring environmental parameters. These challenges can only be overcome with the help of development in the field of technology, improvements in calibration techniques, and improvements in data processing to obtain satisfactory reliability and efficiency of microwave remote sensing under different conditions.

7 Future trends and development

There has always been a need for innovation in technology; microwave remote sensing still has the potential to become well-developed in the future. Some of the trends seem to be toward making sensors smaller and more sensitive in the future to take even more precise readings. These enhancements are expected to increase the accuracy of active and passive microwave sensing for better measurement of the Earth's surface and atmosphere [30]. In the area of passive microwave sensing, advances in the development of radiometers mean that it will be possible to receive signals with higher sensitivity and thus measure such small changes in the environment as the amount of moisture in the ground or the thickness of sea ice. This will be exceptionally helpful for climate assessments and ecological preservation, especially in areas where data is inadequate or challenging to explore.

Due to the growing incidence of disasters, synthetic aperture radar (SAR), under active microwave sensing, is expected to be applied more frequently. Improved data processing procedures and sophisticated learning tools are projected to augment the analysis of SAR data so that more profound changes in land use, vegetation, and infrastructure can be identified and closely monitored [31]. Furthermore, combining SAR with other remote sensing systems, including optical and thermal imagery, will offer a better understanding of multifaceted environmental processes. The future will also demand real-time information processing and application. Developments in cloud computing and artificial intelligence to enhance the current real-time interpretation of microwave remote sensing will further develop to offer near real-time interpretation, enhancing instant decision-making across various sectors, including disaster management, farming, and city planning.

Finally, the launch of small satellites, along with the availability of microwave remote sensing data at lower prices and through open sources, will enhance the usage of this technology. This will enable everyone, from scientists to policymakers to the general public, to harness microwave remote sensing for their numerous uses [32]. To sum up, the prospects of microwave remote sensing are rather active, and further research and development of the technology will improve the characterization of the field and expand its applications in various scientific disciplines.

8 Conclusion

Microwave remote sensing, which includes both active and passive sensors, has become one of the key tools of Earth observation and plays an important role in various fields, including agriculture, the environment, oceans, and disasters. This chapter explores the principles, techniques, and various implementations of these remote sensing technologies, as well as their importance and viability in practical contexts.

Whenever radar is concerned, particularly when using SAR or scatterometer, microwave remote sensing is highly active and effective in observing the Earth's surface and detecting shifts in the surface and vegetation structure. Radar has been described using the radar equation and Doppler effect as principles that make this type of measurement accurate in terms of distance, speed, and movement, thus strengthening the technology. On the other hand, passive microwave remote sensing utilizes naturally emitted microwave radiation to gather important information about the state of the atmosphere and the hydrological cycle. While this approach is not characterized by a high level of signal control, it is effectively used in various applications, including soil moisture measurement, sea surface temperature monitoring, and observing atmospheric parameters. The role played by radiometers in sensing emissions across different spectra has been emphasized, and the significance of passive sensing in climate and environmental research has also been explained.

This chapter demonstrates the necessity of dividing and comparing the two types of microwave remote sensing: passive and active. Nevertheless, active systems can display highway data and are useful for performing structural and surface investigations; at the same time, passive systems can provide a significant amount of information concerning the environment and climate. Combining both approaches is not only feasible but also desirable, as they offer a more holistic view of the Earth systems. The proposed method enhances the information and application of both techniques due to their complementarity, enabling more effective decisions in agriculture, resource management, and disaster response. Additionally, advancements in methodologies have enhanced the reliability and utilization of data obtained through microwave remote sensing through improvements such as radiometric and geometric corrections. These processes make it possible to convert the readings recorded by the sensors into meaningful, accurate, and ready-to-use data for numerous scientific and practical fields.

In conclusion, microwave remote sensing represents an interaction of technology, science, and application that is important in the quest to understand the planet, as demonstrated in this study. As with other constantly evolving issues such as climate change, resource scarcities, and environmental degradation, microwave remote sensing aids in the provision of enhanced, timely, and effective data. This chapter is more than just an introduction but rather a guide for readers to help them grasp how these potential technologies can be used to improve our understanding of various domains and create a better and sustainable world.

References

[1] Carver, K.R., Elachi, C., Ulaby, F.T., 1985. Microwave remote sensing from space. Proceedings of the IEEE 73, 970–996. https://doi.org/10.1109/PROC.1985.13230

[2] Tuia, D., Ratle, F., Pacifici, F., Kanevski, M.F., Emery, W.J. 2009. Active learning methods for remote sensing image classification. IEEE Transactions on Geoscience and Remote Sensing, 47, 2218–2232. https://doi.org/10.1109/TGRS.2008.2010404

[3] Lee, J.-S., Miller, A.R., Hoppel, K.W. 1994. Statistics of phase difference and product magnitude of multi-look processed Gaussian signals. Waves in Random Media, 4, 307–319. https://doi.org/10.1088/0959-7174/4/3/006

[4] Isa Bakare, B., Ajaegbu, M. n.d.. A comprehensive review of radar system technology.

[5] Li, H.-J., Kiang, Y.-W. 2005. Radar and Inverse Scattering. In: The Electrical Engineering Handbook, Elsevier, 671–690. https://doi.org/10.1016/B978-012170960-0/50047-5

[6] Xiao, L., Xie, Y., Gao, S., Li, J., Wu, P. 2022. Generalized radar range equation applied to the whole field region. Sensors, 22, 4608. https://doi.org/10.3390/s22124608

[7] Prashar, S., Tiwari, U.K., Singh, S. 2022. Review of microwave fundamentals and its applications. In: Radar Remote Sensing, Elsevier, 65–89. https://doi.org/10.1016/B978-0-12-823457-0.00010-0

[8] Lee, J.S., Jurkevich, L., Dewaele, P., Wambacq, P., Oosterlinck, A. 1994. Speckle filtering of synthetic aperture radar images: A review. Remote Sensing Reviews, 8, 313–340. https://doi.org/10.1080/02757259409532206

[9] Dahiya, N., Singh, G., Gupta, D.K., Kalogeropoulos, K., Detsikas, S.E., Petropoulos, G.P., Singh, S., Sood, V. 2024. A novel deep learning change detection approach for estimating spatiotemporal crop field variations from Sentinel-2 imagery. Remote Sensing Applications, 35, 101259. https://doi.org/10.1016/j.rsase.2024.101259

[10] Akash, M., Mohan Kumar, P., Bhaskar, P., Deepthi, P.R., Sukhdev, A. 2024. Review of estimation of soil moisture using active microwave remote sensing technique. Remote Sensing Applications, 33, 101118. https://doi.org/10.1016/j.rsase.2023.101118

[11] Vyas, N., Sethi, G.K., Singh, S. (2024) Comparative analysis of different classifiers on fusion of sentinel datasets for agriculture land. In 2024 4th International Conference on Technological Advancements in Computational Sciences (ICTACS). 2024 4th International Conference on Technological Advancements in Computational Sciences (ICTACS), IEEE. doi:10.1109/ictacs62700.2024.10840995

[12] Yang, S., Huang, Q., Yu, M. 2024. Advancements in remote sensing for active fire detection: A review of datasets and methods. Science of the Total Environment, 943, 173273. https://doi.org/10.1016/j.scitotenv.2024.173273
[13] Chen, F., Liu, L., & Guo, F. (2019). Sea Surface Height Estimation with Multi-GNSS and Wavelet Denoising. Scientific Reports, 9(1), 15181. https://doi.org/10.1038/s41598-019-51802-9
[14] Njoku, E.G. 1982. Passive microwave remote sensing of the earth from space – A review. Proceedings of the IEEE, 70, 728–750. https://doi.org/10.1109/PROC.1982.12380
[15] Idso, S.B. 1974. The calibration and use of net radiometers. 261–275. https://doi.org/10.1016/S0065-2113(08)60873-1
[16] Nikolaev, V.A., Ilić, R. 1999. Etched track radiometers in radon measurements: A review. Radiation Measurements, 30, 1–13. https://doi.org/10.1016/S1350-4487(98)00086-9
[17] Price, R.M. 1976. 3.1. Radiometer Fundamentals, 201–224. https://doi.org/10.1016/S0076-695X(08)60687-0
[18] Dahiya, N., Singh, S., Gupta, S., Rajab, A., Hamdi, M., Elmagzoub, M., Sulaiman, A., Shaikh, A. 2023. Detection of multitemporal changes with artificial neural network-based change detection algorithm using hyperspectral dataset. Remote Sensing (Basel), 15, 1326. https://doi.org/10.3390/rs15051326
[19] Aguilar, M.A., Aguilar, F.J., del Mar Saldaña, M., Fernández, I. 2012. Geopositioning accuracy assessment of GeoEye-1 panchromatic and multispectral imagery. Photogrammetric Engineering & Remote Sensing, 78, 247–257. https://doi.org/10.14358/PERS.78.3.247
[20] Legleiter, C.J., Roberts, D.A., Marcus, W.A., Fonstad, M.A. 2004. Passive optical remote sensing of river channel morphology and in-stream habitat: Physical basis and feasibility. Remote Sensing of Environment, 93, 493–510. https://doi.org/10.1016/j.rse.2004.07.019
[21] Jia, J., Sun, H., Jiang, C., Karila, K., Karjalainen, M., Ahokas, E., Khoramshahi, E., Hu, P., Chen, C., Xue, T., Wang, T., Chen, Y., Hyyppä, J. 2021. Review on active and passive remote sensing techniques for road extraction. Remote Sensing (Basel), 13, 4235. https://doi.org/10.3390/rs13214235
[22] Toth, C., Jóźków, G. 2016. Remote sensing platforms and sensors: A survey. ISPRS Journal of Photogrammetry and Remote Sensing, 115, 22–36. https://doi.org/10.1016/j.isprsjprs.2015.10.004
[23] Fagan, M.E., DeFries, R.S. 2024. Remote sensing and image processing. In: Encyclopedia of Biodiversity, Elsevier, 432–445. https://doi.org/10.1016/B978-0-12-822562-2.00060-8
[24] Abdullah, H.M., Mohana, N.T., Khan, B.M., Ahmed, S.M., Hossain, M., Islam, K.S., Redoy, M.H., Ferdush, J., Bhuiyan, M.A.H.B., Hossain, M.M., Ahamed, T. 2023. Present and future scopes and challenges of plant pest and disease (P&D) monitoring: Remote sensing, image processing, and artificial intelligence perspectives. Remote Sensing Applications, 32, 100996. https://doi.org/10.1016/j.rsase.2023.100996
[25] Jiang, S., Zhi, X., Zhang, W., Wang, D., Hu, J., Chen, W. 2021. Remote sensing image fine-processing method based on the adaptive hyper-Laplacian prior. Optics and Lasers in Engineering, 136, 106311. https://doi.org/10.1016/j.optlaseng.2020.106311
[26] Wu, Y., Zhao, Q., Li, Y. 2022. Top-to-down segment process based urban road extraction from high-resolution remote sensing image. Progress in Oceanography, 25, 851–861. https://doi.org/10.1016/j.ejrs.2022.08.004
[27] Prudente, V.H.R., Martins, V.S., Vieira, D.C., Silva, N.R.D.F.E., Adami, M., Sanches, I.D. 2020. Limitations of cloud cover for optical remote sensing of agricultural areas across South America. Remote Sensing Applications, 20, 100414. https://doi.org/10.1016/j.rsase.2020.100414
[28] Eckerstorfer, M., Bühler, Y., Frauenfelder, R., Malnes, E. 2016. Remote sensing of snow avalanches: Recent advances, potential, and limitations. Cold Regions Science and Technology, 121, 126–140. https://doi.org/10.1016/j.coldregions.2015.11.001
[29] Babin, M., Bélanger, S., Ellingsen, I., Forest, A., Le Fouest, V., Lacour, T., Ardyna, M., Slagstad, D. 2015. Estimation of primary production in the Arctic Ocean using ocean colour remote sensing

and coupled physical–biological models: Strengths, limitations and how they compare. Progress in Oceanography, 139, 197–220. https://doi.org/10.1016/j.pocean.2015.08.008
[30] Zhu, L., Suomalainen, J., Liu, J., Hyyppä, J., Kaartinen, H., Haggren, H. 2018. A review: Remote sensing sensors. In: Multi-Purposeful Application of Geospatial Data, InTech, https://doi.org/10.5772/intechopen.71049
[31] Goodman, R. 1994. Overview and future trends in oil spill remote sensing. Spill Science and Technology Bulletin, 1, 11–21. https://doi.org/10.1016/1353-2561(94)90004-3
[32] Tomsett, C., Leyland, J. 2019. Remote sensing of river corridors: A review of current trends and future directions. River Research and Applications, 35, 779–803. https://doi.org/10.1002/rra.3479

Syna and Hardik Dhiman*

Essentials of RADAR remote sensing and AI integration

Abstract: This chapter provides a foundational understanding of the integration between radio detection and ranging (RADAR) remote sensing and artificial intelligence (AI). It begins with fundamental RADAR concepts, including system classifications, data acquisition techniques, and signal processing. The chapter explores the role of AI in processing and interpreting remote sensing data, discussing various machine learning and deep learning approaches used to enhance RADAR-based analytics. This chapter evaluates AI's benefits and limitations in RADAR applications, focusing on computational efficiency, data accuracy, and operational challenges. The chapter discusses key applications in environmental monitoring, including deforestation assessment, flood detection, urban mapping, and agricultural advancements such as precision farming and pest control. By outlining the synergy between RADAR and AI, this chapter outlines how these technologies contribute to more efficient and accurate remote sensing solutions.

Keywords: Environmental monitoring, agricultural applications, data acquisition, flood mapping, crop monitoring, pest detection

1 Introduction

Radio detection and ranging (RADAR) remote sensing and artificial intelligence (AI) significantly enhance the Earth observation and data analysis. This chapter provides an overview of RADAR remote sensing technology, the transformation brought about by AI to further enhance RADAR's capabilities, and the importance of integration for various applications.

1.1 Overview of RADAR remote sensing

RADAR remote sensing is a way of measuring objects on the surface using microwave signals [1]. The basic concept involves the emission of a series of radio waves that are reflected by the surface and captured by the sensor. RADAR systems measure the

Corresponding author: Hardik Dhiman, Department of Mechanical Engineering, National Chung Cheng University, Minxiong, Chiayi, Taiwan, e-mail: hardik.dhiman29@gmail.com
Syna, Department of Mechanical Engineering, National Chung Cheng University, Taiwan, e-mail: syna200502@gmail.com

https://doi.org/10.1515/9783111572970-005

time it takes for signals to return and their strength to determine the distance, speed, and characteristics of targets [2, 3]. RADAR remote sensing can operate independently of weather and lighting conditions. While optical sensors rely on visible light, RADAR can see through clouds, fog, and precipitation, making it ideal for prolonged observation in adverse weather conditions [4]. This capability is essential for applications in adverse weather conditions or during natural disasters. RADAR systems are used in various fields, such as mapping [Dingle 5], topographic mapping, environmental study, and rescue operations. For instance, synthetic aperture radar (SAR) generates high-resolution imagery of the Earth's surface to obtain precise information about land cover, ground deformation, and vegetation structure. RADAR technology also identifies various atmospheric conditions, from precipitation and storms to meteorology and climatology.

1.2 The role of AI in remote sensing

Machine learning (ML) and deep learning (DL) are subfields of AI that have significantly boosted the efficiency of RADAR remote sensing [6]. Combining these technologies improves data processing efficiency and decision-making across multiple domains. Classification algorithms, including support vector machines (SVMs) and random forests, have been applied to classify RADAR data and distinguish various land cover types, including forests, urban areas, and water classes [7, 8]. These algorithms learn from labeled training data, which can assist in making predictive conclusions about other new, unlabeled data. In this case, they are used to classify and analyze RADAR images autonomously. RADAR data analysis has progressed to the next phase of digital evolution by employing deeper and more developed forms of ML, referred to as DL. One such example is convolutional neural networks (CNNs), more specifically, which recognize spatial patterns and features in RADAR images. For instance, CNNs have been applied to solve different problems, including the detection of land subsidence, mapping deforestation, and identification of infrastructure damage. The use of AI for RADAR data is also useful for creating other enhanced analytical tools, including the changes in detection systems and predictive models. These tools can detect ongoing environmental changes, assess natural disaster impacts, and forecast future events, making them useful for development strategies and emergency operations.

1.3 Importance of RADAR data in modern AI applications

In the agriculture sector, AI integrated with the analysis of RADAR data can enhance precision farming, which involves assessing the crop's health, the expected yield, and the detection of attacks by pests [9]. This capability makes it easier to target the right people and areas of need, ensuring efficient use of resources for improved agricultural productivity. Another method involves using an image fusion-based framework for detecting agricultural changes with the incorporation of optical and microwave satellite data [10]. Natural hazard identification and assessment in disaster management are enhanced by the application of RADAR and AI [11]. For example, using coordinates from RADAR data, AI algorithms can measure floods and landslides, determine the extent of earthquake effects, and provide real-time details to support rescue and recovery endeavors. In terms of defense, AI in RADAR systems provides more effective monitoring and tracking and, inherently, target identification. Real-time RADAR data analysis improves threat detection and supports informed command decisions [12].

In general, the combination of RADAR remote sensing with AI is an innovative step forward in the area of remote sensing and data analysis. Combining the two methods provides more opportunities to extract valuable and useful information from the described RADAR model environments and achieve better results in a vast majority of applications [13]. When we take a closer look at the opportunities and risks of this integration further, it is expected that the integration of RADAR and AI systems will contribute to innovations and improvements in the ways we explore and explain the world.

2 RADAR remote sensing fundamentals

The RADAR remote sensing technology is one of the most important tools for the Earth observation and environmental surveillance. This section introduces the basic operation of acquiring data through the remote sensing technology employed in RADAR systems, together with the general types of systems. Before considering its potential when combined with AI, it is necessary to comprehend these fundamentals.

2.1 Basic principles of RADAR

RADAR stands for radio detection and ranging [14]. This is a remote sensing technique whereby objects on the Earth's surface are identified and characterized by transmitting electromagnetic waves, typically in the microwave part of the spectrum. The sensor calculates target distance, location, and characteristics from signal delay and strength. The major strength of RADAR is its versatility; RADAR operates effectively independent of the state of darkness [15]. In contrast to optical sensors that require light, whether natural or artificial, RADAR can probe through clouds, rain, and even some densities of vegetation and deliver similar data every time. This makes RADAR exceptionally useful in applications in areas that frequently experience cloudy skies or during serious turbulent weather conditions. The second important aspect of RADAR is its dependence on surface roughness and specific dielectric constants [16, 17]. Resonance frequency and phase can be analyzed to extract information about texture, moisture levels, and the general structure of the surface under observation. This capability is important in soils, moisture measurement, forest structure, and urban classification.

2.2 Types of RADAR systems

RADAR systems can be classified into various types based on the mode of operation, platform, and frequency band in use. The two main modes are imaging and non-imaging RADAR. SAR is one of the examples, and it is extensively utilized in remote sensing applications on the imaging front [18]. As the sensor moves, sequential radar pulses create a synthetic aperture for high-resolution imaging. The technique is promising in enhancing capabilities for observation toward detailed interpretation of the Earth's surface features. SAR systems are increasingly popular in different applications, ranging from topographic mapping, which requires fine elevation data, to disaster monitoring, which is concerned with damage assessment in areas affected by floods, earthquakes, or landslides. In addition, SAR studies address numerous environmental issues, such as changes in deforestation, glacier dynamics, and soil moisture estimates; hence, it is a technology of great importance for modern remote sensing and geospatial analysis.

Non-imaging RADAR is not primarily concerned with detailed imagery but rather with detecting the presence, distance, and speed of objects. Examples of such systems include weather RADAR systems tracking precipitation and Doppler RADAR used in the enforcement of traffic speed [19]. While non-imaging RADAR is not typical for detailed Earth observation, it plays an important role in meteorology, aviation, and military operations. Based on the carrying platform, these systems can be classified as airborne, spaceborne, and ground-based. Airborne RADAR systems, mounted on aircraft, are utilized when higher-resolution data is needed over certain areas and for small-scale applications such as topographic mapping and environmental monitoring. Spaceborne RADAR refers to radar devices installed on satellites that provide global coverage and are highly required in wide range of applications such as climate monitoring and disaster management. It also encompasses landslide and infrastructure-related studies with the use of ground-based RADAR systems.

Another critical factor involves the frequency band of the RADAR system, as various frequencies have different penetration capabilities and sensitivities. Common frequency bands involved in remote sensing include L-band, C-band, X-band, and S-band [20]. Due to its longer wavelength, L-band RADAR can penetrate vegetation and thus has been widely applied in forestry and soil moisture studies. C-band typically finds application in disciplines that require imagery in any weather, such as meteorology and oceanography. X-band RADAR offers high resolution, although it is primarily applied in military and urban applications. S-band RADAR has a moderate wavelength and, therefore, finds common application in weather RADAR systems. Figure 1 shows various types of RADAR systems.

2.3 Data acquisition and processing

The acquisition and processing of RADAR data is a complex process, with many steps involved in transforming raw signal returns into information. First, there is data acquisition, in which the RADAR sensor sends pulses toward the Earth's surface and receives the reflected signals back from the targets. These raw signals are called RADAR backscatter and carry information about the distance and properties of the target. Once data is acquired, it is preprocessed to compensate for distortions caused by platform motion, atmospheric conditions, and sensor characteristics. Data preprocessing encompasses several steps, including radiometric calibration, geometric correction, and speckle filtering. The backscatter intensity is altered by radiometric calibration to account for variations in the sensor's sensitivity. Geometric correction aligns the RADAR image with geographic coordinates and corrects distortions caused by sensor movement or the Earth's curvature.

Preprocessed data is now ready for analysis and interpretation. Depending on the application, various techniques can be employed for information extraction from the acquired RADAR data. Interferometric SAR (InSAR) employs small ground movements by comparing phases corresponding to two different time repetitions of SAR imagery [21]. Polarimetric SAR uses different polarization states of the RADAR waves to carry more information about target properties, such as vegetation type or soil moisture [22]. The basic concepts of RADAR remote sensing essentially mean learning the fundamental principles, systems, and data processing techniques that are effective for using the technology in various applications. The integration of AI with RADAR remote sensing is based on this foundational knowledge in the application of a paradigm, enabling advanced achievement of analytical tools and methods that are capable of extracting useful insights from RADAR data for innovative solutions in environmental monitoring, disaster management, and agriculture, among many other uses.

3 AI in remote sensing

AI integrated with remote sensing has changed the way data is processed and interpreted by different sensors, such as RADAR. The critical access points between AI and remote sensing are considered below in the context of techniques concerning ML and

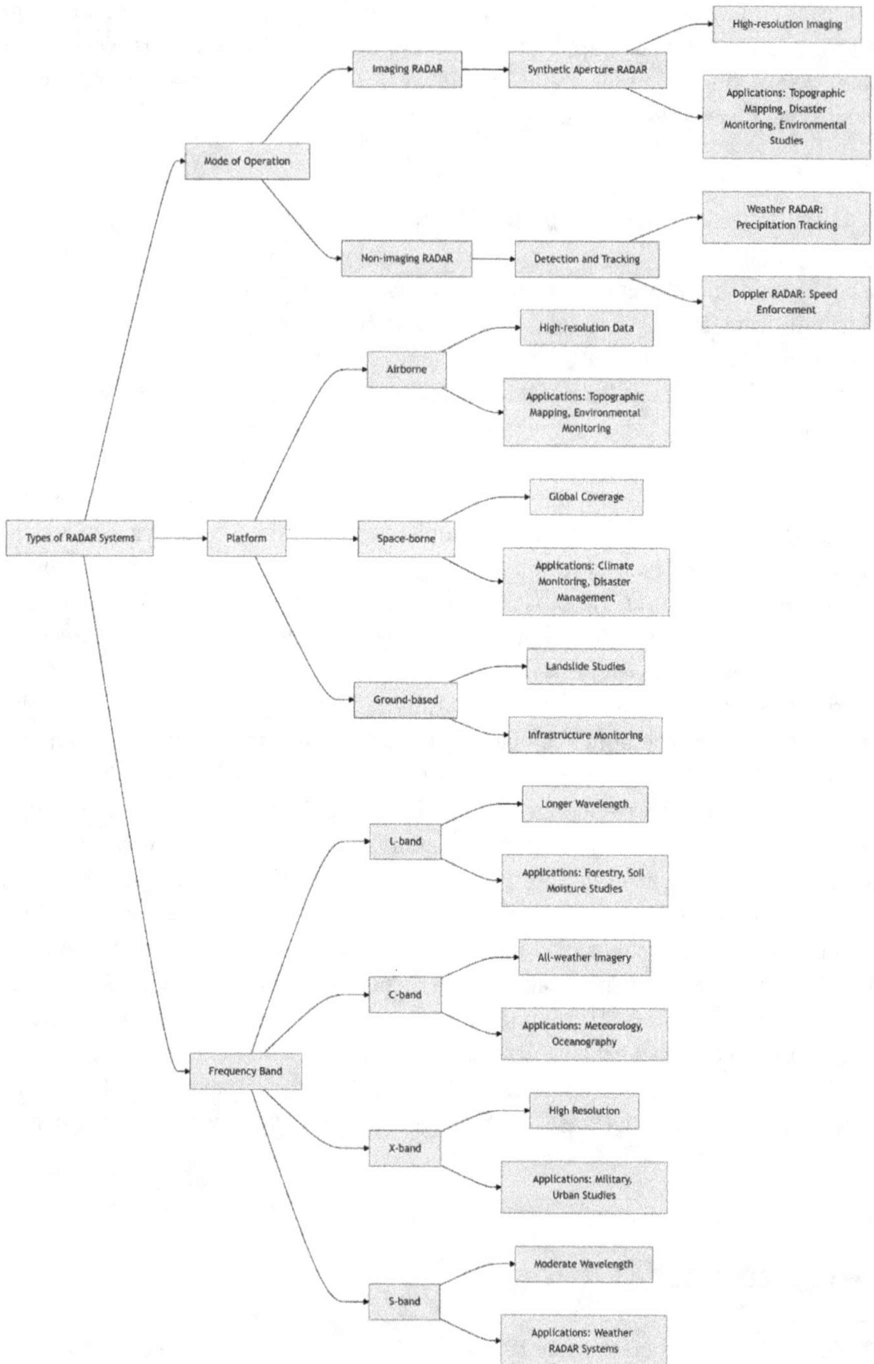

Figure 1: Types of RADAR systems.

DL, their applications in remote sensing, and the benefits and challenges arising from the integration of AI.

3.1 Overview of ML and DL

ML algorithms were used to analyze and interpret the complex datasets obtained from remote sensing sensors, such as those from RADAR sensors [23]. The common ML techniques applied to remote sensing include the classification algorithms of SVMs, decision trees, and random forests. DL is an advanced form of ML based on neural networks with many layered processing units. These deep neural networks can learn hierarchical features from unprocessed input by training them end to end. Normally, this fits perfectly with complicated tasks. The most popular model used in analyzing images in DL is CNNs, which have shown outstanding performance in object detection, segmentation, and classification in various remote sensing applications.

3.2 AI techniques for remote sensing data

The AI techniques provide effective tools for RADAR data analysis, which enhance their utility and effectiveness [24]. The following sections briefly describe some key AI techniques applied to remote sensing data.

3.2.1 Algorithms of classification

ML classification algorithms are applied to classify the data obtained through RADAR into their respective predefined classes. For instance, one will be able to segregate land cover classes such as forests, urban areas, and water bodies by using different supervised classification methods such as SVMs and random forest. These algorithms are trained on a labeled dataset where each point represents data from a particular known class. The trained model uses this knowledge to classify new, previously unseen data.

3.2.2 Change detection

Change detection is one of the most basic applications of remote sensing, considering the changes on the Earth's surface over a period of time. AI techniques enhance this process by automating the processing and comparison of RADAR images acquired at different times. ML algorithms enhance traditional techniques such as image differencing and change vector analysis, improving subtle change detection and reducing false positives. For instance, DL models leverage routines in time to allow for land use, vegetation, and infrastructure changes with high accuracy.

4 Object detection and segmentation

Object detection and segmentation involve identifying and delineating features of interest in RADAR images. DL models have been successfully performed by active learning of spatial hierarchies and feature representation from RADAR images using CNNs. Examples include object detection algorithms such as YOLO (You Only Look Once) and faster R-CNN, which can identify and geolocate objects within an image. In contrast, segmentation algorithms like U-Net determine the exact boundaries and pixels that distinguish one region from another. By leveraging these techniques, applications considered critical today include monitoring urban expansion, detecting deforestation, and identifying infrastructure damage.

5 Feature extraction

Feature extraction, in this case, involves deriving meaningful information from raw data. AI, more so DL, can abstract this level of features automatically without human intervention. For example, CNNs can autonomously learn texture, shape, and spatial patterns from RADAR images for use in further analysis. This capability reduces manual feature engineering workloads and also improves accuracy for successive analyses. The integration of AI with remote sensing data has enormous advantages and a significant number of associated challenges. Understanding these aspects will help optimize the use of AI for remote sensing applications. The use of AI algorithms in analyzing large volumes of RADAR data enhances the precision of results. This is particularly helpful for applications that demand minute details, such as environmental change monitoring and disaster damage assessment. AI methods automate the processing and analysis of data from RADAR, enhancing effectiveness by reducing the man-hours needed to do such tasks. It enhances workflow through automatic classification, change detection, and object recognition for near real-time analysis. AI algorithms can process volumes of data, hence being ideal for applications that require massive scalability. Satellite-based RADAR systems generate extremely large datasets that can be efficiently processed using AI techniques; thus, such approaches enable monitoring and analysis on a global scale. AI, by providing accurate and timely insights, improves decision-making in many spheres [25].

In disaster management, for instance, such AI analytics using RADAR data inform response strategies and resource allocation for more effective interventions. AI and

ML models need quality training data to learn adequately. It is a very difficult task in a remote sensing context, requiring tremendous manpower and time. Besides, there will be variations in the quality of the RADAR data related to environmental states or limitations of the sensor used, which have the potential to affect model performance. Most AI models, especially DL models, require huge computational resources for training and deployment. High-performance hardware with specialized software is needed to manage big datasets and complex algorithms, which acts as a deterrent for some organizations.

6 Applications in environmental monitoring

The integration of RADAR remote sensing with AI has drawn a new perspective on monitoring the environment [26]. This section reflects on how these technologies find applications in deforestation monitoring, flood mapping, soil moisture estimation, and urban area classification. By leveraging the properties of RADAR for penetrating environmental conditions and AI for information processing, environmental monitoring could be done more accurately, timely, and scalable.

6.1 Deforestation and forest monitoring

Deforestation threatens ecosystems, biodiversity, and the global climate. Regularly monitoring forests is essential to understand deforestation trends, map illicit logging, and assess the performance of conservation policy portfolios. Traditional satellite optical remote sensing techniques are often limited by cloud obscuration and atmospheric interference, especially in the tropics, where high deforestation rates are common. Equipped with cloud penetration by RADAR backed by complex data processing through AI, the device can be an ideal tool for forest monitoring. SAR is suitable for forest monitoring, given its ability to produce high-resolution images in almost all-weather conditions and at any time. SAR data can provide insights into the structure and density of forest cover, which are necessary for distinguishing between intact forests, deforestation, and regrowth. AI algorithms can detect forest cover changes from SAR data, such as clear-cutting or selective logging. In addition, the AI model can be used to predict hotspots of future deforestation by training on historical data and guiding preventive measures.

6.2 Flood mapping and water resource management

Flooding is one of the most catastrophic natural disasters and causes significant loss of human lives, property, and economic resources every year. Accurate flood mapping is of prime importance for disaster preparedness, mitigation, and response. In these aspects, remote sensing by RADAR is widely used in flood monitoring because of its capability to capture imagery regardless of the weather even during storms or heavy rainfall when floods occur [27]. However, with the integration of AI, flood detection has become far more accurate and much quicker, thereby making the satellite technique an indispensable tool in disaster management. It works on the principle of variation detection in surface reflectivity from both the water body and its catchment area. AI algorithms detect flooded areas by comparing pre- and post-event RADAR images.. SVMs and random forest ML algorithms classify the extent of flooded areas based on changes in RADAR backscatter. DL models, especially CNNs, have also emerged to be effective in detecting and delineating flood boundaries with high precision.

Besides real-time detection of flooding, AI-powered RADAR data can be utilized to enable the development of predictive models for assessing flood risks. Such models work on historical flood data, topography, rainfall, and land use to identify areas with a high risk of flooding. This is the most crucial information required for disaster preparedness in terms of good governance, and other organizations should be able to prioritize flood defenses and manage water resources with greater efficiency to minimize the impact a flood could have in the future.

6.3 Soil moisture estimation

Soil moisture is one of the most important factors related to agriculture, hydrology, and climate science because it influences plant growth, water supply for various purposes, and weather conditions. Therefore, accurate estimation is important for drought monitoring, irrigation management, and crop yield prediction. Among remote sensing activities, it is evident that RADAR remote sensing, at the L-band and C-band frequencies, is very sensitive to soil moisture, proving to be useful in large-scale soil moisture mapping [28]. AI techniques, when applied to RADAR data, enhance the accuracy and spatial resolution of soil moisture estimates. For example, most of the well-known algorithms in ML could estimate the soil moisture content by using RADAR backscattered data, topographic data, and meteorological data. These models are trained on ground-truth soil moisture measurements to improve their predictive accuracy.

AI enables the integration of RADAR data with other remotely sensed data, including optical and thermal imaging, to enhance soil moisture estimation. This multisensor approach gives further insight into the status of the soil, overcoming certain limitations that each sensor exhibits [29]. While RADAR informs about surface soil moisture, for instance, thermal sensors can infer subsurface moisture conditions; AI models can integrate these datasets for more accurate results. Typically, this is ideal for agriculture since it uses AI-enhanced RADAR data to determine the soil's moisture content with almost real-time monitoring. This allows farmers to develop an optimum irrigation schedule and reduce the amount of water used while maintaining good crop conditions. Soil moisture monitoring thus helps in the early detection of drought in arid areas and the use of water-saving mechanisms accordingly. In climate science, knowledge about the dynamics of soil moisture helps in better modeling of land-atmosphere interactions for advancing weather prediction models.

6.4 Urban area classification

With increased urbanization in the world, it is important for sustainable development and urban planning that processes of urban growth and land-use changes are observed. In particular, RADAR remote sensing from SAR systems allows for obtaining extremely detailed information on surface structures, such as buildings, roads, and other infrastructures that characterize urban areas [30]. The use of AI, coupled with this, makes the RADAR data even more effective in classifying areas of urban environments and changes over time. AI-based urban classification techniques are performed by supervised ML models, which are trained with labeled datasets consisting of features from both classes, namely urban and non-urban. These models analyze SAR data to classify all types of urban features into residential, industrial, and transport classes. Advanced DL models, including CNNs, allow for more refinement based on complex patterns and spatial relationship learning in the data.

Another important benefit linked to the use of AI in the classification of urban areas is that it can easily facilitate the detection of urban expansion and changes in land use. For example, such automation is very important to governments and urban planners who depend on timely and accurate information for making decisions regarding infrastructure development, zoning, and environmental impact assessments. AI approaches have the potential to integrate RADAR data with other geospatial data, such as optical imagery and demographic data, to develop a more integrated impression of the urban area. This integrated approach allows urban planners to analyze the effect of urbanization on natural resources such as transportation networks and public services to make informed decisions for sustainable development strategies. The integration of RADAR remote sensing and AI has changed environmental observation, making this activity more accurate, timely, and scalable. From deforestation monitoring and flood mapping to soil moisture estimation and urban area classification, these technologies provide essential insights for the effective management of natural resources, disaster mitigation, and sustainable development planning. As AI techniques continue to advance in their integration with RADAR data, so will our ability to monitor and protect the environment in support of global conservation, disaster management, and adaptation to climate change.

7 Applications in agriculture and food security

7.1 Precision agriculture

Smart farming is a method of agribusiness that allows not only the application of water, fertilizers, and pesticides to the field but also the determination of their dose individually for each plant. RADAR remote sensing, given its independence from the current weather and its coverage of large regions, can be useful in precision agriculture [31]. The integration with AI helps RADAR data track soil moisture, crop development, and changes in land usage, where farmers can effectively make informed decisions on managerial impacts. A major use of RADAR in precision agriculture is in estimating the moisture content in the soil. Since RADAR signals depend on the moisture content in the soil, RADAR sensors can give accurate estimates of large-scale soil moisture status. Another example is that, using ML and other AI techniques, the data collected by RADAR can be combined with other environmental parameters, such as temperature and humidity, to model changes in soil moisture over time. This information is very important to coordinate the irrigation periods when crops should be watered. This section discusses two evident problems that farmers encounter in the use of water in agriculture, including over-irrigation and under-irrigation, which both lead to wastage or scarcity of water, low productivity, and loss of arable soil. AI-enhanced RADAR data provides real-time insights into crop water needs, helping farmers overcome irrigation challenges. Figure 2 shows the satellite view of an agricultural area in Taiwan.

The use of AI-built models based on RADAR can produce estimations of crop stress, allowing farmers to distinguish the fields where crops fail due to a lack of water, nutrients, and so on. Stress identification at the initial stage allows farmers to make necessary changes to their growing environment, such as watering or spraying fertilizer. This precision not only increases yields but also reduces the environmental impact of excessive resource use.

7.2 Crop yield estimation

Production forecasting is crucial in food supply chain management, pricing of agricultural products, and food security. The conventional approach to estimating crop yields involves physical appraisal on the ground and, therefore, is time-consuming and, in most cases, provides outdated information. RADAR remote sensing can gather data on

Figure 2: Satellite view of an agricultural area in Taiwan (source: Copernicus Browser).

the growth of crops and the state of the fields over large areas in a relatively quicker and simpler way than using ground-based equipment [32]. When combined with AI, this data can be analyzed to offer accurate yield forecasts. The information gathered by the RADAR sensor can be processed by applying ML, DL, or other AI techniques to calculate the biomass, developmental stage, and health condition of crops. For instance, using a CNN, images captured by remote agricultural asset detection through RADAR can be used to identify various crop types and forecast their production from records. These models are trained to identify structures in RADAR backscatter, as such patterns can relate to the structure and density of vegetation. By using data gathered from planting up to the time of harvest, AI-driven RADAR analysis can generate real-time yield predictions that adapt to current conditions.

Apart from the fact that enhanced RADAR data with the help of AI can lead to more accurate yield forecasts, the information acquired can assist farmers in adjusting their input. This approach to the allocation of resources assists in farming that can be embraced as a sustainable farming system that reduces the negative impacts of agriculture on the environment. Other stakeholders, such as governments and agricultural organizations, also stand to gain from appropriate yield forecasts, which help with food shortfall predictions, resource distribution, and international trade planning in the market system. Through RADAR technology and applications of AI, the framework can examine agricultural yields in real time and quickly identify regions that are likely to fail in producing crops due to climate challenges such as drought, flooding, or unfavorable weather conditions. This systemic process empowers a timely prevention of compromise of the food security strength.

7.3 Pest and disease detection

Pests and diseases are some of the biggest challenges to food security in the contemporary world, mainly because they can cause significant losses to farmers. It is important to identify pests and plant diseases early to reduce losses in cultivation. The use of RADAR remote sensing in combination with AI provides a new approach to monitoring crop health and identifying possibilities of stress from pests or diseases [33]. While RADAR sensors effectively measure structural properties and moisture content to help with damage determination, AI can fuse this data with other remote sensing information, including optical and thermal imagery, to identify patterns that could suggest pest or disease outbreaks. For instance, ML models can help identify irregularities in the growth or reflectivity of crops that could be associated with pests or diseases. Even more accurate detection of stresses within crops may be achieved by exploring DL representations such as CNN, which are capable of mapping intricate spatial relationships within data collected by RADAR.

By using AI to improve the RADAR data, it is also possible to analyze environmental factors for disease and pest outbreaks. For example, certain temperatures and humidity levels might cause illness and pests, in addition to weather conditions that are conducive to these issues. Combining these variables with the use of crop monitoring through the RADAR system, AI models can predict the probability of pest outbreaks and prescribe measures, including, apart from pesticide use, the deployment of biocontrol agents. Also, early detection of pests and diseases facilitates the development of efficient control measures in a limited section of a field to prevent the need for generic sprays across a whole field. Furthermore, it reduces the cost that farmers have to incur over time to buy chemicals and reduces the negative effects on the environment caused by the use of chemicals.

7.4 Irrigation management

Effective use of water for irrigation is very important in enhancing productivity among farming activities, particularly where water is scarce. When used in excess, water essential for agriculture activities causes soil depletion, decreases yields, and has long-term impacts on the environment. On the other hand, over-irrigation leads to crop stress, resulting in low yields, while under-irrigation leads to low production [34]. As has been pointed out earlier, radar data is highly responsive to the moisture content of the soil. Thus, it is used to map the moisture content in large tracts of agricultural land. Weather data can be combined with topographical data and crop type data and fed into AI models to set an appropriate irrigation schedule. With the help of AI technologies, farmers can predict when and where water is necessary for crop growth, save water, and ensure proper crop conditions. Another advantage of using

AI and RADAR for irrigation management is the potential to implement site-specific practices.

8 Conclusion

AI, combined with RADAR remote sensing, significantly boosts agriculture and supports food security amid global challenges. These technologies amplify efficiency in farming, an area traditionally facing challenges in effective resource utilization. Degradation of the environment through traditional methods leads to poor crop yield estimates, pest/disease identification, and irrigation techniques, all of which can be improved with modern technologies. With the world's population increasing constantly and the need for food growing year by year, the applications of RADAR and AI in agriculture will become more critical to advancing efforts to feed people and ensure the sustainability of agriculture.

References

[1] Gupta, D.K., Prashar, S., Singh, S., Srivastava, P.K., Prasad, R. 2022. Introduction to RADAR remote sensing. In: Radar Remote Sensing, Elsevier.

[2] Bakare, B.I., Ajaegbu, M., Idigo, V. 2022. A comprehensive review of radar system technology. J. Q. J. J. E. C. E. R, 8, 2321–5941.

[3] Zohuri, B. (2020) "Fundaments of Radar," Radar Energy Warfare and the Challenges of Stealth Technology. Springer International Publishing. doi:10.1007/978-3-030-40619-6_1.

[4] Vargas, J., Alsweiss, S., Toker, O., Razdan, R., Santos, J. 2021. An overview of autonomous vehicles sensors and their vulnerability to weather conditions. J. S, 21, 5397.

[5] Dingle Robertson, L., Davidson, L., Mcnairn, A., Hosseini, H., Mitchell, M., de Abelleyra, S., Verón, D., Cosh, M.H. 2020. Synthetic aperture radar (SAR) image processing for operational space-based agriculture mapping. J. I. J. O. R. S., 41, 7112–7144.

[6] Chen, Y.-N. et al. (2023) "Special Issue Review: Artificial Intelligence and Machine Learning Applications in Remote Sensing," Remote Sensing. MDPI AG. doi:10.3390/rs15030569.

[7] Paheding, S., Saleem, A., Siddiqui, M.F.H., Rawashdeh, N., ESSA, A., Reyes, A.A. 2024. Advancing horizons in remote sensing: A comprehensive survey of deep learning models and applications in image classification and beyond. J. N. C. & APPLICATIONS, 36, 16727–16767.

[8] Sheykhmousa, M., Mahdianpari, M., Ghanbari, H., Mohammadimanesh, F., Ghamisi, P., Homayouni, S. 2020. Support vector machine versus random forest for remote sensing image classification: A meta-analysis and systematic review. J. I. J. O. S. T. I. A. E. O. & Sensing, R., 13, 6308–6325.

[9] Mohyuddin, G. et al. (2024) "Evaluation of Machine Learning Approaches for Precision Farming in Smart Agriculture System: A Comprehensive Review," IEEE Access. Institute of Electrical and Electronics Engineers (IEEE). doi:10.1109/access.2024.3390581.

[10] Vyas, N., Singh, S., Sethi, G.K. 2025. A novel image fusion-based post classification framework for agricultural variations detection using Sentinel-1 and Sentinel-2 data. J. E. S. I, 18, 1–26.

[11] Albahri, A., Khaleel, Y.L., Habeeb, M.A., Ismael, R.D., Hameed, Q.A., Deveci, M., Homod, R.Z., Albahri, O., Alamoodi, A., Alzubaidi, L. 2024. A systematic review of trustworthy artificial intelligence applications in natural disasters. J. C. & Engineering, E., 118, 109409.
[12] Valle, A. 2021. Bilby Rover autonomous mobile robot in the context of Industry 4.0-Survey on sensor-enabled applications through Webots simulations and implementation of Hector-SLAM algorithm for autonomous navigation, Politecnico di Torino.
[13] Zhang, J.A., Liu, F., Masouros, C., Heath, R.W., Feng, Z., Zheng, L., Petropulu, A. 2021. An overview of signal processing techniques for joint communication and radar sensing. J. I. J. O. S. T. I. S. P, 15, 1295–1315.
[14] Skolnik, M.I. 1962. Introduction to radar. J. R. H., 2, 21.
[15] Kingsley, S., Quegan, S. 1999. Understanding radar systems, SciTech Publishing.
[16] Plaut, J.J. (2019) "Radar Remote Sensing of Planetary Bodies," Remote Compositional Analysis. Cambridge University Press. doi:10.1017/9781316888872.033.
[17] Mancini, M., Hoeben, R., Troch, P.A. 1999. Multifrequency radar observations of bare surface soil moisture content: A laboratory experiment. J. W. R. R, 35, 1827–1838.
[18] Moreira, A., Prats-iraola, P., Younis, M., Krieger, G., Hajnsek, I., Papathanassiou, K.P. 2013. A tutorial on synthetic aperture radar. J. I. G. & Magazine, R. S, 1, 6–43.
[19] Valin, P., Jouan, A., Bosse, E. 1999. Fusion of imaging and nonimaging sensor information for airborne surveillance. In: Sensor Fusion: Architectures, Algorithms, and Applications III, SPIE, 126–138.
[20] Ye, Z., Long, J., Zhang, T., Lin, B., Lin, H. 2024. L-Band synthetic aperture radar and its application for forest parameter estimation, 1972 to 2024: A review. J. P, 13, 2511.
[21] Pepe, A., Calò, F. 2017. A review of interferometric synthetic aperture RADAR (InSAR) multi-track approaches for the retrieval of Earth's surface displacements. J. A. S, 7, 1264.
[22] Yamaguchi, Y. (2020) Polarimetric SAR Imaging. CRC Press. doi:10.1201/9781003049753.
[23] Haut, J.M., Paoletti, M.E., Moreno-Álvarez, S., Plaza, J., Rico-Gallego, J.-A., Plaza, A. 2021. Distributed deep learning for remote sensing data interpretation. J. P. O. T. I, 109, 1320–1349.
[24] Zhang, L., Zhang, L. 2022. Artificial intelligence for remote sensing data analysis: A review of challenges and opportunities. J. I. G. & Magazine, R. S., 10, 270–294.
[25] Blasch, E., Pham, T., Chong, C.-Y., Koch, W., Leung, H., Braines, D., Abdelzaher, T. 2021. Machine learning/artificial intelligence for sensor data fusion – opportunities and challenges. J. I. A. & Magazine, E. S, 36, 80–93.
[26] Paul, P., Aithal, P., Bhuimali, A., Tiwary, K., Saavedra, R., Aremu, B. 2020. Geo Information systems & remote sensing: Applications in environmental systems & management. J. I. J. O. M., Technology & Sciences, S, 5, 11–18.
[27] Singh, G., Rawat, K.S. 2024. Mapping flooded areas utilizing Google Earth Engine and open SAR data: A comprehensive approach for disaster response. J. D. G, 2, 5.
[28] Edokossi, K., Calabia, A., Jin, S., Molina, I. 2020. GNSS-reflectometry and remote sensing of soil moisture: A review of measurement techniques, methods, and applications. J. R. S, 12, 614.
[29] Janga, B. et al. (2023) "A Review of Practical AI for Remote Sensing in Earth Sciences," Remote Sensing. MDPI AG. doi:10.3390/rs15164112.
[30] Yin, J., Dong, J., Hamm, N.A., LI, Z., Wang, J., Xing, H., Fu, P. 2021. Integrating remote sensing and geospatial big data for urban land use mapping: A review. J. I. J. O. A. E. O. & Geoinformation, 103, 102514.
[31] Sishodia, R.P., Ray, R.L., Singh, S.K. 2020. Applications of remote sensing in precision agriculture: A review. J. R. S, 12, 3136.
[32] Jafarbiglu, H., Pourreza, A. 2022. A comprehensive review of remote sensing platforms, sensors, and applications in nut crops. J. C. & Agriculture, E. I., 197, 106844.

[33] Abdullah, H.M., Mohana, N.T., Khan, B.M., Ahmed, S.M., Hossain, M., Islam, K.S., Redoy, M.H., Ferdush, J., Bhuiyan, M., Hossain, M.M. 2023. Present and future scopes and challenges of plant pest and disease (P&D) monitoring: Remote sensing, image processing, and artificial intelligence perspectives. J. R. S. A. S. & Environment, 32, 100996.
[34] Bwambale, E., Naangmenyele, Z., Iradukunda, P., Agboka, K.M., Houessou-dossou, E.A., Akansake, D.A., Bisa, M.E., Hamadou, -A.-A.H., Hakizayezu, J., Onofua, O.E. 2022. Towards precision irrigation management: A review of GIS, remote sensing and emerging technologies. J. C. E, 9, 2100573.

Rajinder Kaur*, Sartajvir Singh, and Ganesh Kumar Sethi

Fusion of scatterometer and optical remote sensing: enhanced classification and change detection

Abstract: Earth observation via high or enhanced resolution remote sensing satellite imagery is necessary to observe the Earth's resources accurately. Nevertheless, a single satellite sensor's remote sensing images do not offer significant information. Pansharpening techniques have become more common in producing multispectral images with great spatial resolution. The optical and microwave datasets are fused using pan-sharpening techniques to provide high-resolution products with substantial spectral and spatial information. These datasets were combined using the Brovey transform to create high-resolution pictures. A support vector machine classifier was used first to classify the photos, and a change detection model was then used to classify images to create change maps. Finally, using MODIS data as the validation reference, an accuracy study was conducted to gauge the outcomes. This research aims to enhance natural hazard monitoring and forecasting in mountainous regions.

Keywords: Remote sensing, pan-sharpening, snow mapping, change detection, satellite imagery

1 Introduction

Satellite images from remote sensing have shown their flexibility in a range of Earth observation applications. These images aid in gathering information from hazardous and inaccessible locations. Due to the quick development of satellite sensors such as SCATSAT-1 and MODIS, remote sensing images are widely employed in many different fields, including predictive maintenance [1], monitoring [2], and management [3] of natural resources. Satellite images with a high spatial resolution are necessary for remote sensing imaging systems. Nevertheless, a single satellite sensor's remote sensing images do not offer a significant amount of information. There are basically two types of sensors: optical and microwave. Both optical and microwave sensors provide the

***Corresponding author: Rajinder Kaur**, Department of Computer Science, Punjabi University, Patiala, Punjab, India; Department of Computer Applications, Baba Farid College, Bathinda, Punjab, India, e-mail: rajindersidhu654@gmail.com, ORCID: 0009-0008-2780-4187
Sartajvir Singh, University Institute of Engineering, Chandigarh University, Mohali, India, e-mail: sartajvir.dhillon@gmail.com, ORCID: 0000-0002-4451-4949
Ganesh Kumar Sethi, Department of Computer Science, Multani Mal Modi College, Punjab, India, e-mail: ganeshsethi147@gmail.com, ORCID: 0000-0003-2903-6712

https://doi.org/10.1515/9783111572970-006

essential information with respect to their spectral or microwave bands [4]. The optical sensors obtain high-quality images across various spectral bands. In contrast, the microwave dataset offers the advantage of capturing data both day and night in multiple polarization modes (HH, VV, HV, and VH), unaffected by atmospheric conditions [5]. To generate high-resolution products for various purposes, the data is collected from two or more sensors and combined to get adequate information [6].

Pan-sharpening is a possible solution to combine data from two or more sensors to generate high-resolution images [7]. There are several types of pan-sharpening methods at different levels: pixel, feature, and decision levels [8]. At the pixel level, the images are combined by substituting values of pixels, and new images are generated by calculating the values of pixels from input images. At the feature level, the features are extracted to create the pan-sharpened image. At the decision level, the final output is obtained by combining the various decisions from the input datasets. However, the pixel-level methods are commonly chosen to provide pan-sharpened imagery due to the advantage of simple processing compared to the others [9].

There are two types of pixel-level techniques: component substitution (CS) and multiresolution analysis (MRA) [10]. Several researchers implement these image fusion techniques to achieve both high spectral and spatial quality [3, 11]. Gram-Schmidt (GS), Brovey Transform (BT), Principal Component Analysis (PCA), Intensity Hue Saturation (IHS) [12, 13], Elhers fusion [14], and nearest neighbor diffusion [15] are the pixel-level techniques. The pan-sharpened data is used for various purposes, like classification and change detection.

In snow cover mapping, the pan-sharpened data is utilized to develop the snow maps [15]. The classification techniques are used to identify class categories from high-resolution data. The classification algorithms are categorized as supervised, unsupervised, and semisupervised [3]. Some of the well-known classification algorithms are support vector machine (SVM), random forest, spectral angle mapper, maximum likelihood classifier, and K-means clustering [16]. These are the most widely used classification techniques in various scientific domains [1]. Change detection allows the identification of changes occurring between two different periods. It is more suitable for identifying seasonal and multitemporal changes [17]. The snow cover change detection can help avalanche forecasting models better predict and mitigate avalanche dangers in mountainous regions [18].

This study investigates the use of pan-sharpening algorithms to improve optical and microwave datasets: (a) preprocessing; (b) using BT to apply pan-sharpening techniques to MODIS optical and SCATSAT-1 microwave images; (c) using SVM classifier for image classification; and (d) change detection. Lastly, accuracy assessment approaches are used to evaluate these methods' performance. Performance analysis is carried out on a portion of the Himalayas that is primarily covered in snow as part of the study.

2 Study site and data

The study is carried out over the North Indian region (Ladakh, Jammu and Kashmir) as shown in Figure 1 (a) Map of India, and (b) MODIS Image over study site". There is a lot of snowfall in this mostly mountainous region. On February 16, 2017, and February 16, 2020, data were acquired from the optical-based MODIS (500 m) and the microwave-based SCATSAT-1 (2 km). With its several dual-polarization modes [14], ISRO's SCATSAT-1 allows for very fine surface feature differentiation [11]. The research makes use of backscattered data (Sigma-naught) from the Level 4 India (S1L4) product SCATSAT-1. The NASA web portal's MOD02 product served as the source of MODIS data.

In order to record reflected energy without considering surface roughness into account, SCATSAT-1 sends out microwave pulses toward the Earth and record the backscattered signals. Active microwave sensors, such as scatterometers, provide wide worldwide coverage, surpassing 90% of the Earth's surface every day, and are not impacted by atmospheric sunlight, in contrast to passive sensors [14]. Furthermore, scatterometers can penetrate cloud cover to measure sigma-nought (σ) over the Earth's surface at night and during the day [19]. MODIS data for the same day was obtained from the MOD10A2 product on the NASA web portal for validation reasons.

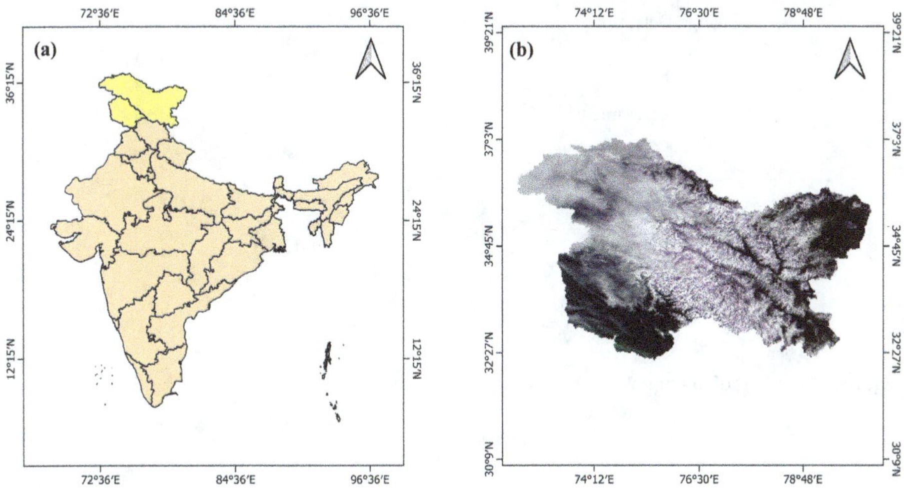

Figure 1: (a) Map of India and (b) MODIS image.

3 Methods

The method to perform pan-sharpening is shown in Figure 2: (a) preprocessing, (b) pan-sharpening, (c) classification, (d) change detection, and (e) accuracy assessment.

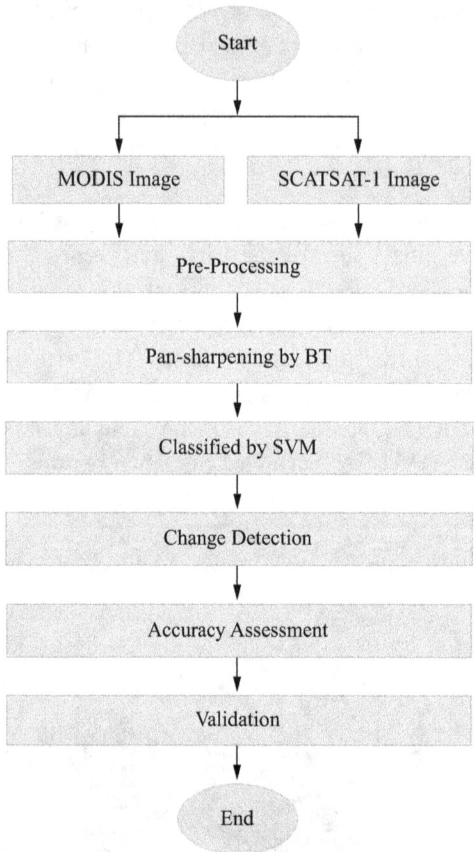

Figure 2: Flowchart of methodology.

3.1 Preprocessing

The preprocessing is required because when sensors capture images from the Earth, some artifacts, such as noise, are present in the raw image. Therefore, preprocessing is applied to the raw data to improve spatial resolution. Both MODIS and SCATSAT-1 images must be processed to the required corrections for geometric, radiometric, and atmospheric parameters in order for pan-sharpening to be successful. These factors can affect the quality and brightness of the images. As a result, using eq. (1) [10, 15]

improves the accuracy of spectral reflectance (SR) determination, leading to more high-quality images during the pan-sharpening process. The pre-processing is essential for creating high-resolution pan-sharpened images that are reliable and of high quality, which are important for several applications:

$$\mathrm{SR} = \frac{\pi R \curlywedge ES^2}{E_0 + \cos\theta_z} \tag{1}$$

where R is the radiance between the sensor and the path, ES is Earth-Sun distance, E_0 is the exo-atmospheric spectral value, and θ_z is the zenith angle.

3.2 Pan-sharpening

It is a process of creating high-resolution images from optical and panchromatic (microwave) images. The pan-sharpening techniques are applied to merge both optical and microwave datasets to generate high-resolution products that preserve a substantial amount of both spectral and spatial information. In this study, the Brovey transform technique is implemented to combine the features of both datasets to generate high-resolution images. Bob Brovey [12] developed the Brovey transform technique, which consists of multiplying each pixel values. To apply the Brovey transform for the fusion of both MS and PAN images, both images need to be normalized before fusion. Next, for each pixel, determine the ratio by dividing its value in the PAN image by the total of its values across multispectral spectral bands, as follows:

$$I_{\text{pan-sharpened}}(x,y) = \frac{I_{\text{PAN}}(x,y) \times I_{\text{MS}}(x,y)}{\sum_i^0 \mathrm{I}_{\mathrm{MS_i}}(x,y)} \tag{2}$$

where $I_{\text{pan-sharpened}}(x,y)$ is the fused value at coordinates (x, y). $I_{\text{PAN}}(x,y)$ represents the panchromatic. The multispectral image is denoted as $I_{\text{MS}}(x,y)$. The pixel value at the ith band is denoted as $I_{\text{MS}_i}(x,y)$. The total of the pixel values for all bands of the multispectral images is $\sum_i^0 I_{\text{MS}_i}(x,y)$.

3.3 Classification

After pan-sharpening, the pan-sharpened data is used for classification. Several classification algorithms have been used by various researchers [20]. In this study, the SVM classifier is implemented to generate classified maps from pan-sharpened images. Both linear and nonlinear data can be handled by the SVM classification method [21]. Classification is achieved by first translating the original training data into a higher-dimensional space and then creating a hyperplane within that enlarged space. To distinguish one set of data from another, the decision plane, also known as a hyperplane, is essential [22]. It identifies particular information points called support vectors, that aid in defining the decision boundary and ensure a substantial margin of separation between the various classes [23]. Within this decision plane, it focuses on increasing the separation between the class categories [24, 25]. It has the lowest error rate for classifying items. According to Pal and Foody [22], SVM can be mathematically expressed by eqs. (3) and (4) if the training set consists of n examples:

$$\{ a_i, b_i \};\ i = 1, \ldots, n \tag{3}$$

where $b \in R^t$ denotes the t classes and $a \in R^z$ denotes the z input characteristics. The classes in a binary classification issue are designated as $y \in \{-1, +1\}$. When there is a weight vector "w" that specifies the discriminating plane's orientation and a scalar "y" that indicates the discriminating plane's offset from the origin [22],

$$b_i(wa_i + y) - 1 \geq 0 \tag{4}$$

3.4 Change detection

The technique of identifying the variations that occur during multitemporal dates is known as change detection. It allows us to determine the seasonal variations throughout a specific time frame. The procedure compares and examines the variations between images taken at different intervals [17].

3.4.1 Change magnitude

In the two fractional change maps that correspond to dates 1 and 2, the class categories (snow and non-snow) are represented by $P = (x_0, x_1, \ldots, x_n)^{T1}$ and $Q = (y_0, y_1, \ldots, y_n)^{T2}$, respectively, where n is the number of fractional maps. Furthermore, eq. (5) is utilized to compute the change magnitude $|H|$ from two fractional maps [26, 27]:

$$|H| = \sqrt{\sum_{k=1}^{n} (y_n - x_n)} \tag{5}$$

3.4.2 Change direction

Change direction allows the identification of the types of changes that occurred during the multitemporal dates, such as base change vectors [28] and cosine-based methods [29]. To identify the direction of change, the change-combination approach will be employed [30]. Shift direction represents the accumulation or melting of snow during the multitemporal dates as follows:

- Positive change (snow accumulation): If $y_k > x_{k'}$ indicates the snow accumulation in pixel k.
- Negative change (snow melt): If $y_k < x_{k'}$ indicates the snow melt in pixel k.
- Stable (no change): If $y_k = x_{k'}$ indicates the no-change in snow cover in pixel k.

3.5 Validation

The validation process measures the accuracy of change and classified maps generated from fused images [10]. The accuracy is generally evaluated by cross-referencing with the reference dataset. To perform the evaluation, MOD10A2 has been acquired to carry out the validation process. The user's accuracy (UA) represents how well each class category in the image is identified, whereas the producer's accuracy (PA) measures the degree of agreement between the classification findings and the reference data. Important factors are taken into account in this work.

Table 1: Accuracy assessment of two multitemporal images by using the SVM classifier.

Date	Class	RT	CT	NC	PA	UA	Classified OA	Change detection OA
Date 1 (Feb 16, 2017)	Snow	52,102	40,703	33,556	64.40%	82.44%	85.67%	94.45%
	Non-snow	127,238	138,637	120,091	–	–		
Date 2 (Feb 16, 2020)	Snow	52,197	45,717	3,810	73.01%	83.36%	87.84%	
	Non-snow	126,297	132,777	118,688	–	–		

Notes: RT, reference totals; CT, classified totals; NC, number of correct; PA, producer's accuracy; UA, user's accuracy; OA, overall accuracy.

4 Results and discussion

The effectiveness and temporal variance of the classification and change detection procedure are evaluated by determining the classification accuracy for snow and non-snow regions using pan-sharpening of SCATSAT-1 and MODIS datasets. A comprehensive summary of the performance measures for 2017 (date 1) and 2020 (date 2) is given in Table 1. Two multitemporal images (February 16, 2017, and February 16, 2020) of Ladakh and Jammu and Kashmir were obtained from MODIS and SCATSAT-1 Landsat-8 in order to detect changes. First, preprocessing was done on the MODIS and SCATSAT-1 datasets to perform the various corrections. Following that, the BT approach was chosen as a pan-sharpening method based on previous research and applied to the MODIS and SCATSAT-1 datasets, as shown in Figure 3(a–g). The efficiency

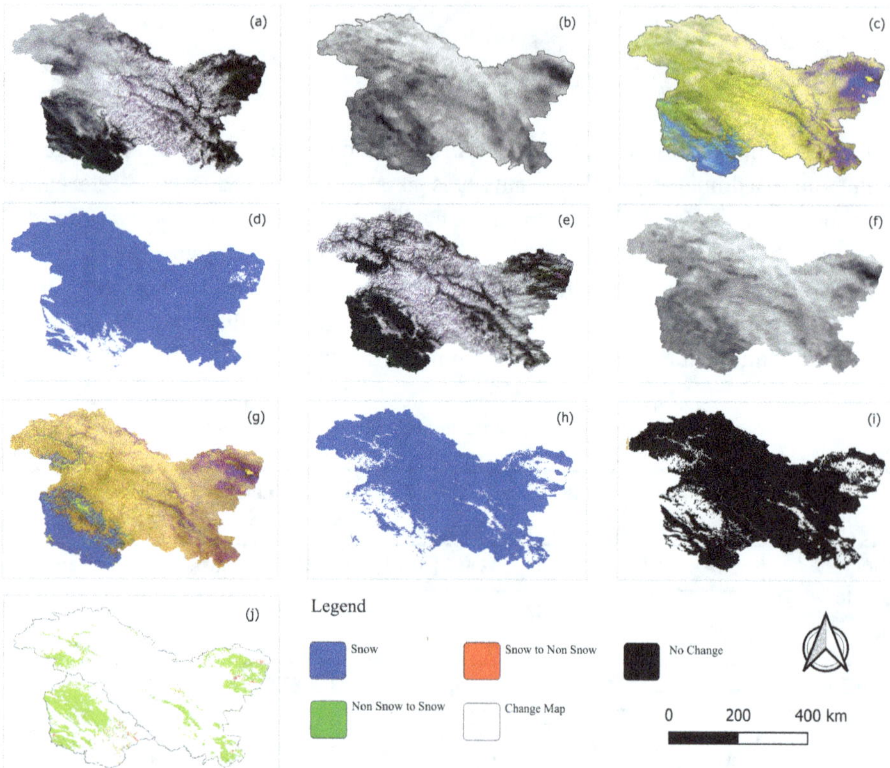

Figure 3: (a) MODIS 2017 image, (b) SCATSAT-1 2017 image, (c) BT pan-sharpened 2017, (d) SVM classified 2017, (e) MODIS 2020 image, (f) SCATSAT-1 2020 image, (g) BT pan-sharpened 2020, (h) SVM classified 2020, (i) change/no change, and (j) "from-to" change.

of the BT pan-sharpening technique has been evaluated by classifying pan-sharpened images using the SVM. The classified images are shown in Figure 3(d) and (h).

Snow and non-snow fraction classes, for example, can be visually interpreted in this image from Figure 3(d) and (h), respectively. Table 1 displays the accuracy evaluation that has been calculated for each fractional map. An overall accuracy of 85.67% (kappa = 1.6481) for the snow in date 1 (February 16, 2017) image and 87.84% (kappa = 1.3390) for the snow in date 2 (February 16, 2020) image has been attained, according to the results. Subsequently, using the change detection methodology, "change/no-change" and "from-to" change maps were generated. Figure 3(i) and (j) shows the resulting change maps: (i) a "change/no-change" map based on change magnitude, and (j) a "from-to" change map based on change direction.

The MODIS and SCATSAT-1 datasets were effectively utilized in the study for change detection over Ladakh and Jammu and Kashmir by employing SVM classification and BT pan-sharpening. The preprocessing steps successfully managed both atmospheric and radiometric impacts, producing high-quality data for study. Pan-sharpening process was enhanced using the BT technique, and pan-sharpened data is classified by using SVM and these classified images led to show precise snow cover change maps.

5 Conclusion

In this study, for experimental purposes, data is acquired from the MODIS and SCATSAT-1 datasets, which covered the geographical areas in Ladakh and Jammu and Kashmir, to assess the effectiveness of the BT pan-sharpening technique and SVM classification in detecting snow cover changes. The preprocessing applies to enhanced image quality, while BT pan-sharpening is used to combine both MODIS and SCATSAT-1 datasets to generate high spatial resolution images. These pan-sharpened high-resolution images are used to classify snow and non-snow areas in mountain region. Changes are detected from classified images that can be used for various purposes such as prediction of natural hazards, hydrological research, water cycle, and agricultural supply. From the experimental outcomes, BT pan-sharpened-based classified image shows 87.84% overall accuracy and change detection model achieved 94.45% overall accuracy. The SVM classifier produced clear classifications like snow and non-snow. The results show that advanced pan-sharpening technique in combination with SVM classification approaches can be applied to precise environmental monitoring and risk prediction of natural hazards and water mass balance of glacier. To increase its generalizability and accuracy in identifying changes, future studies should look at more satellite datasets and machine learning methods while expanding them to different areas or time periods.

References

[1] Carvalho, T.P., Soares, F.A.A.M.N., Vita, R., Francisco, R.D.P., Basto, J.P., Alcalá, S.G.S. 2019. A systematic literature review of machine learning methods applied to predictive maintenance. Computers & Industrial Engineering 137, 106024. doi: 10.1016/j.cie.2019.106024

[2] Jagalingam, P., Hegde, A.V. 2015. A review of quality metrics for fused image. Aquatic Procedia 4, 133–142. doi: 10.1016/j.aqpro.2015.02.019

[3] Sharma, R., Kamble, S.S., Gunasekaran, A., Kumar, V., Kumar, A. 2020. A systematic literature review on machine learning applications for sustainable agriculture supply chain performance. Computers & Operations Research 119, 104926. doi: 10.1016/j.cor.2020.104926
[4] Largeron, C., Dumont, M., Morin, S., Boone, A., Lafaysse, M., Metref, S., Cosme, E., et al. 2020. Toward snow cover estimation in mountainous areas using modern data assimilation methods: A review. Frontiers in Earth Science 8, 325. doi: 10.3389/feart.2020.00325
[5] Sun, W., Chen, B., Messinger, D.W. 2014. Nearest-neighbor diffusion-based pan-sharpening algorithm for spectral images. Optical Engineering 53(1), 013107. doi: 10.1117/1.OE.53.1.013107
[6] Gusain, H.S., Mishra, V.D., Arora, M.K., Mamgain, S., Singh, D.K. 2016. Operational algorithm for generation of snow depth maps from discrete data in Indian Western Himalaya. Cold Regions Science and Technology 126, 22–29. doi: 10.1016/j.coldregions.2016.02.012
[7] Du, P., Liu, S., Xia, J., Zhao, Y. 2013. Information fusion techniques for change detection from multi-temporal remote sensing images. Information Fusion 14(1), 19–27. doi: 10.1016/j.inffus.2012.05.003
[8] Joshi, N., Baumann, M., Ehammer, A., Fensholt, R., Grogan, K., Hostert, P., Jepsen, M., et al. 2016. A review of the application of optical and radar remote sensing data fusion to land use mapping and monitoring. Remote Sensing 8(1), 70. doi: 10.3390/rs8010070
[9] Shah, E., Jayaprasad, P., James, M.E. 2019. Image fusion of SAR and optical images for identifying Antarctic ice features. Journal of the Indian Society of Remote Sensing 47(12), 2113–2127. doi: 10.1007/s12524-019-01040-3
[10] Vivone, G., Alparone, L., Chanussot, J., Dalla Mura, M., Garzelli, A., Licciardi, G.A., Restaino, R., et al. 2015. A critical comparison among pansharpening algorithms. IEEE Transactions on Geoscience and Remote Sensing 53(5), 2565–2586. doi: 10.1109/TGRS.2014.2361734
[11] Snehmani, Gore, A., Ganju, A., Kumar, S., Srivastava, P.K., R P, H.R. 2017. A comparative analysis of pansharpening techniques on QuickBird and WorldView-3 images. Geocarto International 32(11), 1268–1284. doi: 10.1080/10106049.2016.1206627
[12] Su, S.-C. 2001. Efficient intensity-hue-saturation-based image fusion with saturation compensation. Optical Engineering 40(5), 720. doi: 10.1117/1.1355956
[13] Tu, T.-M., Huang, P.S., Hung, C.-L., Chang, C.-P. 2004. A fast intensity–hue–saturation fusion technique with spectral adjustment for IKONOS imagery. IEEE Geoscience and Remote Sensing Letters 1(4), 309–312. doi: 10.1109/LGRS.2004.834804
[14] Amarsaikhan, D., Blotevogel, H.H., Van Genderen, J.L., Ganzorig, M., Gantuya, R., Nergui, B. 2010. Fusing high-resolution SAR and optical imagery for improved urban land cover study and classification. International Journal of Image and Data Fusion 1(1), 83–97. doi: 10.1080/19479830903562041
[15] Meng, X., Shen, H., Li, H., Zhang, L., Fu, R. 2019. Review of the pansharpening methods for remote sensing images based on the idea of meta-analysis: Practical discussion and challenges. Information Fusion 46, 102–113. doi: 10.1016/j.inffus.2018.05.006
[16] Vyas, N., Singh, S., Sethi, G.K. 2024. A novel image fusion-based post classification framework for agricultural variations detection using Sentinel-1 and Sentinel-2 data. Earth Science Informatics 18(1), 40. doi: 10.1007/s12145-024-01506-0
[17] Sood, V., Gusain, H.S., Gupta, S., Taloor, A.K., Singh, S. 2021. Detection of snow/ice cover changes using subpixel-based change detection approach over Chhota-Shigri glacier, Western Himalaya, India. Quaternary International 575–576, 204–212. doi: 10.1016/j.quaint.2020.05.016
[18] Das, I., Sarwade, R.N. 2008. Snow depth estimation over north-western Indian Himalaya using AMSR-E. International Journal of Remote Sensing 29(14), 4237–4248. doi: 10.1080/01431160701874595
[19] Sharma, V., Mishra, V.D., Joshi, P.K. 2014. Topographic controls on spatio-temporal snow cover distribution in Northwest Himalaya. International Journal of Remote Sensing 35(9), 3036–3056. doi: 10.1080/01431161.2014.894665

[20] Amancio, D.R., Comin, C.H., Casanova, D., Travieso, G., Bruno, O.M., Rodrigues, F.A., Da Fontoura Costa, L. 2014. A systematic comparison of supervised classifiers. In: Shen, H.-B.. (Ed.). PLoS ONE, 9 (4). e94137. doi: 10.1371/journal.pone.0094137
[21] Jayadeva, Khemchandani, R., Chandra, S. 2017. Twin Support Vector Machines (TWSVM) for classification. In; Twin Support Vector Machines, vol. 659. Cham: Springer International Publishing, 43–62. doi: 10.1007/978-3-319-46186-1_3
[22] Pal, M., Foody, G.M. 2012. Evaluation of SVM, RVM and SMLR for accurate image classification with limited ground data. IEEE Journal of Selected Topics in Applied Earth Observations and Remote Sensing 5(5), 1344–1355. doi: 10.1109/JSTARS.2012.2215310
[23] Guyon, I., Weston, J., Barnhill, S., Vapnik, V. 2002. Gene selection for cancer classification using support vector machines. Machine Learning 46(1/3), 389–422. doi: 10.1023/A:1012487302797
[24] Kuo, B.-C., Ho, -H.-H., Li, C.-H., Hung, -C.-C., Taur, J.-S. 2014. A kernel-based feature selection method for SVM with RBF kernel for hyperspectral image classification. IEEE Journal of Selected Topics in Applied Earth Observations and Remote Sensing 7(1), 317–326. doi: 10.1109/JSTARS.2013.2262926
[25] Prajapati, G.L., Patle, A. 2010. On performing classification using SVM with radial basis and polynomial kernel functions. In: 2010 3rd International Conference on Emerging Trends in Engineering and Technology, presented at the Third International Conference on Emerging Trends in Engineering and Technology (ICETET 2010), Goa: IEEE, 512–515. doi: 10.1109/ICETET.2010.134
[26] Singh, S., Talwar, R. 2015. Performance analysis of different threshold determination techniques for change vector analysis. Journal of the Geological Society of India 86(1), 52–58. doi: 10.1007/s12594-015-0280-x
[27] Singh, S., Talwar, R. 2017. Response of fuzzy clustering on different threshold determination algorithms in spectral change vector analysis over Western Himalaya, India. Journal of Mountain Science 14(7), 1391–1404. doi: 10.1007/s11629-016-4248-0
[28] Chen, J., Chen, X., Cui, X., Chen, J. 2011. Change vector analysis in posterior probability space: A new method for land cover change detection. IEEE Geoscience and Remote Sensing Letters 8(2), 317–321. doi: 10.1109/LGRS.2010.2068537
[29] Chen, J., Gong, P., He, C., Pu, R., Shi, P. 2003. Land-use/land-cover change detection using improved change-vector analysis. Photogrammetric Engineering & Remote Sensing 69(4), 369–379. doi: 10.14358/PERS.69.4.369
[30] Dewi, R., Bijker, W., Stein, A. 2017. Change vector analysis to monitor the changes in fuzzy shorelines. Remote Sensing 9(2), 147. doi: 10.3390/rs9020147

Inderjeet Singh, Ajay Pal Singh, Yash Mahajan*, Eakansh, and Devansh Saxena

AI-powered urban infrastructure monitoring using RADAR-based remote sensing

Abstract: This chapter explores how artificial intelligence (AI) drives a paradigm shift in RADAR-based remote sensing for urban infrastructure monitoring. Urban monitoring has shifted toward a predictive and proactive approach by harnessing RADAR's ability to penetrate materials and AI's advanced data processing techniques. This chapter examines how AI can be applied to RADAR data for tracking changes in infrastructure, including roads, bridges, and underground facilities, and identifying risks related to ground subsidence. The discussion includes AI-driven methodologies for structural assessment, urban expansion analysis, and predictive infrastructure maintenance. Case studies illustrate the practical applications of this technology in smart city initiatives, disaster management, and predictive maintenance. The chapter also addresses key challenges in applying AI for infrastructure monitoring, including data accuracy, empirical limitations, and ethical concerns. Finally, the future potential of AI in shaping smart, sustainable cities is discussed.

Keywords: AI-powered urban monitoring, RADAR remote sensing, infrastructure health monitoring, urban infrastructure, predictive maintenance, structural health monitoring, change detection

1 Introduction

1.1 Urban infrastructure monitoring: a growing necessity

Early detection of deterioration, wear, or failure signs in these assets is very critical. These methods also require a significant amount of human intervention, which may

***Corresponding author: Yash Mahajan**, Department of Computer Science and Engineering, Chandigarh University, Mohali, Punjab, India, e-mail: gyash724@gmail.com, ORCID: 0009-0000-2530-0366
Inderjeet Singh, Department of Computer Science and Engineering, Chandigarh University, Mohali, India, e-mail: er.inderjeetsingh1989@gmail.com
Ajay Pal Singh, Department of Computer Science and Engineering, Chandigarh University, Mohali, India, e-mail: apsingh3289@gmail.com
Eakansh, Department of Computer Science and Engineering, Chandigarh University, Mohali, India, e-mail: bhardwaj09e@gmail.com
Saxena Devansh, Department of Computer Science and Engineering, Chandigarh University, Mohali, India, e-mail: illuminatidevansh@gmail.com

https://doi.org/10.1515/9783111572970-007

expose workers to the risk of human error as well as pose safety concerns for those inspecting deteriorating or hazardous structures [1].

Modern cities are complex systems, and without real-time data on their infrastructure's health, delays in maintenance can cause minor issues to escalate into major failures. As a result, there has been a growing emphasis on advanced remote sensing technologies and data-driven methods that provide more comprehensive, accurate, and actionable insights [2]. RADAR-based remote sensing has emerged as an effective solution. It is noninvasive, scalable, and independent of weather conditions, making it ideal for assessing urban infrastructure health. Integrating artificial intelligence (AI) with RADAR enhances this process, enabling real-time, autonomous, and predictive monitoring, which offers deeper insights into efficiency compared to traditional methods.

1.2 Role of RADAR-based remote sensing in urban monitoring

Indeed, using RADAR technology, especially synthetic aperture radar (SAR), has become an important tool in remote sensing of the urban environment. The principle of RADAR involves detecting objects and changes on the Earth's surface through radio waves, which makes it effective in monitoring significant elements of urban infrastructure such as roads, bridges, buildings, and utilities. In addition to that, the signals have the capacity to penetrate clouds, fog, or precipitation. For this reason, such observations are possible in cases with various changes in weather conditions, which may often be quite an issue in urban regions where these frequently occur and could interrupt other forms of remote sensing. The time delay for signal transmission and reception, as well as the frequency shift caused by movement, facilitates measuring accurate distances, characteristics of objects, and changing properties over time. Such data can provide critical information relating to the integrity of infrastructure, which, even to the naked eye, cannot be visualized.

For instance, subsidence or structural integrity can be monitored [3]. In roads and bridges, signs of tilt or damage may be surveyed on buildings. Underground utilities, such as pipelines, can also have displacements or leaks assessed. Unlike ground-based sensors, which yield point-specific data, RADAR provides a more holistic view of infrastructure health and is highly scalable in large and densely populated urban areas. The monitoring of changes over time is particularly significant for the advantages offered by RADAR, which explains why it is of utmost interest in urban expansion monitoring and disaster management, as many unplanned infrastructure developments go together with rapid urbanization and expose people to an increased risk of structural failure or environmental degradation. Moreover, by tracking land-use change and continuing to monitor the impact of human activities on infrastructure, city planners and engineers find valuable information for sustainable urban development [4].

2 Overview of RADAR technology in urban monitoring

Monitoring in the case of cities poses a very demanding problem due to the high concentration of infrastructure as well as the complexity of urban landscapes. Advanced technologies, such as radar, can be very useful in ensuring that the cities are safe, resilient, and maintained. Radar is now a very viable option for acquiring high-resolution, large-area data over urban environments without invading them. This section [5] discusses the basics of radar technology, the specific capabilities of this technology for monitoring infrastructure in urban areas, the associated challenges in densely populated environments, and how AI-driven enhancements have overcome these weaknesses to provide better accuracy for real-time monitoring of the urban environment.

2.1 RADAR fundamentals for urban applications

RADAR is a remote sensing technology that uses radio waves for the detection of objects, determination of distance, and measurement over time. By measuring the time of return for the reflected signals and the Doppler effect from changes in frequency, systems with RADAR determine distance, velocity, and other physical properties of objects under observation. Figure 1 represents the fundamentals of RADAR for urban applications.

SAR is one of the most critical improvements made in RADAR technology for applications in urban areas. SAR is based on taking advantage of antenna motion to simulate a much larger aperture than is physically available. This translates to higher-resolution images. This will be very useful in the detection of small-scale changes in the infrastructure in urban monitoring. SAR can return resolved images that outline displacement and deformation in detailed images, even in dense urban environments. It involves sending a sequence of pulses as the RADAR sweeps along a flight path, in the case of airborne or satellite-based SAR. Then, the reflected signals are processed to produce high-resolution images of the target area. Using SAR technology, InSAR is a technique through which the difference in various timescales of SAR images is used to separate minor differences, such as subsidence, deformation, or movement. InSAR is highly applicable for monitoring urban infrastructure, as, for example, it may vary measurements of millimeters in buildings, roads, and other structures. For example, subsidence occurring beneath a town could be monitored with InSAR technology, indicating problems' underlying infrastructure or the stability of building foundations. The most important aspect of utilizing this technology is its early detection capabilities because it can quantify changes over time.

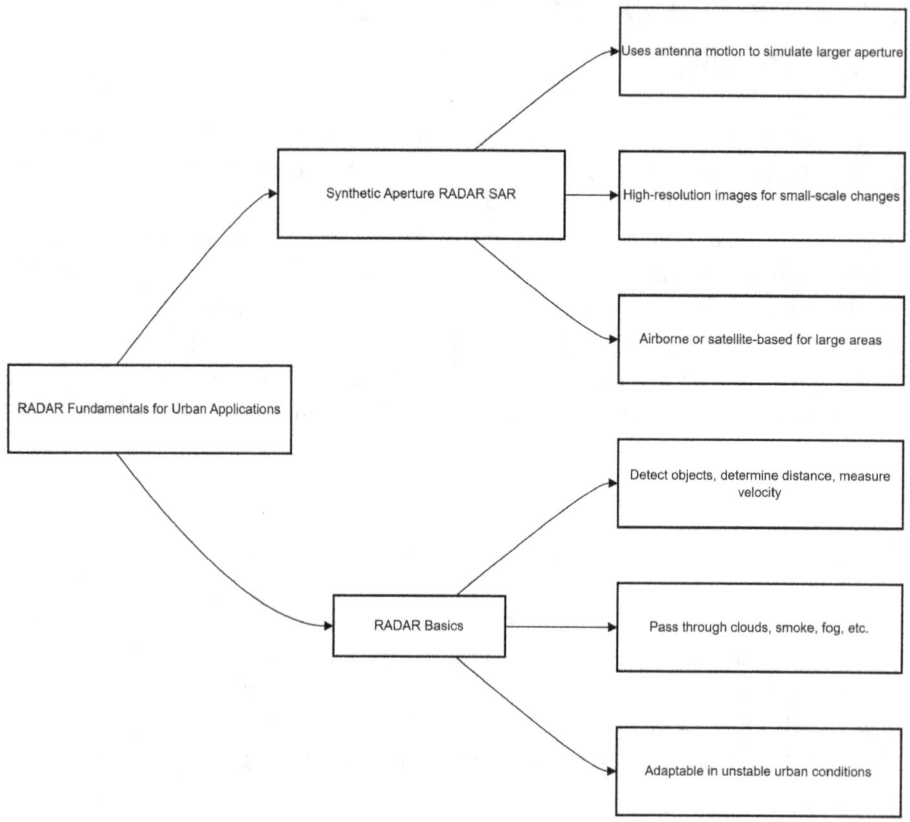

Figure 1: RADAR fundamentals for urban applications.

2.2 RADAR capabilities in urban settings

It has been realized that the employment of RADAR technology in urban ecosystems is profoundly efficient for several reasons. This chapter gives an overview of how RADAR detects urban infrastructure and some advantages, particularly monitoring a densely populated urban setting. Several RADAR-based urban monitoring applications are shown in Figure 2.

In an urban environment, infrastructure can be detected and tracked in parts, through roads, buildings, bridges, and utilities. Structural and surface deformation changes can now be identified accurately with the capability of high-resolution images in RADAR, which makes it possible to monitor any structural shift, crack, or subsidence within a building over time. These are crucial indicators of failure. The technique of InSAR is very effective in monitoring surface deformation in urban areas and can turn out to be a very useful technique to detect land subsidence that, if it is

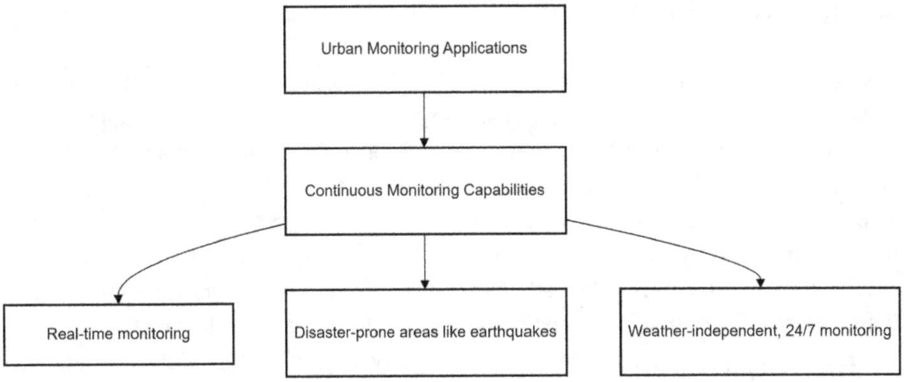

Figure 2: RADAR-based urban monitoring applications.

not monitored, may lead to structural collapses in infrastructure. The dense fabric of an urban setting requires close monitoring so that small movements in the complex networks of roads, bridges, and buildings may not lead to major structural failures. A major advantage of RADAR technology is that it enables an overview of small-scale, detailed data over vast areas. A key advantage of RADAR in monitoring urban areas is continuous observation. The most common methods for monitoring infrastructure are directly limited by time, cost, and scope: they require human input, and manual inspections and ground-based sensors introduce delays in the detection of infrastructural failure. In contrast, with the assistance of RADAR, almost real-time information is possible over entire urban areas, enabling quick identification of potential issues and timely interventions. Continuous monitoring is highly relevant in disaster-prone areas [6].

The high spatial resolution provided by SAR and InSAR technologies enables the detection of even minute changes in infrastructure, allowing for early identification of wear and tear in roads, buildings, and bridges. RADAR is also resilient to weather and lighting conditions, unlike optical sensors, which makes it suitable for operation in any weather and at any time of day – crucial for consistent monitoring in the unpredictable urban environment. Furthermore, RADAR can generate detailed 3D maps of urban areas, providing a comprehensive assessment of infrastructure health, which is particularly useful for monitoring tall structures like high-rise buildings or bridges that require precise data for structural integrity. RADAR technology is particularly well-suited for monitoring urban infrastructure because it provides continuous, high-resolution data in a noninvasive manner. However, while providing many benefits, RADAR technology also poses several challenges when applied in urban settings, notably related to signal interference and the complexity of the urban environment [7].

2.3 RADAR limitations in urban environments

Despite the wide array of benefits associated with RADAR technology, its application in urban settings has several limitations. The level of infrastructure complexity in a densely populated urban environment may influence data reliability and accuracy. It is, therefore, critical to understand the limitations associated with the effective use of RADAR in monitoring infrastructural usage within an urban setup. This chapter presents the challenges associated with the use of RADAR technology within the urban environment and how AI-backed advancements make efforts to overcome these limitations. Figure 3 shows how AI can be used to tackle the limitations of RADAR.

High-density infrastructure in an urban city comprises tall buildings, bridges, roads, and utilities. This high-density infrastructure could cause signal interference due to waves from RADAR being scattered off many surfaces, leading to cluttered or distorted signals. Specifically, multipath effects often occur in the case of tall buildings, as RADAR signals bounce off structures and cause misleading readings. For instance, in a city canyon from which at least two building walls confine it, signal reflections from the towers may bounce back several times to the sensor [8].

Another challenge in urban environments is the high reflectivity of certain materials commonly used in buildings and infrastructure. Glass, steel, and concrete surfaces can cause strong reflections that overwhelm the RADAR sensor, making it difficult to extract meaningful data. These reflections can create artifacts in the RADAR imagery, leading to false positives or obscuring important infrastructure features. The complex geometries of urban environments, including irregularly shaped buildings and infrastructure, present another challenge for RADAR. For example, curved roads, bridges with unusual angles, and irregularly shaped buildings may not be fully captured by RADAR systems that are optimized for simpler, more uniform environments. While RADAR technology faces several challenges in urban environments, AI-driven advancements have emerged as powerful tools for addressing these limitations. AI, particularly machine learning (ML) and deep learning (DL) algorithms, can process and analyze RADAR data more effectively, filtering out noise and improving the accuracy of the results:

- Noise reduction and signal processing: AI algorithms can be trained to recognize and filter out noise caused by signal interference and reflections through the urban environment. Through the analysis of RADAR data patterns, AI can distinguish the relevant infrastructure features from noise caused by reflections, such as high-rise buildings or moving cars. DL models, like convolutional neural networks (CNNs), have been highly effective in enhancing RADAR image processing so that features of urban infrastructure can be more precisely detected.
- Improved data interpretation through AI: AI models can be trained on massive data collections of urban infrastructure to better interpret complex geometries. For example, feeding AI models with data from diverse urban environments with buildings having complex shapes or roads with complex configurations would

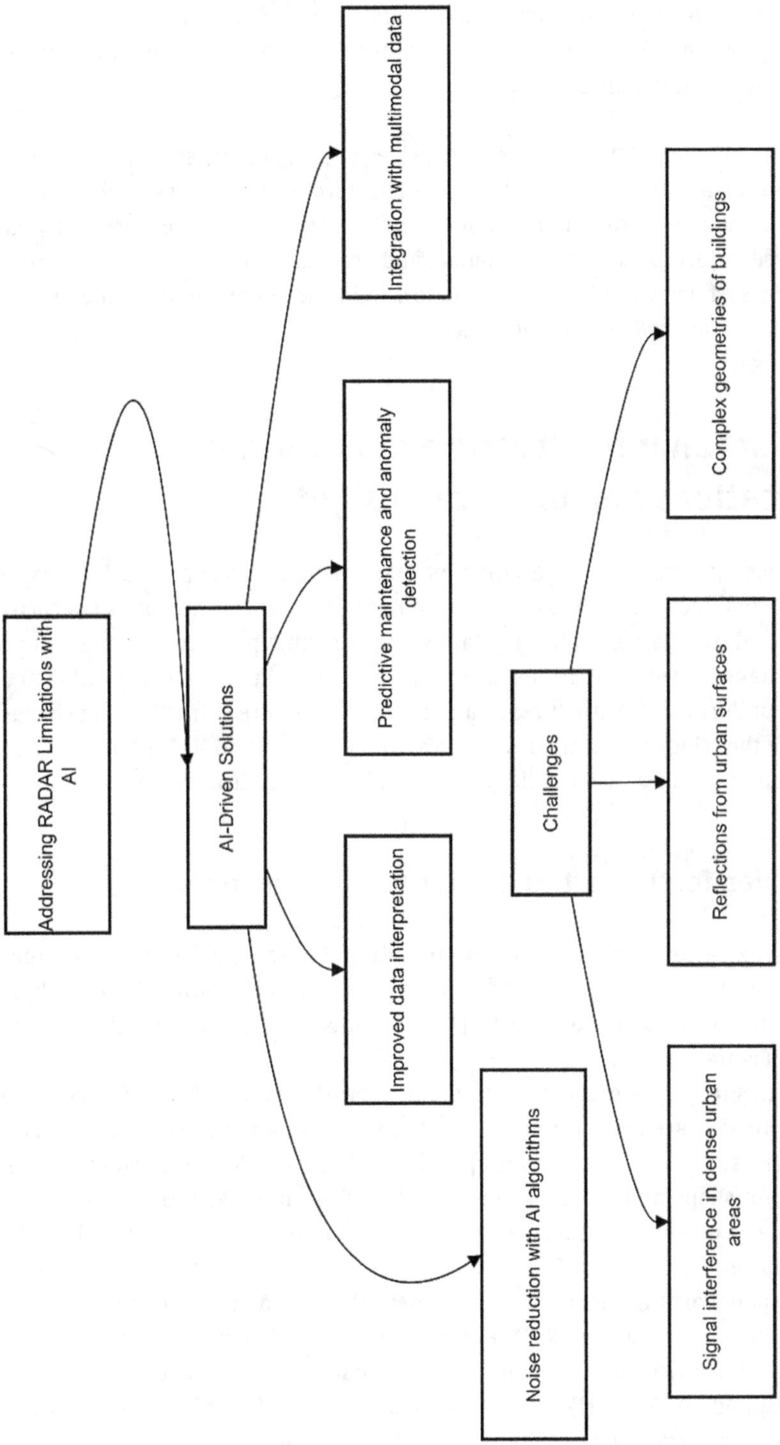

Figure 3: Addressing RADAR limitations with AI.

help them understand these features and, thus, analyze them better. This would make it possible to better monitor the infrastructure in places where different geometries cause difficulties.

In conclusion, although there are a few downsides to using radar technology in monitoring urban infrastructures regarding signal interference, reflections, and complexity within geometries, AI-driven development will overcome such weaknesses by enhancing noise reduction, data interpretation, and predictive analysis [9]. The future of AI and radar systems will play a paramount role in the success of continued safety and resilience of all urban infrastructures.

3 AI in urban infrastructure monitoring: applications and practical insights

AI has completely changed the paradigm of monitoring urban infrastructure, especially when combined with RADAR-based remote sensing. This is because AI is correlated with analyzing large, complex datasets and detecting patterns, anomalies, and structural changes over time. In this chapter, we discuss the main AI algorithms involved in monitoring infrastructures in an urban area, feature extraction and change detection methodology using AI, and practical applications in AI-RADAR-based roads and bridge monitoring systems, buildings, and underground infrastructures.

3.1 AI-driven feature extraction for urban structures

The feature extraction process is predominantly followed in urban infrastructure monitoring, where the features of the data acquired through RADAR could include buildings, roads, bridges, and utilities [10]. The AI-powered RADAR monitoring system is shown in Figure 4.

Hence, this feature is extracted with the help of AI from RADAR data since some types of ML models are being trained to identify special types of urban infrastructure patterns. For example, it then becomes possible to have a CNN be trained on the determination of shape and texture in images derived from the RADAR data of buildings, roads, and other infrastructure characteristics. Features can be learned by the model based on their unique RADAR signatures, such as reflectivity and texture, along with spatial arrangement. Once the model gets trained, it can automatically extract those features in the new RADAR images. This would enable fast and accurate monitoring of infrastructure in urban areas. Automatically, it can detect road boundaries, cracks, and potholes [11]. In a RADAR image, a model that sees buildings will track signs of structural deformations such as tilting or cracks.

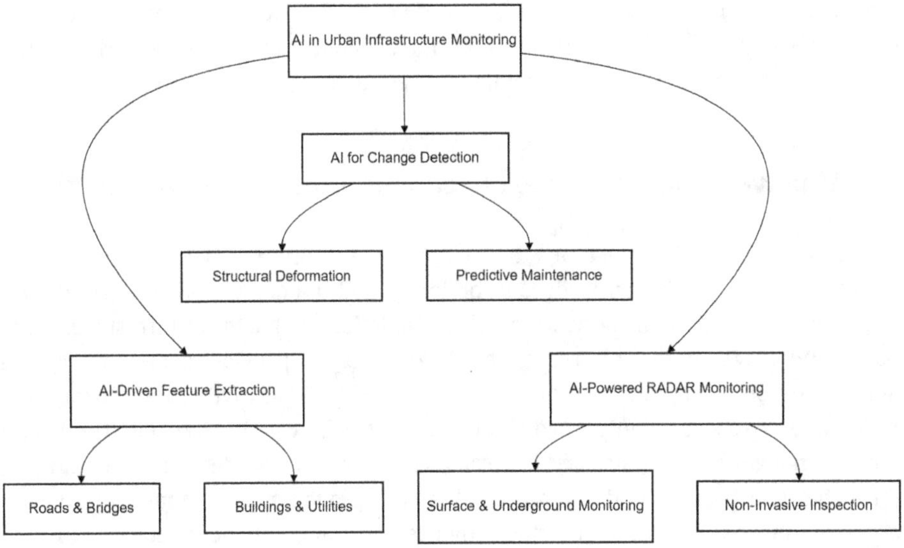

Figure 4: AI-powered urban infrastructure monitoring.

3.2 AI for change detection in urban infrastructure

Change detection is probably the most significant application of AI in monitoring urban infrastructure. Change detection refers to comparing RADAR data obtained at various points in time to identify shifts, deformations, or other structural changes in a system that may be indicators of the failure or degradation of infrastructure. AI excels in the area by automating the analysis of time-series data to spot even the mildest changes that might slip through the macroscopic view of eyeballing. AI-driven analysis from time-series RADAR data points out trends and anomalies in infrastructure behavior. For example, AI may be trained to identify gradual subsidence under a building as indicative of a problem with the foundation. Similarly, AI may identify the progressive deformation of a bridge or the gradual crack development on a road. General or overall, urban environments will suffer from some form of constant stress on infrastructure from traffic, weather, and environmental factors and change detection, which then comes into play in preventing these failures. AI models can continuously monitor these pieces of infrastructure for signs of deterioration, showing early intervention that could prevent costly repairs or even catastrophic failure. Some of the most common among these include time-series analysis and anomaly detection. Time-series analysis of collected data compared at various intervals determines changes over time [12]. It performs well for such gradual degradation in infrastructure, for example, in roads, bridges, or buildings. For example, an AI model can be trained on a time-series set of RADAR images of a bridge. An AI model analyzing changes in the structure of the bridge over time may identify early deformation signs or stress and thus perform proactive maintenance. Continuous monitoring will make urban infrastructure less likely to encounter sudden failures and last longer as well.

3.3 AI-powered RADAR-based urban monitoring: key applications

As it has hundreds of applications in monitoring very different types of urban infrastructure – from roads and bridges to buildings and underground utilities – the AI-powered RADAR monitoring will make it possible for the health of infrastructure to be continuously monitored in real time [13]. This chapter provides some practical examples of monitoring key components with AI and RADAR. Given these factors that make urban roads constantly worn and routed by traffic, weather, and environmental forces, among others that are less controllable, the traditional methods of monitoring through eye inspections and ground-based sensors prove time and labor-intensive. Instead, AI-powered RADAR monitoring provides much more efficient detection of road damages such as cracks, potholes, and surface deformations. For example, AI can be trained with historical RADAR data and traffic patterns to predict road degradation. A CNN model can recognize early signs of wear on roads in their images, such as surface cracks or deformations caused by heavy traffic. Using time-series analysis, AI can predict the progression of such problems, thus enabling city authorities to schedule road repairs before they become critical.

The AI monitored continuous roads through RADAR monitoring in an instance of a smart city. It was trained on images captured by RADAR on the city's roads related to common defects like cracks, potholes, and wear patterns [14]. This system was incorporated into the city's traffic management platform to provide real-time monitoring of road conditions. When the AI system detected road damage, it automatically generated maintenance reports and prioritized repairs based on the severity of the damage. This proactive approach to road maintenance proved beneficial in reducing repair costs and promoting safer roads for the city's residents. Bridges and other elevated structures in a city's infrastructure are critical, and their collapse can prove very devastating in its impact. AI-powered RADAR monitoring can help detect structural anomalies in bridges, such as displacements, cracks and overload stress on the structures.

The system was trained to identify changes in the loadbearing components, such as the girders and piers of a bridge. After detecting all forms of stress or deformation, the system was able to inform city authorities, who could investigate and make the appropriate targeted repairs. This technique greatly minimized the chance of a bridge [15] collapsing and extended the lifespan of the bridges. Urban buildings, especially skyscrapers, undergo various kinds of stress that can potentially challenge their stability. With the help of AI and RADAR technology, buildings are inspected for deformation, cracks, and tilting. AI RADAR equipment can detect slight angular changes in structures, such as leaning or foundation settling. Such systems may be part of early warning systems that alert building managers to potential structural issues, so that intervention occurs at the earliest possible moment. An AI-enabled RADAR monitoring system was installed to keep track of the structural integrity of some skyscrapers in a densely populated urban area. An AI system could deduce any signs of tilting or deformation due to foundation settlement using RADAR images of the buildings. Once such anomalies were detected by the system, early warnings were issued, and the building managers could inspect the buildings and rectify issues before they turned out to be major problems. Underground infrastructure, including pipelines and utili-

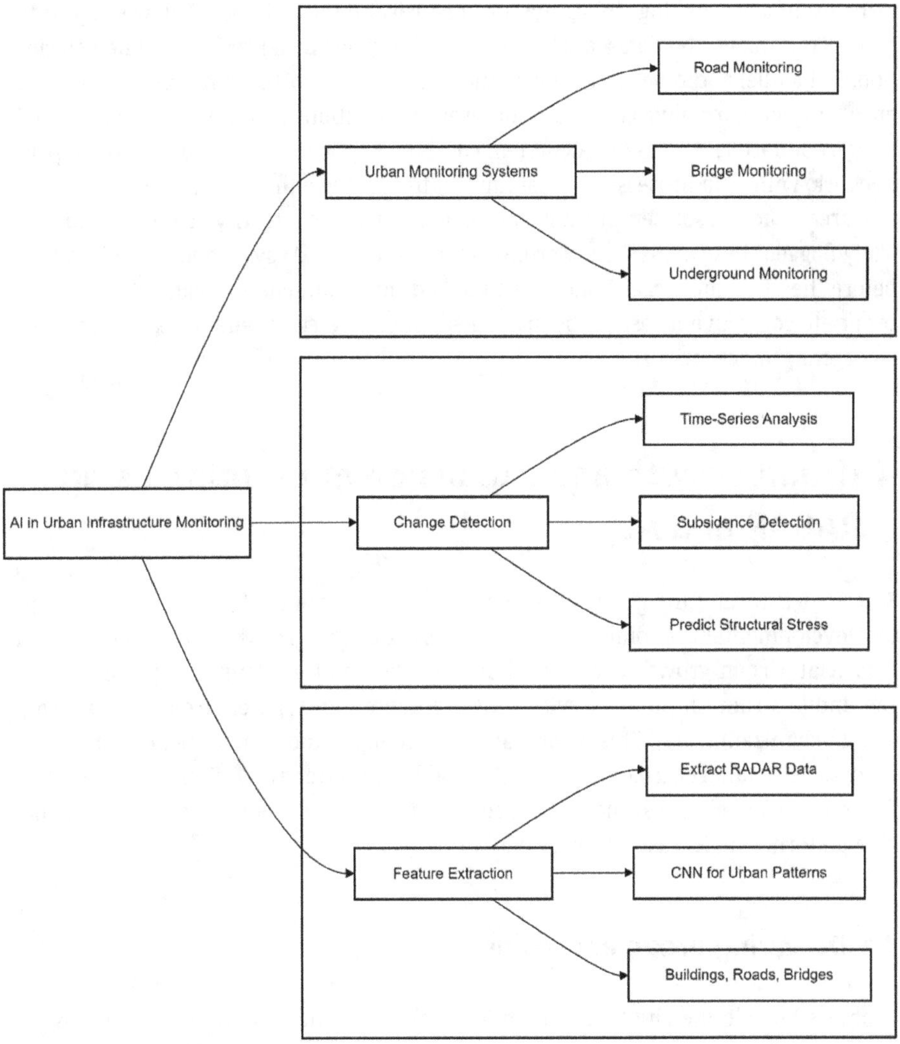

Figure 5: AI in urban infrastructure monitoring.

ties, poses significant access challenges for monitoring. AI-powered RADAR monitoring is a noninvasive leak detection strategy to detect leaks, shifts, or degradation in the underground infrastructure [16]. By analyzing time-series RADAR data, AI can predict the future progression of these issues, enabling pre-emptive maintenance efforts. Figure 5 shows how AI can be used in urban infrastructure monitoring.

In an application deployment in a real-world urban environment, an AI-enhanced RADAR system was employed to detect potential failures in the underground water pipeline network. It used high-resolution data from the AI system to identify minor changes in the ground next to the pipes, which could serve as early indicators of leaks or structural deterioration. The AI captured these trends as anomalies: normal data patterns established during the analysis of historical data had been followed up to this point. Training on the dataset, which consisted of prior instances of pipeline deterioration, soil shifts, and other related conditions, allowed the AI system to learn the difference between normally occurring underground conditions and those that might predict a future failure [17]. The RADAR system continuously scanned a portion of the pipeline network, with data processed in real time by the AI. Once the system detected potential risk areas, such as soil settling that could compromise the integrity of a pipe, it automatically flagged these areas for closer inspection. Often, the AI system identified problems before they become larger issues. This implied that maintenance teams could take appropriate corrective measures by making specific targeted repairs instead of expensive emergency interventions.

4 Urban growth and expansion monitoring using RADAR and AI

Since cities around the globe are still growing to accommodate more people and foster developmental economic growth, monitoring urban growth and land-use changes is crucial. Urban growth can lead to uncontrolled and unplanned expansion due to the undue strain on public services, infrastructure, and the environment caused by rapid urbanization [18]. This helps track such changes and enables better data for city planners to manage urban growth sustainably and effectively. Rather than using AI for monitoring, cities can now track current growth rates and predict future expansion patterns and infrastructure needs.

4.1 Detecting urban expansion

It occurs outside the city limits, often in rural or uninhabited areas. Sometimes, it is expressed through developing new residential, commercial, and industrial venues. At the same time, it may represent an expansion of transport systems such as roads and railway lines. Normally, this growth is not well planned and occurs very quickly; hence, it presents several problems, such as transport congestion, increasing demands on public services, and environmental deterioration. A good monitoring tool remains the high-resolution constant scan of large areas by the RADAR system, which processes data to detect changes in land cover and new infrastructures. As AI models are data-trainable from RADAR, these patterns indicate growth in urban sprawl, including new networks of roads, developments, or even construction sites, or earlier less developed residential or commercial developments. The integration of RADAR and AI facilitates real-time urban growth monitoring. This offers a more detailed, dynamic view of how cities expand and a more vivid presentation of how cities grow. Proper information management for addressing the impacts of urban sprawl on existing infrastructures and services is only possible with this information [19]. It is very valuable for city planners, as they can use the data to allocate resources better and avoid infrastructure bottlenecks that usually come with rapid urbanization. AI-assisted RADAR can identify patterns of uncontrolled or unlawful expansion. In others, expansions occur without following the required paperwork procedures in the formal system, leading to the emergence of informal settlements that lack basic services. AI systems can identify such unauthorized developments early so that the authorities can intervene to stop the construction or ensure that the infrastructure that would ensure effective facility use is established.

4.2 Monitoring changes in land use

Cities expand over areas formerly zoned for agricultural purposes, conservation, or forestry. Thus, the land-use pattern is significantly altered in these areas [20]. Such land-use changes seriously affect urban planning, resource utilization, and environmental sustainability. These AI models, which have been trained on data from a RADAR, are most successful when tracking the changes that occur in land usage. For example, AI will determine whether agricultural land is being converted to residential or commercial land based on changes in vegetation patterns, soil conditions, and surface features. This helps city planners track whether development aligns with the zoning regulations created.

AI-driven monitoring, in cases where encroachment needs to be made into protected or sensitive environmental areas due to urban expansion, can provide sufficient early warnings. For instance, based on RADAR data, the encroachment of deforestation or clearing of lands that were supposed to be conserved can be detected with enough time to act before significant environmental destruction occurs. Consequently, AI systems support urban planning and contribute critically to protecting natural resources and the sustainable growth of urban development [21]. This versatility of AI in processing large amounts of data at high speeds also adds flexibility to its applications in zoning and development plans. As new developments occur, AI models can evaluate in real time how such changes may impact the demand on infrastructure, such as water, energy, and transportation. A more comprehensive analysis by AI can be achieved by integrating the datasets of RADAR data with demographic and traffic datasets so that where the new developments will demand resources and services ahead of time. This can be particularly useful for urban development, such as constructing new commercial or industrial districts. In this regard, AI monitoring would greatly support planners in optimizing the location of new infrastructure so that roads, utilities, and other public services are constructed in areas that will readily meet greater demands.

4.3 Tracking environmental impacts of urbanization

Coastal urban areas face unique environmental challenges regarding sea level rise, erosion, and storm surges. In one example, a city on the coast utilized AI-powered RADAR systems to monitor its urban structure and assess how it interacts with environmental features. The AI system was incorporated with the city's flood management program; it processed the RADAR data about changes in topography, soil conditions, and flood defenses. The AI model monitored coastal erosion and land subsidence using RADAR data, which increased the risk of flooding in low-lying urban areas. The AI automatically alerted city officials whenever areas were identified as subsiding or where coastal erosion had compromised flood defenses. This enabled the city to act proactively by upgrading sea walls, improving drainage systems, or moving the exposed infrastructure before extreme weather events occurred. On the other hand, using the AI system tracked the city's infrastructure during storms. As storm surges affect coastal areas, RADAR provided real-time data on water levels and the effectiveness of flood defenses. This combination of RADAR and AI helped the city manage immediate risks of coastal flooding while providing long-term data for such decisions in the future. For example, a larger area could be designated where future development must be severely restricted due to risks of erosion or flooding. That information played a crucial role in guiding the city's expansion, ensuring that infrastructure resilience and environmental sustainability were highly emphasized.

5 Case studies

5.1 AI-driven RADAR monitoring of a city's road network

This serves to underline that monitoring and maintaining urban roads is one of the major challenges for cities, primarily because this tends to correlate with the growth of urban populations and higher traffic volumes. Traditional road inspection methods are usually conducted via manual surveys or ground-based sensors and are quite time-consuming and expensive, as well as possibly scope-dependent. A progressive city seeking to elevate the maintenance of its vast network of roads commissioned an AI-driven RADAR system to monitor the condition of its road network. AI-enhanced RADAR systems were fitted onto vehicles and drones operating across roads in the city regularly, collecting high-resolution data through RADAR. The AI processed the data in real time to identify common issues associated with the roads, including cracking or potholing, surface deformations, or deterioration resulting from traffic and environmental factors. It could automatically raise areas identified to be in a state of deterioration or likely to deteriorate soon.

With the automation of the detection of road issues, the system allowed city authorities to focus on the most urgently needed repairs – that is, the worst damage detected. This was good for the road network's general state, but the maintenance cost was also reduced since preventive repair was much cheaper than after-road failure interventions. Lastly, it helped properly allocate resources so that road crews concentrated on high-risk areas first, consequently delivering better services and improving road safety for the city's residents. The predictive abilities of the AI model made it possible to achieve long-term planning. The AI analyzed historical and real-time data, determining which parts of the road network were more susceptible to future wear and tear the city could plan its preventions. This case study shows the great potential of AI-driven RADAR systems in optimizing road network management toward cost savings and improved quality and safety in urban infrastructure.

5.2 AI-powered RADAR surveillance for urban bridge health monitoring

Bridges are an integral part of urban infrastructure, and failure at places often brings heavy loss in traffic and loss of life. To address this issue, AI-powered RADAR monitoring is applied in one city to assess the health of a major urban bridge that saw heavy traffic and other environmental factors indicating wear and structural fatigue. The system is based on SAR, which provides clear images of the bridge's structure. AI has been trained to identify diverse structural elements such as cables, beams, and joints, and programmed to note slight shifts, cracks, and displacements that may signal weakness or stress. The system relies on continuous real-time monitoring by analyzing RADAR data within a 24-h clock to look for anomalies likely to indicate probable failure.

The monitoring period saw the AI machine detect several microstructural movements in the bridge's load-bearing structure. These movements are not harmful at an initial glance but mark the onset of fatigue in the sensitive sections of the bridge. The AI system flagged these changes and warned the city's infrastructure management team early, enabling them to inspect the affected parts of the bridge and undertake reinforcing work. Thus, an issue that might have otherwise grown into a major structural problem was detected well in advance, and extensive repairs with considerable safety risks were avoided. Thirdly, with its early warning system using AI, the city avoided high-cost, reactionary repairs and traffic-flow disruptions by scheduling maintenance work during low-traffic hours. The real-time monitoring also provided city officials with topline information regarding the health of the bridge so they could make more data-driven decisions regarding investments in future bridge maintenance and upgrades. This case study demonstrates the power of AI-powered RADAR surveillance, which provides real-time, actionable insights into the health of bridges, thereby enhancing public safety and extending the lifespan of important infrastructures in urbanized settings.

5.3 Using AI and RADAR for monitoring urban flood defenses

Managing and maintaining flood defenses in urban areas within flood-prone regions are extremely challenging. The intensification of extreme climatic changes has increased, and hence, the role of flood barriers, levees, and drainage systems in urban planning and disaster preparation is highly significant. For example, regarding an impending coastal city that faces a risk of storm surges aside from normal seasonal flooding, an AI-powered RADAR system was mounted to monitor the city's flood defenses continuously. With the AI algorithms coupled with the RADAR system, the city's flood barriers, levees, and drainage networks were continuously scanned to provide high-resolution data on the systems' structural integrity. It was designed to recognize the evidence of erosion, subsidence, and signs of material degradation that might render the flood defenses ineffective. Besides its role in structural monitoring, the AI followed and monitored aspects such as water levels and storm patterns, which is subsequently used to predict the impressing weather conditions that would develop to affect flood defenses.

It certainly came in very handy during the stormy season. As soon as a storm surge caused a rise in water levels, it identified some areas on the levees of the city that were experiencing accelerated erosion and flagged them for immediate reinforcement. This ensured that there was no adequate thorough flooding; thus, thousands of houses and businesses did not experience damage. The AI also ensured that the rescue teams received live data concerning the areas likely to breach or fail. With the capability to post-storm AI reporting, assessments of long-term impacts on flood defenses could be provided, hence prioritizing where their repairs would be needed. The system would provide constant real-time monitoring so that the city's flood defense system is always ready for yet another storm, enhancing disaster preparedness and resilience to storm events.

This case study is an example of how such a system becomes more useful by including AI and RADAR technologies to enhance the monitoring of urban flood defenses, thus providing cities with tools, and the proper risk management of which is possible that goes along with the environment. Real-time data analysis with predictive capabilities in an AI-powered system gives insight to cities concerning safeguarding infrastructure, preventing further escalation of disaster costs, and safeguarding communities against the growing risks brought on by climate change.

6 Conclusion

The future of urban infrastructure monitoring will increasingly rely on the integration of multiple remote sensing technologies to create a more comprehensive and accurate picture of infrastructure health. While RADAR provides critical insights into structural stability, surface deformation, and subsurface conditions, its effectiveness can be enhanced with other tools such as light detection and ranging (LiDAR), optical sensors, and thermal imaging. LiDAR is particularly effective at capturing detailed surface geometry, while RADAR excels in detecting subsurface changes and monitoring infrastructure under varying weather conditions. By combining these data sources, AI-driven systems can produce highly accurate and comprehensive models of urban environments, allowing for more informed decision-making and predictive analysis. One of the most promising applications of this integrated approach is the creation of urban digital twins, virtual replicas of urban environments that mirror real-time conditions of physical infrastructure. Digital twins allow city planners and engineers to simulate and predict how infrastructure will respond to various stresses, such as increased traffic, natural disasters, or long-term wear and tear. These simulations, powered by AI and data from RADAR, LiDAR, and other sensors, provide critical insights into infrastructure health and help cities plan maintenance and upgrades more effectively. Smart cities increasingly adopt these integrated systems to improve infrastructure management, disaster preparedness, and urban planning. AI-driven multimodal monitoring not only enhances infrastructure resilience but also enables smarter, more responsive urban environments that can adapt to the needs of their populations in real time.

References

[1] Sharma, K., Shivandu, S.K. 2024. Integrating artificial intelligence and Internet of Things (IoT) for enhanced crop monitoring and management in precision agriculture. Sensors International 5, 100292. https://doi.org/10.1016/j.sintl.2024.100292

[2] Yang, C., Li, Q., Hu, Z., Chen, J., Shi, T., Ding, K., Wu, G. 2019. Spatiotemporal evolution of urban agglomerations in four major bay areas of US, China and Japan from 1987 to 2017: Evidence from remote sensing images. Science of the Total Environment 671, 232–247. https://doi.org/10.1016/j.scitotenv.2019.03.154

[3] Lee, Y., Son, B., Im, J., Zhen, Z., Quackenbush, L.J. 2024. Two-step carbon storage estimation in urban human settlements using airborne LiDAR and Sentinel-2 data based on machine learning. Urban For Urban Green 94, 128239. https://doi.org/10.1016/j.ufug.2024.128239
[4] Liang, R., AL-Huqail, A.A., Elhosiny Ali, H., Ponnore, J.J., Alkhalifah, T., Alturise, F., Assilzadeh, H. 2023. Wireless water consumption sensing system for building energy efficiency: A visual-based approach with self-powered operation. Energy and Buildings 301, 113584. https://doi.org/10.1016/j.enbuild.2023.113584
[5] Kumar, A., Nanthaamornphong, A., Selvi, R., Venkatesh, J., Alsharif, M.H., Uthansakul, P., Uthansakul, M. 2023. Evaluation of 5G techniques affecting the deployment of smart hospital infrastructure: Understanding 5G, AI and IoT role in smart hospital. Alexandria Engineering Journal 83, 335–354. https://doi.org/10.1016/j.aej.2023.10.065
[6] Southworth, J., Herrero, H.V., Gibbes, C., Bunting, E.L., Hassan, M.M. 2024. Remote sensing of savanna vegetation. In: Reference Module in Earth Systems and Environmental Sciences, Elsevier. https://doi.org/10.1016/B978-0-443-13220-9.00006-8
[7] Tehrani, A.A., Veisi, O., Fakhr, B.V., Du, D. 2024. Predicting solar radiation in the urban area: A data-driven analysis for sustainable city planning using artificial neural networking. Sustainable Cities and Society 100, 105042. https://doi.org/10.1016/j.scs.2023.105042
[8] Aslanoğlu, R., Kazak, J.K., Szewrański, S., Świąder, M., Arciniegas, G., Chrobak, G., Jakóbiak, A., Turhan, E. 2025. Ten questions concerning the role of urban greenery in shaping the future of urban areas. Building and Environment 267, 112154. https://doi.org/10.1016/j.buildenv.2024.112154
[9] Li, Z., Chen, B., Wu, S., Su, M., Chen, J.M., Xu, B. 2024. Deep learning for urban land use category classification: A review and experimental assessment. Remote Sensing of Environment 311, 114290. https://doi.org/10.1016/j.rse.2024.114290
[10] Almouctar, M.A.S., Wu, Y., An, S., Yin, X., Qin, C., Zhao, F., Qiu, L. 2024. Flood risk assessment in arid and semi-arid regions using multi-criteria approaches and remote sensing in a data-scarce region. Journal of Hydrology: Regional Studies 54, 101862. https://doi.org/10.1016/j.ejrh.2024.101862
[11] Neupane, B., Aryal, J., Rajabifard, A. 2024. CNNs for remote extraction of urban features: A survey-driven benchmarking. Expert Systems with Applications 255, 124751. https://doi.org/10.1016/j.eswa.2024.124751
[12] Aela, P., Chi, H.-L., Fares, A., Zayed, T., Kim, M. 2024. UAV-based studies in railway infrastructure monitoring. Automation in Construction 167, 105714. https://doi.org/10.1016/j.autcon.2024.105714
[13] Dharmarathne, G., Waduge, A.O., Bogahawaththa, M., Rathnayake, U., Meddage, D.P.P. 2024. Adapting cities to the surge: A comprehensive review of climate-induced urban flooding. Results in Engineering 22, 102123. https://doi.org/10.1016/j.rineng.2024.102123
[14] Sirmacek, B., Vinuesa, R. 2022. Remote sensing and AI for building climate adaptation applications. Results in Engineering 15, 100524. https://doi.org/10.1016/j.rineng.2022.100524
[15] Garcia-del-real, J., Alcaráz, M. 2024. Unlocking the future of space resource management through satellite remote sensing and AI integration. Resources Policy 91, 104947. https://doi.org/10.1016/j.resourpol.2024.104947
[16] Chen, H., Cifelli, R., Xie, P. 2024. Active and passive remote sensing of precipitation. In: Reference Module in Earth Systems and Environmental Sciences, Elsevier. https://doi.org/10.1016/B978-0-443-13220-9.00034-2
[17] Tu, W., Chen, D., Cao, R., Xia, J., Zhang, Y., Li, Q. 2024. Towards SDG 11: Large-scale geographic and demographic characterisation of informal settlements fusing remote sensing, POI, and open geo-data. ISPRS Journal of Photogrammetry and Remote Sensing 217, 199–215. https://doi.org/10.1016/j.isprsjprs.2024.08.014
[18] Chen, G., Zhou, Y., Voogt, J.A., Stokes, E.C. 2024. Remote sensing of diverse urban environments: From the single city to multiple cities. Remote Sensing of Environment 305, 114108. https://doi.org/10.1016/j.rse.2024.114108

[19] Ramesh Naidu, P., Kawale, S.R., Dankan Gowda, V., Hussain, N., Samal, A. 2024. Design and Implementation of Single to Multi-cloud Securities in Network, 591–603. https://doi.org/10.1007/978-981-99-7622-5_42

[20] Bhati, N., Duggar, R., Saber, A. 2023. Empowering Safety by Embracing IoT for Leak Detection Excellence, 231–251. https://doi.org/10.4018/979-8-3693-1194-3.ch012

[21] Singh, S., Talwar, R. 2013. Review on different change vector analysis algorithms based change detection techniques. In: 2013 IEEE Second International Conference on Image Information Processing (ICIIP-2013), IEEE, 136–141. https://doi.org/10.1109/ICIIP.2013.6707570

Bhavneet Kaur*, Raman Maini, and Sartajvir Singh

Fusion of the optical and microwave images for cloud removal

Abstract: The presence of clouds in optical images is a notable threat that needs to be dealt with since it tampers the accuracy of the observation and analysis process. The cloud-contaminated pixels can be identified and eradicated by the fusion techniques. Microwave and optical images are fused to leverage their respective strengths. Optical images offer the advantage of providing detailed high-resolution multispectral information, whereas microwave images provide benefits such as better penetration, independence from weather conditions, and longer wavelengths. This chapter reviews state-of-the-art strategies for fusing optical and microwave images to enhance their capabilities in supporting effective cloud removal. The work also covers some significant challenges encountered during the fusion of images to remove clouds. In this work, we have taken the optical and microwave images from standard datasets obtained from the Copernicus source and merged them using the NNDiffuse pansharpening technique. The resulting fused image provides improved visualization with cloud pixels effectively removed. Additionally, it also highlights some future substitutes and refinements that could enhance the overall process.

Keywords: Remote sensing, microwave and optical images, fusion, pansharpening, cloud removal

1 Introduction

1.1 Remote sensing

Remote sensing (RS) is an accurate method for capturing information about the surface of the Earth from a distance using various sensors. Optical and microwave sensors have their respective attributes, such as different wavelengths and the impact of the environment on their execution in different ways. There are several hindrances in the atmosphere affecting these sensors, such as aerosols (dust and smoke), water

***Corresponding author: Bhavneet Kaur,** Department of Computer Science and Engineering, Punjabi University, Patiala, Punjab, India; Department of Computer Science and Engineering, Chandigarh University, Mohali, Punjab, India, e-mail: sethi.bhavneet37@gmail.com, ORCID: 0000-0001-8648-3880
Raman Maini, Department of Computer Science and Engineering, Punjabi University, Patiala, India, e-mail: research.raman@gmail.com
Sartajvir Singh, University Institute of Engineering, Chandigarh University, Mohali, India, e-mail: sartajvir.dhillon@gmail.com, ORCID: 0000-0002-4451-4949

https://doi.org/10.1515/9783111572970-008

vapor, atmospheric gases, etc. Among these, clouds pose a significant challenge when collecting RS images [1, 2]. Since it act as a major obstacle in collecting and perceiving images through sensors, they need to be addressed to improve results.

1.2 Fusion and its need

There is a need for a technique where the information gathered can be enhanced by utilizing the best features of different sensors [3]. Fusion is one way through which data from multiple sensors is integrated to provide more comprehensive data [4]. Optical RS images have the property of holding multispectral information but are affected by the presence of clouds. On the other hand, microwave RS images acquire information in the absence of light as well but have low resolution [5]. Table 1 summarizes some of the significant comparisons between optical and microwave images [6–9].

Table 1: Comparison of microwave and optical RS images.

Parameter	Microwave imaging	Optical imaging
Radiation source	Active	Passive
Spectral range	1 mm to 1 m	0.4 to 2.5 μm
Weather independence	All-weather	Weather-dependent
Day/night operation	Day and night	Day-only
Surface penetration	Deep	Limited
Spatial resolution	Lower resolution	Higher resolution
Atmospheric effects	Minimal impact	Highly affected
Applications	Terrain mapping	Land cover
Data availability	Less frequent	More frequent
Cost	High	Lower

The process of fusion utilizes the benefits of both images and extracts a fused image with enhanced visualization (Zhang, 2010). Figure 1 shows various attributes that are used in the fusion process. Spatial resolution holds detailed information from the optical band and also represents image sharpness. Elevation data provides a visualization of the earth's terrain relative to a specific point, and textual features are used to quantify the texture characteristics of an image [10]. In addition to these, polarization attributes used in the fusion process include RADAR wave modes, which reveal surface properties such as HH (horizontal-horizontal), HV (horizontal-vertical), and VV (vertical-vertical) [11]. RADAR backscatter intensity refers to the strength of surface reflection from RADAR [12]. By blending these complementary features, fusion enhances many RS applications. It also overcomes the limitations of various sensors and improves the usability of images with better spatial-temporal resolution [13]. By removing clouds from original images, fused images provide better insights for different domains, including disaster management, urban planning, snow monitoring, etc. [14, 15].

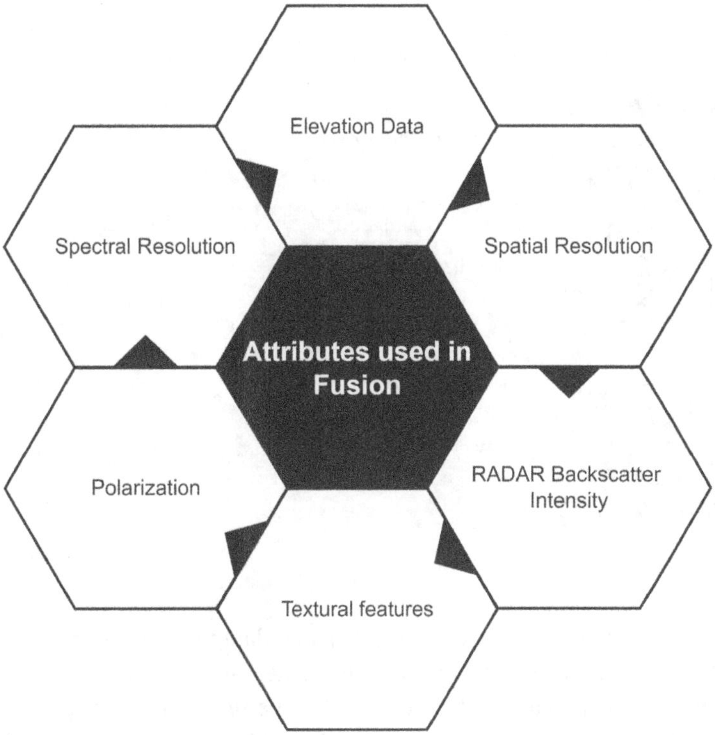

Figure 1: Attributes used in fusion.

1.3 Fusion algorithms for microwave and optical images

There are several fusion techniques developed to combine the information from optical and microwave RS images. By performing this process, complementary information can be extracted from the fused image obtained. Microwave images use radar sensors, while optical images use visible/infrared sensors to capture images from a distance [16, 17]. Multiple methods exist for the fusion of optical and microwave images. Pansharpening is a method that merges a panchromatic single wide-range band with a multispectral band of lower resolution to obtain an image with higher resolution [18]. Figure 2 highlights some of the fusion methods that are commonly implemented. Various pansharpening methods are designed to minimize spatial distortions in RS images. The Gram-Schmidt (GS) pansharpening algorithm uses an orthogonalization process where the multiple spectral bands are decorrelated, and the first principal component is replaced with a panchromatic image [19, 20]. This method effectively sharpens the multispectral image (MI) without distorting the spectral information of the image.

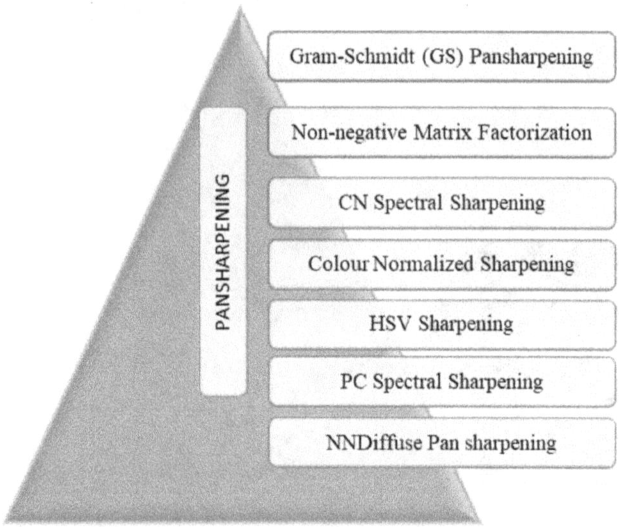

Figure 2: Fusion techniques.

NNDiffuse (NND) pansharpening technique diffuses spatial data taken from the panchromatic image (PI) into a multispectral image by using neural network techniques. It intelligently integrates PI spatial details into the MI while preserving the spectral characteristics of multispectral bands (Liu, Huang & Zhao, 2006) [22]. The algorithm estimates the missing high-frequency details in multispectral bands by using PI and diffusively transfers this information to enhance spatial resolution. This method has the benefits of reducing color distortions, improving spatial resolution, and not compromising spectral information [23]. Non-negative matrix factorization is another fusion technique that decomposes high-dimensional multispectral or hyperspectral image data into non-negative components to enhance the interpretability of images [24]. The input optical image is broken down into initial nonnegative matrices and a co-efficient matrix whose elements are also nonnegative. This process helps preserve the reflectance as well as the radiance of input pixel values [25]. Another fusion method to improve spatial and spectral image quality is CN spectral sharpening. In this method, a MI is analyzed using a noise-adjusted principal component and transformed into its uncorrelated components. These components are then substituted by high-resolution PI, most likely the one most highly correlated with a panchromatic band. Noise reduction from the input image is also performed during this process [26, 27].

The color normalized (CN) sharpening method is another pansharpening technique that normalizes multispectral image colors to eliminate variations in intensity.

It then uses high-resolution data from the PI to sharpen these normalized color components. This technique attempts to balance color information with panchromatic data [28]. The hue, saturation, value (HSV) fusion technique transforms the MI from the RGB (red, green, blue) color space to the HSV color space. Following this, the value (V) component is substituted with high-resolution PI containing the brightness information. Finally, the fused image obtained is converted back to the RGB model, combining color information from the original MI with high-resolution spatial details from the PI [29]. This technique preserves the color accuracy of the original image and also enhances the spatial resolution [30]. Another method known as principal component spectral (PCS) sharpening, uses principal component (PC) analysis for fusing PI with MIs. Initially, the transformation of MIs is performed into a group of uncorrelated PCs, with the most variant first PC. In the substitution step, the high-resolution PI is substituted for the first PC containing the highest spatial information. After this, inverse PC analysis is performed to return to the original spectral space, creating a fused image [31, 32].

In comparison to the existing methods discussed above, NND pansharpening ensures more natural image reconstruction with minimal spectral distortions. It requires tuning for specific datasets as a prerequisite. The objectives of our work include: (a) preprocessing the images taken from two data sets, that is, Sentinel-1 and Sentinel-2, (b) performing fusion of these images using the NND pansharpening technique; and (c) conducting a visual comparison of the original image (without fusion) and the resultant image (with fusion). The fusion process aims to remove clouds from the input image to enhance interpretation and analysis.

2 Dataset and area of interest

The input images have been taken from two standard data sets, Sentinel-1 for microwave images and Sentinel-2 for multispectral optical images (https://dataspace.copernicus.eu/). The study area chosen for our implementation is located in the Himachal Pradesh state. The study area covers an area of 47,681.88 km^2. Figure 3(a) shows the study site in yellow, and Figure 3(b) shows the details highlighting the cloud coverage of 20% and terrain with snow traces. The input images for both datasets have been taken on February 6, 2024 for analysis. The justification for choosing this specific area of interest is due to the presence of snow, which can be further used for predictive analysis during the classification of snow-covered and snow-uncovered regions.

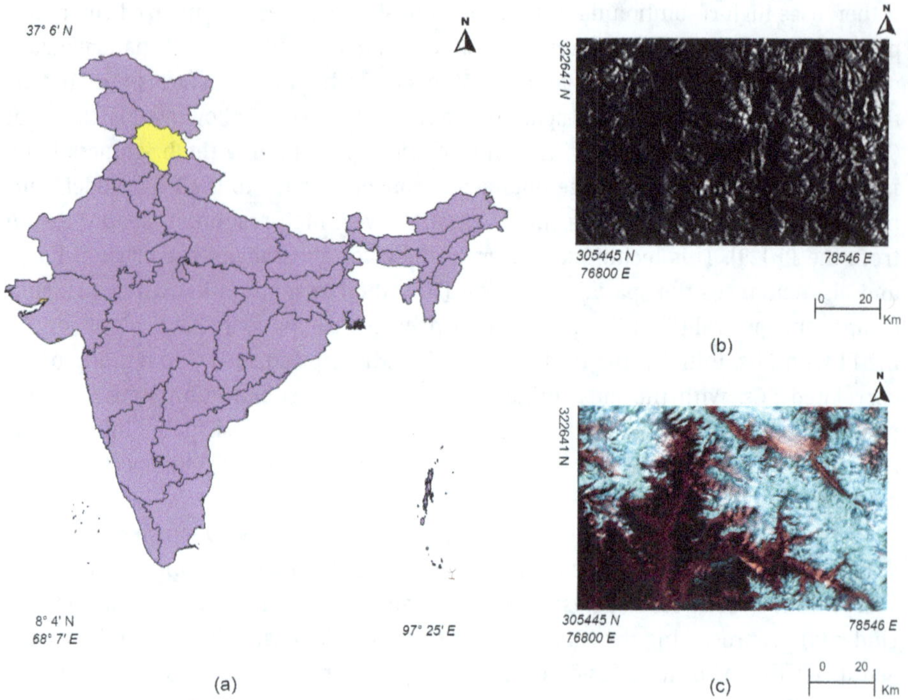

Figure 3: (a) Area under study in Himachal Pradesh,. (b) Sentinel-1 image of the area under study with cloud and snow cover. (c) Sentinel-2 image of the area under study with cloud and snow cover.

3 Methodology: process followed for fusion

The methodology shown in Figure 4, followed for the fusion of microwave and optical images, is as follows: the selection of the area of interest, based on which microwave and optical images will be extracted from the given dataset. In the next step, input raw images will be pre-processed, which includes stacking and sub-stacking of the corresponding images. In the final step, the fusion of stacked images of the respective datasets will be performed using the NND pansharpening technique to obtain a fused, enhanced image.

3.1 Input raw images

The input microwave and multispectral optical images are taken from their respective datasets, Sentinel-1 and Sentinel-2, in the same area of interest and on a specific date. The images have similar cloud coverage and the presence of snow content. Figure 5 depicts true input images taken from the datasets. The Sentinel-2 image is composed of 13

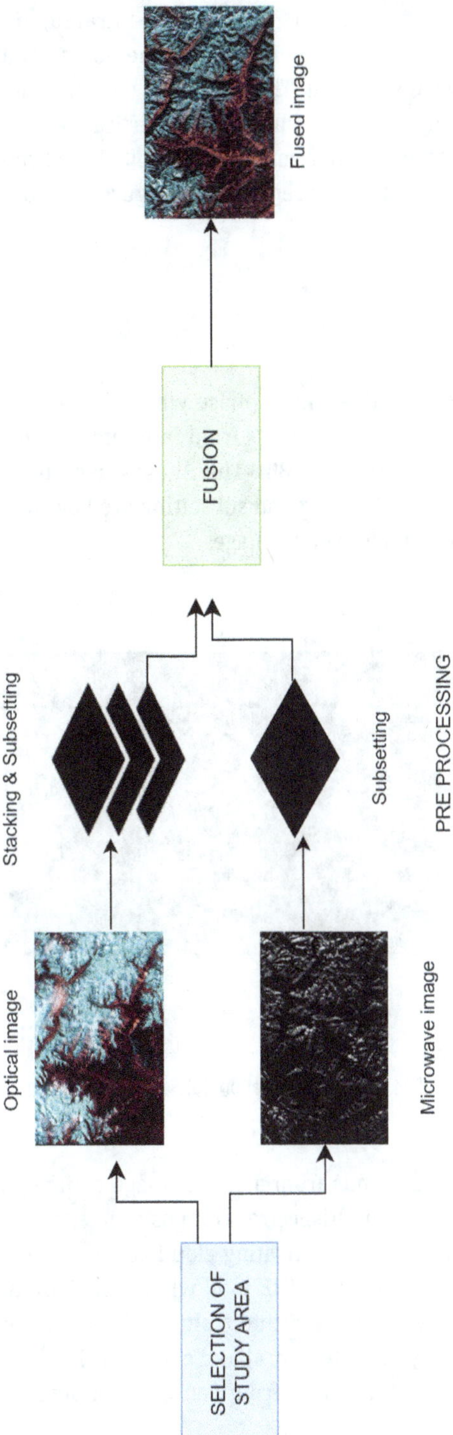

Figure 4: Methodology of the proposed framework.

spectral bands with different spatial resolutions. It covers visible, near-infrared, and shortwave infrared regions of the electromagnetic spectrum [33]. On the other hand, Sentinel-1 covers the C-band of the microwave spectrum. The radar imagery provided by Sentinel-1 has two key polarizations, named VV (vertical transmit, vertical receive) polarization and VH polarization (vertical transmit, horizontal receive) [34]. The raw images taken as inputs from Sentinel-1 and Sentinel-2 are shown in Figures 5 and 6, respectively.

3.2 Preprocessing

Preprocessing is a critical phase following the initial input phase when working on the RS process. This exercise is required to remove distortions from input images that may have been introduced during data acquisition [35, 36]. The images need to be aligned with each other to enhance the analysis. Stacking and subsetting are key steps before performing a fusion of these optical and microwave images.

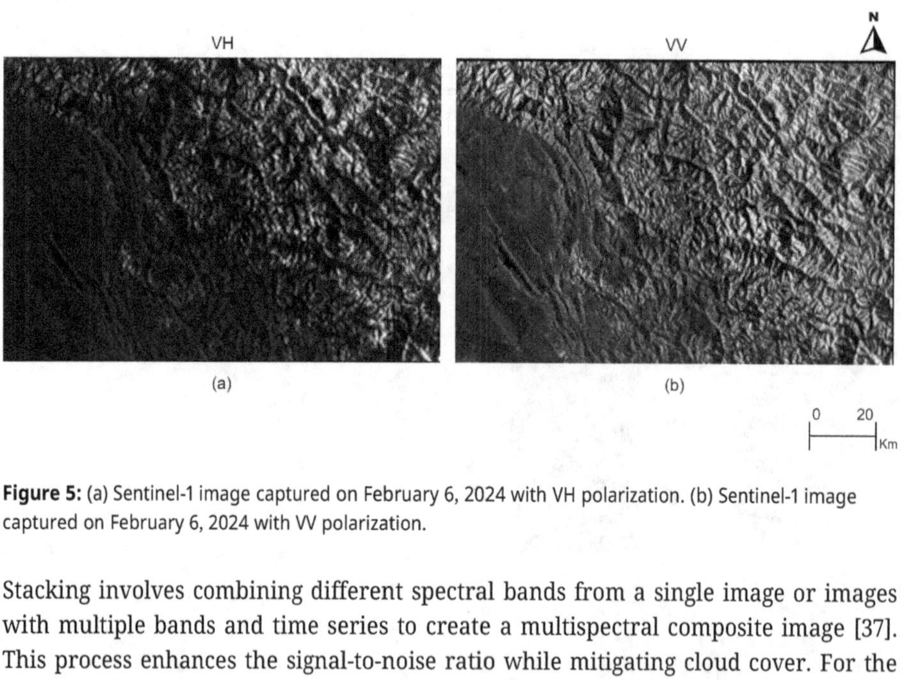

Figure 5: (a) Sentinel-1 image captured on February 6, 2024 with VH polarization. (b) Sentinel-1 image captured on February 6, 2024 with VV polarization.

Stacking involves combining different spectral bands from a single image or images with multiple bands and time series to create a multispectral composite image [37]. This process enhances the signal-to-noise ratio while mitigating cloud cover. For the stacking of Sentinel-2 images, we used the ERDAS IMAGINE tool, where all 13 input images with their respective spectral bands were stacked into a single MI, as shown in Figure 7(a). Sentinel-1 images are inherently multi-temporal and coherent. The synthetic aperture radar capabilities of the dataset acquired from Sentinel-1 allow it to

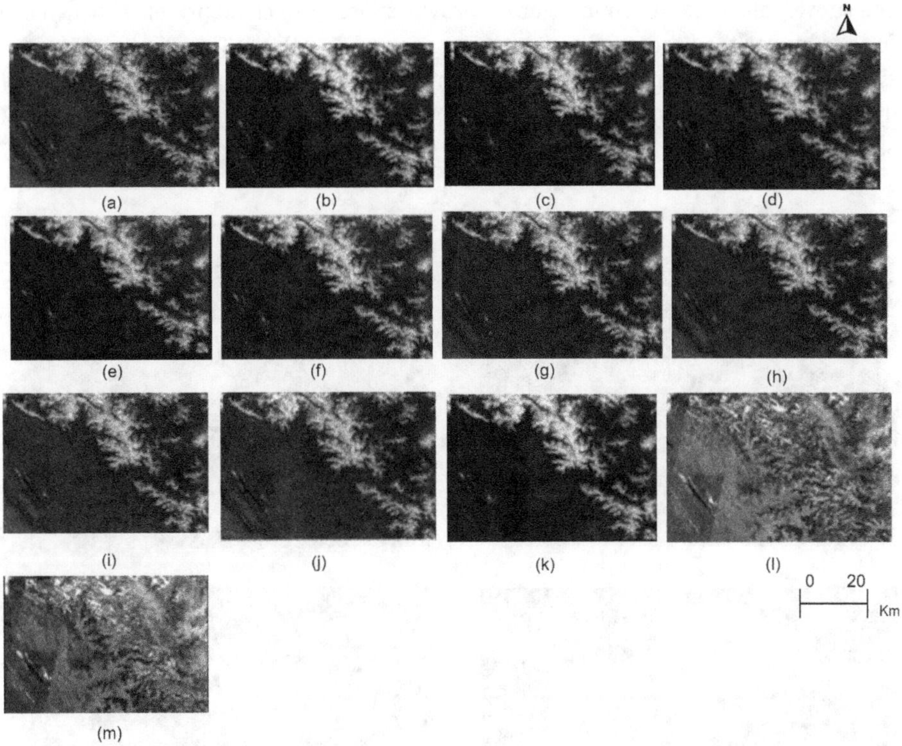

Figure 6: Sentinel-2 image captured on February 6, 2024 with 13 spectral bands.

capture data through clouds and various weather conditions, thus making it less critical for the stacking process [38].

After obtaining the co-registered and stacked image, which is multi-band, we performed subsetting on two images from the above-mentioned datasets [39]. Subsetting is another major part of preprocessing, where a specific region of interest is extracted from a larger geographical region for deeper analysis. We used the created area of interest (AOI) for both Sentinel-1 and the stacked image of Sentinel-2 using Raster [40] in the ERDAS IMAGINE tool. Figure 7(b) shows the subset image of Sentinel-2, and Figures 7 (c) and (d) display the subset images of Sentinel-1, which were obtained by applying the same AOI to different polarized images.

3.3 Fusion technique used: NNDiffuse pansharpening

The subset images (radar and optical) fetched as an outcome of preprocessing need to be enhanced. The objective is to eliminate the flaws that occur in the processed images due to the inherent differences in data types, resolutions, incompatibilities, etc.

The subset image, as shown in Figure 7, provides visuals of cloud presence, which can further hinder the process of data interpretation and analysis. This can hamper decision-making at the application level. To improve it, we need to perform a fusion of the stacked and subset images of Sentinel-2 (optical imagery) and the subset image of Sentinel-1 (microwave imagery).

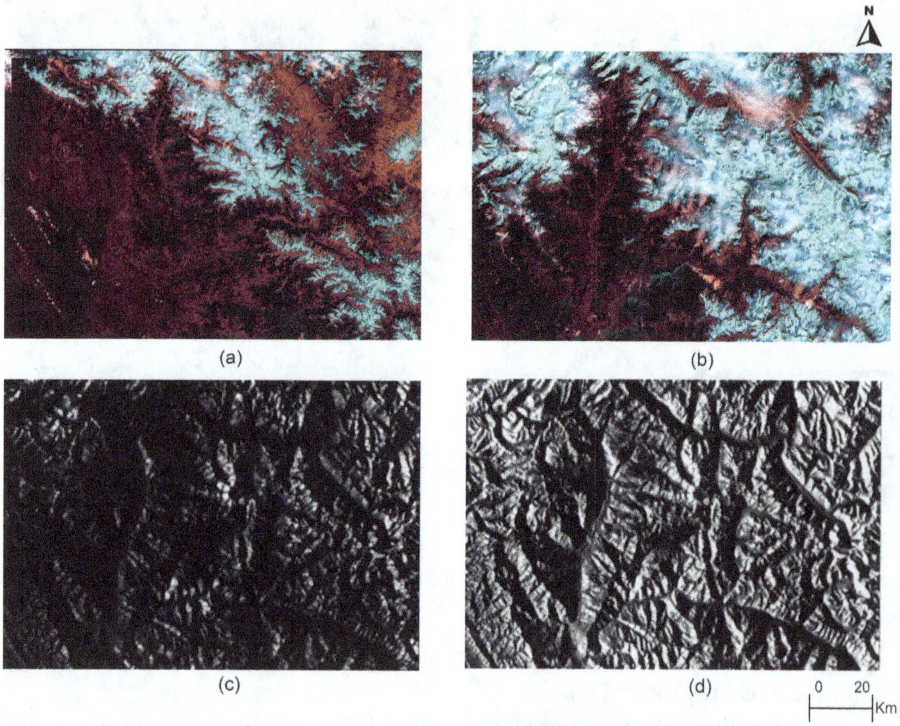

Figure 7: (a) Stacked image of Sentinel-2,, (b) subset image of Sentinel-2, (c) subset image of Sentinel-1 with VH polarization, and (d) subset image of Sentinel-1 with VV polarization.

The fusion technique followed here is NNDiffuse pansharpening since it provides better spatial resolution of multispectral images while preserving their spectral properties. It sharpens multispectral data using the nearest neighbor diffusion method [22]. Figure 8 provides a diagrammatic representation of the NNDiffuse pansharpening technique. The process initially begins with two input images, including a high-resolution PI taken from Sentinel-1 and a low-resolution MI from Sentinel-2. The pixels of these images are geometrically aligned and co-registered spatially.

It is then resampled to resolve the image similar to the PI. Next, a neural network-based diffusion procedure is applied to merge the spatial information from the panchromatic microwave image with the spectral information of the multispectral optical image. The resultant image is a high-resolution pan-sharpened image that retains

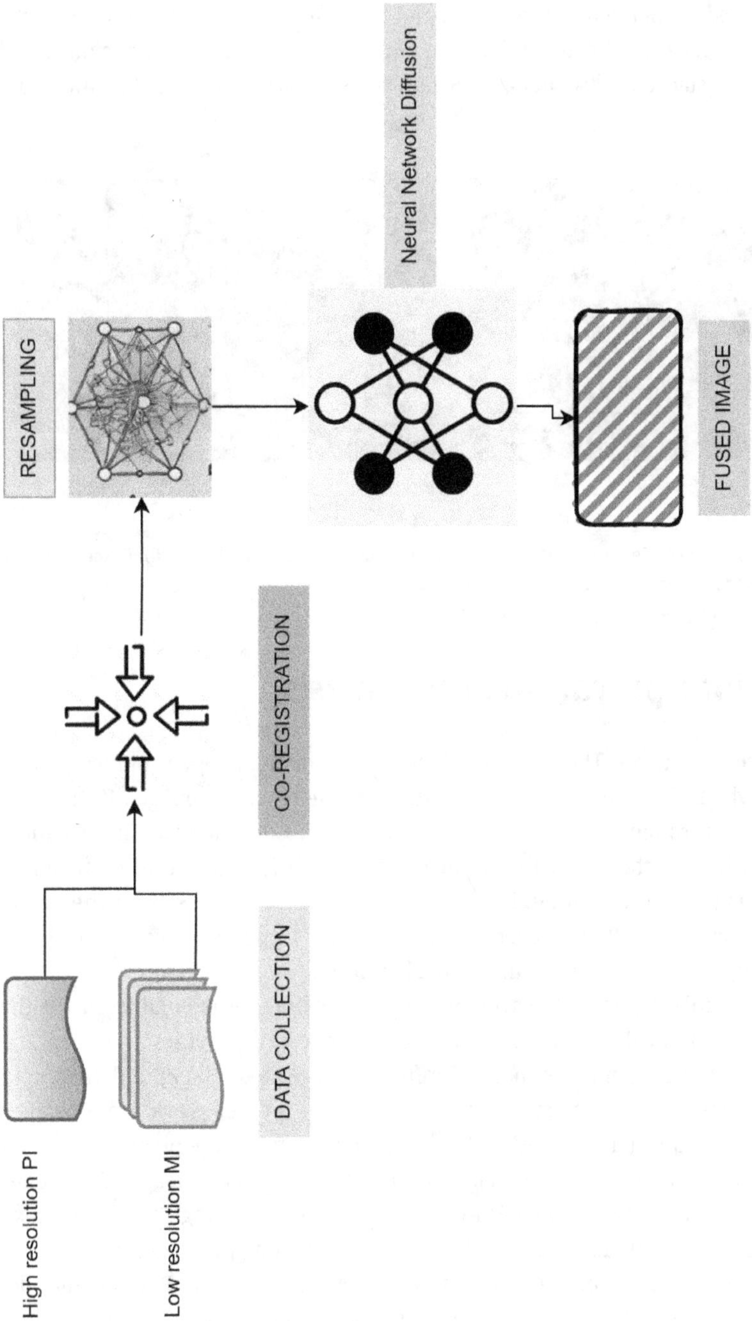

Figure 8: NNDiffuse pansharpening.

both the enhanced spatial detail from the PI and the rich spectral information from the MI. The fusion is performed consecutively on two different polarized subset images of Sentinel-1 with the stacked subset image of Sentinel-2, as depicted in Figure 9(a) and 9(b).

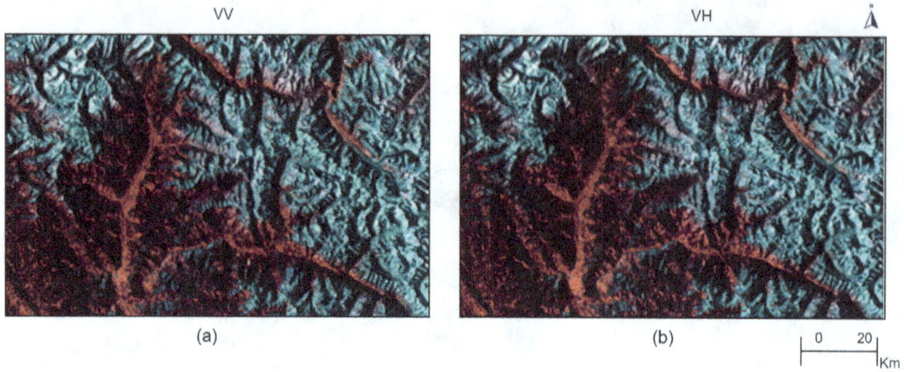

Figure 9: (a) Fused image of Sentinel-1 VV polarization and subset image of Sentinel-2. (b) Fused image of Sentinel-1 VH polarization and subset image of Sentinel-2.

4 Result interpretation and analysis

a. **Visual interpretation:** The implementation of the methodology provides a fused image in which the cloud pixels are eliminated. The resultant image offers better visualization through enhanced resolution without losing the exact information. The visual interpretation of the input image before fusion and after fusion is shown in Figure 10, which depicts the removal of cloud pixels from the actual image. This can be further utilized for classification purposes in specific decision-making for the particular area under consideration.
b. **Statistical analysis:** The objective of the statistical analysis conducted for the fused image is to evaluate its quality and effectiveness. It provides an interpretation regarding the extent of enhanced information related to spatial details, content, and accuracy. The metrics of assessment used for this work are R^2 values and root mean squared error (RMSE) values. We have taken the pixel values of all the bands corresponding to the original image and the fused image. The values considered are of different polarizations, i.e., VV and VH. Using these values, we calculated the R^2 value for each band of the corresponding polarization, as shown in Table 2. The results obtained are visualized in Figure 11. The RMSE values depict the overall spectral distortions of the source image and the NNDiffusion-based fused image. Figure 12 visualizes the RMSE values of different bands with their respective polarizations. From the results we analyzed, band 1 shows the

maximum error in the range of 0.2442–0.2448, and band 9 shows the minimum error in the range of 0.0375–0.0491. The overall R^2 value of VH polarization is greater than that of VV polarization, which indicates that the proposed model is satisfactory.

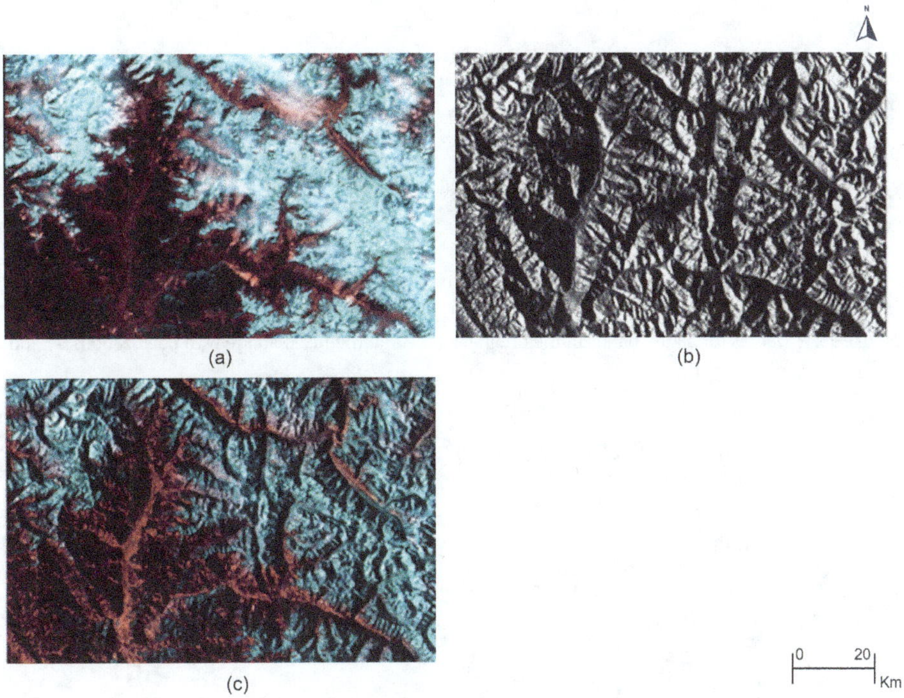

Figure 10: (a) Subset image of Sentinel-2 captured on February 6, 2024. (b) Subset image of Sentinel-1 captured on February 6, 2024. (c) Fused image with eliminated clouds.

Table 2: R^2 values of VV and VH polarizations across bands.

Bands	VH	VV
B1	0.2448	0.2442
B2	0.2219	0.2218
B3	0.2059	0.2054
B4	0.189	0.1882
B5	0.1494	0.1509
B6	0.0805	0.0848
B7	0.0576	0.0623
B8	0.0608	0.0653
B9	0.0375	0.0491
B10	0.0938	0.0938
B11	0.0817	0.1098

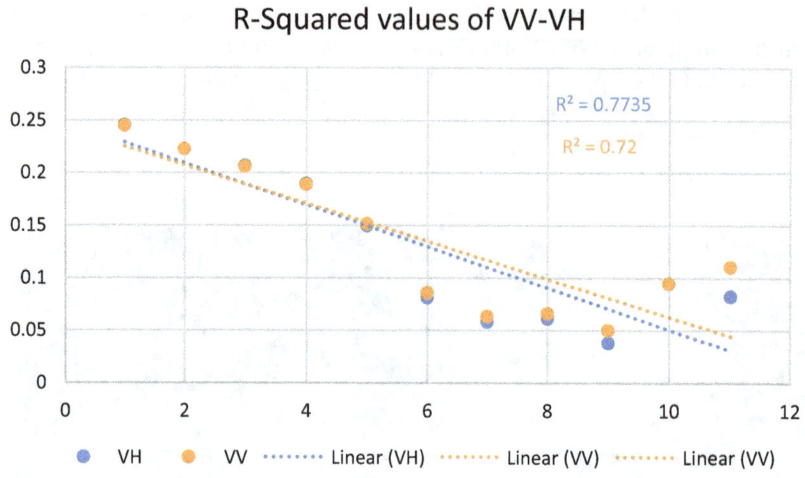

Figure 11: R^2 values for all the bands of the original image and the fused image with polarizations VV and VH.

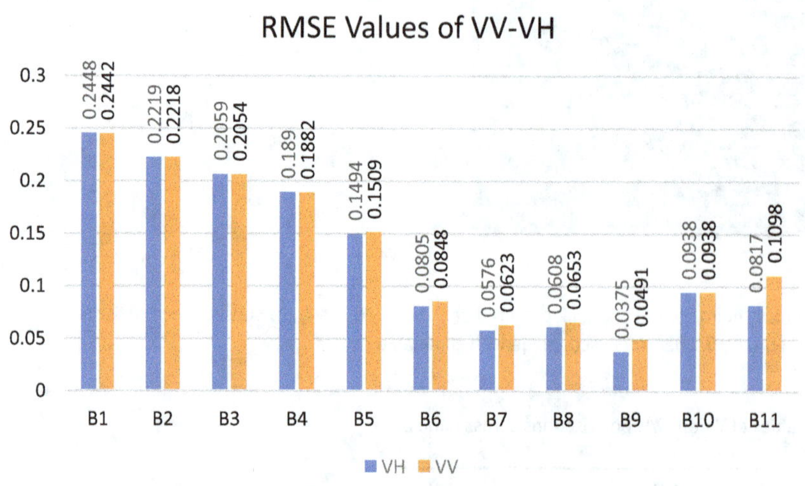

Figure 12: RMSE values for all the bands of the original image and the fused image with polarizations VV and VH.

5 Conclusion

Fusion, or pansharpening, is a method to improve the quality of RS images by incorporating the beneficial attributes of input images and producing an output image with better quality. The issues encountered while collecting and processing RS images are addressed through fused images. In our work, we have highlighted the importance of fusion algorithms and summarized a few of the most commonly used techniques. Furthermore, a methodology has been developed to eliminate clouds from optical and microwave images collected in a specific area of interest in the Himachal Pradesh state. The fusion technique employed here is NNDiffusion, which produces a resultant image where cloud pixels have been eliminated, as demonstrated through visualization. The statistical analysis of the output image identifies errors in all the bands with their respective polarizations. The cloud removal approach implemented here can also be further utilized to classify different domains.

References

[1] Mertikas, S.P., Partsinevelos, P., Mavrocordatos, C., Maximenko, N.A. 2021. Environmental applications of remote sensing. In: Pollution Assessment for Sustainable Practices in Applied Sciences and Engineering, Elsevier, 107–163. https://doi.org/10.1016/B978-0-12-809582-9.00003-7

[2] Ramachandran, S. 2018. Aerosols and Climate Change: Present Understanding, Challenges, and Future Outlook, 341–378. https://doi.org/10.1007/978-3-319-67474-2_17

[3] Ghamisi, P., Gloaguen, R., Atkinson, P.M., Benediktsson, J.A., Rasti, B., Yokoya, N., Wang, Q., Hofle, B., Bruzzone, L., Bovolo, F., Chi, M., Anders, K. 2019. Multisource and multitemporal data fusion in remote sensing: A comprehensive review of the state of the art. IEEE Geoscience and Remote Sensing Magazine 7, 6–39. https://doi.org/10.1109/MGRS.2018.2890023

[4] Kashinath, S.A., Mostafa, S.A., Mustapha, A., Mahdin, H., Lim, D., Mahmoud, M.A., Mohammed, M.A., Al-Rimy, B.A.S., Fudzee, M.F.M., Yang, T.J. 2021. Review of data fusion methods for real-time and multi-sensor traffic flow analysis. IEEE Access 9, 51258–51276. https://doi.org/10.1109/ACCESS.2021.3069770

[5] Vyas, N., Singh, S., Sethi, G.K. 2024. A novel image fusion-based post classification framework for agricultural variations detection using Sentinel-1 and Sentinel-2 data. In: Earth Science Informatics, Media LLC: Springer Science and Business. doi: 10.1007/s12145-024-01506-0

[6] Chang, Z., Fan, L., Wigneron, J.-P., Wang, Y.-P., Ciais, P., Chave, J., Fensholt, R., Chen, J.M., Yuan, W., Ju, W., Xin, L., Jiang, F., Wu, M., Chen, X., Qin, Y., Frappart, F., Xiaojun, L., Wang, M., Liu, X., Tang, X., Hobeichi, S., Yu, M., Ma, M., Wen, J., Xiao, Q., Shi, W., Liu, D., Yan, J. 2023. Estimating aboveground carbon dynamic of china using optical and microwave remote-sensing datasets from 2013 to 2019. Journal of Remote Sensing 3. https://doi.org/10.34133/remotesensing.0005

[7] Darbaghshahi, F.N., Mohammadi, M.R., Soryani, M. 2022. Cloud removal in remote sensing images using generative adversarial networks and SAR-to-optical image translation. IEEE Transactions on Geoscience and Remote Sensing 60, 1–9. https://doi.org/10.1109/TGRS.2021.3131035

[8] Woodhouse, I.H. 2017. Introduction to Microwave Remote Sensing, CRC Press. https://doi.org/10.1201/9781315272573

[9] Zhang, Q., Tang, J., Zheng, H., Lin, C. 2022. Efficient object detection method based on aerial optical sensors for remote sensing. Displays 75, 102328. https://doi.org/10.1016/j.displa.2022.102328

[10] Rahman, M.M., Tetuko Sri Sumantyo, J., Sadek, M.F. 2010. Microwave and optical image fusion for surface and sub-surface feature mapping in Eastern Sahara. International Journal of Remote Sensing 31, 5465–5480. https://doi.org/10.1080/01431160903302999

[11] Kulkarni, S.C., Rege, P.P. 2020. Pixel level fusion techniques for SAR and optical images: A review. Information Fusion 59, 13–29. https://doi.org/10.1016/j.inffus.2020.01.003

[12] Liu, X., Zheng, Q., Liu, R., Wang, D., Duncan, J.H., Huang, S. 2016. A study of radar backscattering from water surface in response to rainfall. Journal of Geophysical Research: Oceans 121, 1546–1562. https://doi.org/10.1002/2015JC010975

[13] Shao, Z., Wu, W., Li, D. 2021. Spatio-temporal-spectral observation model for urban remote sensing. Geo-spatial Information Science 24, 372–386. https://doi.org/10.1080/10095020.2020.1864232

[14] Ebel, P., Meraner, A., Schmitt, M., Zhu, X.X. 2021. Multisensor data fusion for cloud removal in global and all-season sentinel-2 imagery. IEEE Transactions on Geoscience and Remote Sensing 59, 5866–5878. https://doi.org/10.1109/TGRS.2020.3024744

[15] Shen, H., Wu, J., Cheng, Q., Aihemaiti, M., Zhang, C., Li, Z. 2019. A spatiotemporal fusion based cloud removal method for remote sensing images with land cover changes. IEEE Journal of Selected Topics in Applied Earth Observations and Remote Sensing 12, 862–874. https://doi.org/10.1109/JSTARS.2019.2898348

[16] Joseph, G. 1996. Imaging sensors for remote sensing. Remote Sensing Reviews 13, 257–342. https://doi.org/10.1080/02757259609532307

[17] Wu, Y., Tan, S., Zhao, Y., Liang, L., Zhou, M., Ji, G. 2023. Broadband multispectral compatible absorbers for radar, infrared and visible stealth application. Progress in Materials Science 135, 101088. https://doi.org/10.1016/j.pmatsci.2023.101088

[18] Dadrass Javan, F., Samadzadegan, F., Mehravar, S., Toosi, A., Khatami, R., Stein, A. 2021. A review of image fusion techniques for pan-sharpening of high-resolution satellite imagery. ISPRS Journal of Photogrammetry and Remote Sensing 171, 101–117. https://doi.org/10.1016/j.isprsjprs.2020.11.001

[19] Abdulwahab, R.A., Al-Ani, L.A., Shaban, A.H. 2023a. Hyperspectral Pansharpening Improvement using MNF Transformation, 020052. https://doi.org/10.1063/5.0171978

[20] Cánovas-García, F., Pesántez-Cobos, P., Alonso-Sarría, F. 2020. fusionImage: An R package for pan-sharpening images in open source software. Transactions in Geographic Information Systems 24, 1185–1207. https://doi.org/10.1111/tgis.12676

[21] Liu, W., Huang, J. and Zhao, Y. (2006) "Multisensor Image Fusion with the Undecimated Discrete Wavelet Transform," 2006 8th international Conference on Signal Processing. 2006 8th international Conference on Signal Processing, IEEE. https://doi:10.1109/icosp.2006.345604.

[22] Rokni, K. 2023. Investigating the impact of Pan Sharpening on the accuracy of land cover mapping in Landsat OLI imagery. Geodesy and Cartography 49, 12–18. https://doi.org/10.3846/gac.2023.15308

[23] Ducay, R., Messinger, D.W. 2022. Hyperspectral-multispectral image fusion using nearest-neighbor diffusion-based sharpening algorithm. In: Messinger, D.W., Velez-Reyes, M. (Eds.). Algorithms, Technologies, and Applications for Multispectral and Hyperspectral Imaging XXVIII. SPIE, 22. https://doi.org/10.1117/12.2619267

[24] Khader, A., Yang, J., Xiao, L. 2022. NMF-DuNet: nonnegative matrix factorization inspired deep unrolling networks for hyperspectral and multispectral image fusion. IEEE Journal of Selected Topics in Applied Earth Observations and Remote Sensing 15, 5704–5720. https://doi.org/10.1109/JSTARS.2022.3189551

[25] Chen, H., Ma, Y., Zhu, A., Wang, Z., Zhao, G., Wei, Y. 2021. Soil salinity inversion based on differentiated fusion of satellite image and ground spectra. International Journal of Applied Earth Observation and Geoinformation 101, 102360. https://doi.org/10.1016/j.jag.2021.102360

[26] Kumar, U., M, C., R, T.V. 2009. Pixel based fusion using IKONOS imagery. International Journal of Recent Trends in Engineering 1, 173.

[27] Vibhute, A.D., Gaikwad, S.V., Dhumal, R.K., Nagne, A.D., Varpe, A.B., Nalawade, D.B., Kale, K.V., Mehrotra, S.C. 2019. Hyperspectral and Multispectral Remote Sensing Data Fusion for Classification of Complex-Mixed Land Features using SVM, 345–362. https://doi.org/10.1007/978-981-13-9181-1_31

[28] Rehman, A.U., R, A. 2024. Comparison of different image fusion methods using Gaofen-6 and Sentinel-2 Imagery of Beijing City, China. The Sciencetech 5, 70–86.

[29] Xu, Z., Latif, M.A., Madni, S.S., Rafiq, A., Alam, I., Habib, M.A. 2021. Detecting white cotton bolls using high-resolution aerial imagery acquired through unmanned aerial system. IEEE Access 9, 169068–169081. https://doi.org/10.1109/ACCESS.2021.3138847
[30] Zhang, S., Zhang, Y., Chou, Y., Wang, Z., Shi, Y., Sun, Z. 2021. Analysis of the multispectral and SAR image. In: 2021 IEEE 6th International Conference on Computer and Communication Systems (ICCCS), IEEE, 312–315. https://doi.org/10.1109/ICCCS52626.2021.9449213
[31] Abdulwahab, R.A., Al-Ani, L.A., Shaban, A.H. 2023b. Fused Images Based on Division of Hyperspectral Images into Spectral Groups, 020009. https://doi.org/10.1063/5.0171974
[32] Sharma, K.V., Kumar, V., Singh, K., Mehta, D.J. 2023. LANDSAT 8 LST Pan sharpening using novel principal component based downscaling model. Remote Sensing Applications 30, 100963. https://doi.org/10.1016/j.rsase.2023.100963
[33] Spoto, F., Sy, O., Laberinti, P., Martimort, P., Fernandez, V., Colin, O., Hoersch, B., Meygret, A. 2012. Overview of sentinel-2. In: 2012 IEEE International Geoscience and Remote Sensing Symposium, IEEE, 1707–1710. https://doi.org/10.1109/IGARSS.2012.6351195
[34] Zhao, Y., Longépé, N., Mouche, A., Husson, R. 2021. Automated rain detection by Dual-Polarization Sentinel-1 data. Remote Sensing (Basel) 13, 3155. https://doi.org/10.3390/rs13163155
[35] Han, R., Liu, P., Wang, G., Zhang, H., Wu, X. 2020. Advantage of Combining OBIA and classifier ensemble method for very high-resolution satellite imagery classification. Journal Sensors 2020, 1–15. https://doi.org/10.1155/2020/8855509
[36] Alparone, L. et al. (2015) "Remote Sensing Image Fusion." CRC Press. https://doi:10.1201/b18189.
[37] Das, B., Rathore, P., Roy, D., Chakraborty, D., Jatav, R.S., Sethi, D., Kumar, P. 2022. Comparison of bagging, boosting and stacking algorithms for surface soil moisture mapping using optical-thermal-microwave remote sensing synergies. Catena (Association of Meat Scientists and Technologists) 217, 106485. https://doi.org/10.1016/j.catena.2022.106485
[38] Jiao, X., McNairn, H., Yekkehkhany, B., Dingle Robertson, L., Ihuoma, S. 2022. Integrating Sentinel-1 SAR and Sentinel-2 optical imagery with a crop structure dynamics model to track crop condition. International Journal of Remote Sensing 43, 6509–6537. https://doi.org/10.1080/01431161.2022.2142077
[39] Schulz, D., Yin, H., Tischbein, B., Verleysdonk, S., Adamou, R., Kumar, N. 2021. Land use mapping using Sentinel-1 and Sentinel-2 time series in a heterogeneous landscape in Niger, Sahel. ISPRS Journal of Photogrammetry and Remote Sensing 178, 97–111. https://doi.org/10.1016/j.isprsjprs.2021.06.005
[40] Shafique, A., Cao, G., Khan, Z., Asad, M., Aslam, M. 2022. Deep learning-based change detection in remote sensing images: A review. Remote Sensing (Basel) 14, 871. https://doi.org/10.3390/rs14040871

Dankan Gowda V.*, V. Nuthan Prasad, Christian Rafael Quevedo Lezama, Srinivas D., Prasanna Kumar Lakineni

Integrating AI in RADAR remote sensing: enhancing data processing, interpretation, and decision-making

Abstract: This chapter focuses on using artificial intelligence (AI) in RADAR remote sensing, with applications such as enhanced target detection and noise reduction. Various advanced techniques in the field of AI, including convolutional neural networks (CNNs) and recurrent neural networks, have improved the efficiency of RADAR systems. Autoencoders and generative adversarial networks can be used to enhance the quality of images. These techniques also accelerate real-time data processing, improving RADAR system responsiveness in disaster monitoring and autonomous navigation. This chapter addresses these challenges, explores methods to enhance AI models for RADAR applications, and outlines future research directions. Integrating AI into RADAR systems enhances their intelligence, autonomy, and ability to address climate monitoring, defense, and smart city application challenges.

Keywords: Artificial intelligence, RADAR remote sensing, machine learning, deep learning, target detection, environmental monitoring, SAR, big data, data processing, cloud computing, real-time applications

1 Introduction

The quantity of data generated by modern RADAR systems and the variety of data processing tasks pose significant challenges. Processing large volumes of data in real-time using manual or conventional methods is highly challenging [1]. This is where artificial intelligence (AI) can be utilized, as it offers effective ways of handling and interpreting vast amounts of data. As a result, advanced AI and machine learning

***Corresponding author: Dankan Gowda V.**, Department of Electronics and Communication Engineering, BMS Institute of Technology and Management, Bangalore, Karnataka, India, e-mail: dankan.v@bmsit.in
V. Nuthan Prasad, Department of Electronic and Communication, M S R I T, Bangalore, Karnataka, India, e-mail: nuthan.v@msrit.edu
Christian Rafael Quevedo Lezama, Electrical and Electronics Engineer, Universidad Nacional Mayor de San Marcos, Cercado de Lima, Peru, e-mail: christian.quevedo1@unmsm.edu.pe
Srinivas D., School of Business, SR University, Warangal, Telangana, India, e-mail: srinivas.d@sru.edu.in
Prasanna Kumar Lakineni, Department of Computer Science and Engineering, Koneru Lakshmaiah Education Foundation, Vaddeswaram, Andhra Pradesh, India, e-mail: lpk.lakineni@gmail.com

https://doi.org/10.1515/9783111572970-009

(ML) techniques can automate features, including object identification, categorization, and real-time processing or analysis [2]. This chapter examines the latest developments and innovation trends in AI algorithms applied to RADAR remote sensing. It discusses how AI advances the remote sensing application landscape and the challenges faced by traditional remote sensing approaches.

RADAR remote sensing uses electromagnetic waves to gather information about the physical attributes of objects or locations on Earth or in the atmosphere [3]. RADAR remote sensing is particularly beneficial because it can operate regardless of weather or local lighting conditions and is highly suitable for continuous monitoring [4]. The common types of RADAR systems include synthetic aperture radar (SAR), interferometric SAR (InSAR), and Doppler radar, which are widely used in today's society. These systems are applied in various areas, such as environmental monitoring, military surveillance, land use planning, and the evaluation of natural disasters [5]. Multisensor data fusion is also becoming increasingly popular, integrating data from various satellite sensors and achieving high accuracy in classification [6]. However, because of its relatively recent origin, collection analysis, and interpretation of the RADAR data, which, with the improvements in volume and resolution, are more difficult tasks, leading to the incorporation of AI technologies in present-day RADAR systems.

As shown in Figure 1, the RADAR data processing can be performed sequentially, with the utilization of AI further improving the data processing. AI is also used to enhance each stage, starting from pre-processing, where, for example, noise is removed from the data. Both feature extraction and target detection have leveraged ML and

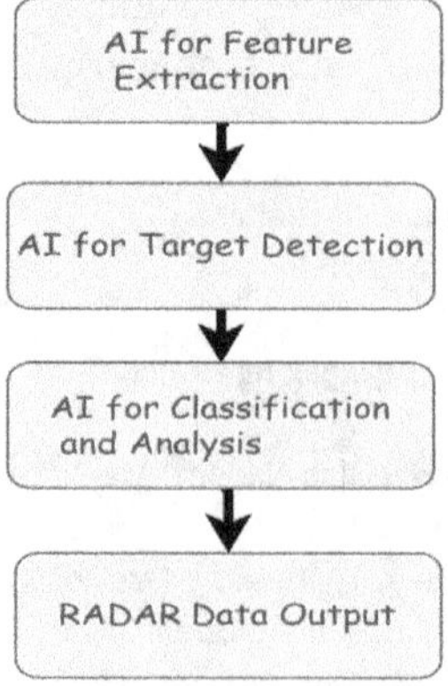

Figure 1: Overview of AI integration in RADAR remote sensing.

deep learning (DL) models, which help in the identification of objects in a significantly improved manner [7]. Using AI in the final step to make a classification and analysis of the situation makes RADAR systems more effective in decision-making. In the context of the framework stated above, it is clear how incorporating AI can enhance the evident high-value RADAR remote sensing applications.

2 Fundamentals of RADAR remote sensing

RADAR remote sensing is a technology that uses electromagnetic waves to identify, determine the position of, and map objects or features on the Earth's surface or in the atmosphere [8]. This characteristic makes RADAR systems suitable for continuous wide-area surveillance without the influence of environmental variables [9]. RADAR systems are especially applied in topographic mapping, disaster monitoring, environmental monitoring and surveillance, and military applications [10]. Since RADAR remote sensing can gather information over large areas and 'see through' clouds, it is also invaluable when optical sensors are not feasible. However, processing RADAR data is challenging due to the nature of signals and their interaction with the surfaces of the intended target [11].

RADAR systems generally employ two key modes: real-aperture RADAR (RAR) and synthetic-aperture RADAR (SAR). In the case of RAR, resolution is defined by the physical size of the antenna as well as the range to the intended target. However, the best way to enhance RADAR imaging technology is SAR, where the real width of the antenna is artificially enlarged by integrating the results from the sent-out pulses as the sensor moves along a course. SAR provides high-resolution imagery, which may be of greater value than optical imagery for many applications, such as geographical mapping, surveillance of infrastructure, etc [12]. Radio waves are transmitted in horizontal or vertical planes, a process known as polarization, to penetrate or construct images of the target area. Wave polarization supplies additional data concerning the examined surface, for instance, distinguishing between wet and dry portions or varying types of vegetation. The frequency shift of the returned signal, through Doppler techniques, is also used to identify the movement of objects, such as the speed of moving vehicles and ocean currents.

3 AI integration in RADAR remote sensing

The incorporation of AI into RADAR remote sensing systems is a major step up in terms of data processing, analysis, and interpretation. Many advances in RADAR data analysis have benefited from AI, especially ML and DL techniques [13]. This integration allows the processing of large amounts of data by incorporating otherwise time-consuming and intensive tasks such as, feature extraction, object detection, or classification, eliminating the need for human intervention, or the involvement of slow conventional algorithms [14]. The first major shift in RADAR remote sensing enabled by AI is real-time data analysis for disaster monitoring, military reconnaissance, and autonomous navigation applications [15].

Figure 2 presents a comparative analysis of four AI techniques, supervised, unsupervised, DL, and reinforcement learning, based on three key performance metrics: accuracy, precision, and recall. The grouped bar chart illustrates the performance of the individual AI methods in target detection within RADAR data. According to the results, DL provides the highest accuracy and precision, benefiting from more detailed target identification. Supervised learning and reinforcement learning are among the highest overall performers, albeit with moderate recall, while, conversely, unsupervised learning performs slightly lower across the assortment [16]. This type of visualization highlights the appropriateness of specific AI techniques for various RADAR applications while emphasizing the efficiency of DL in RADAR target identification.

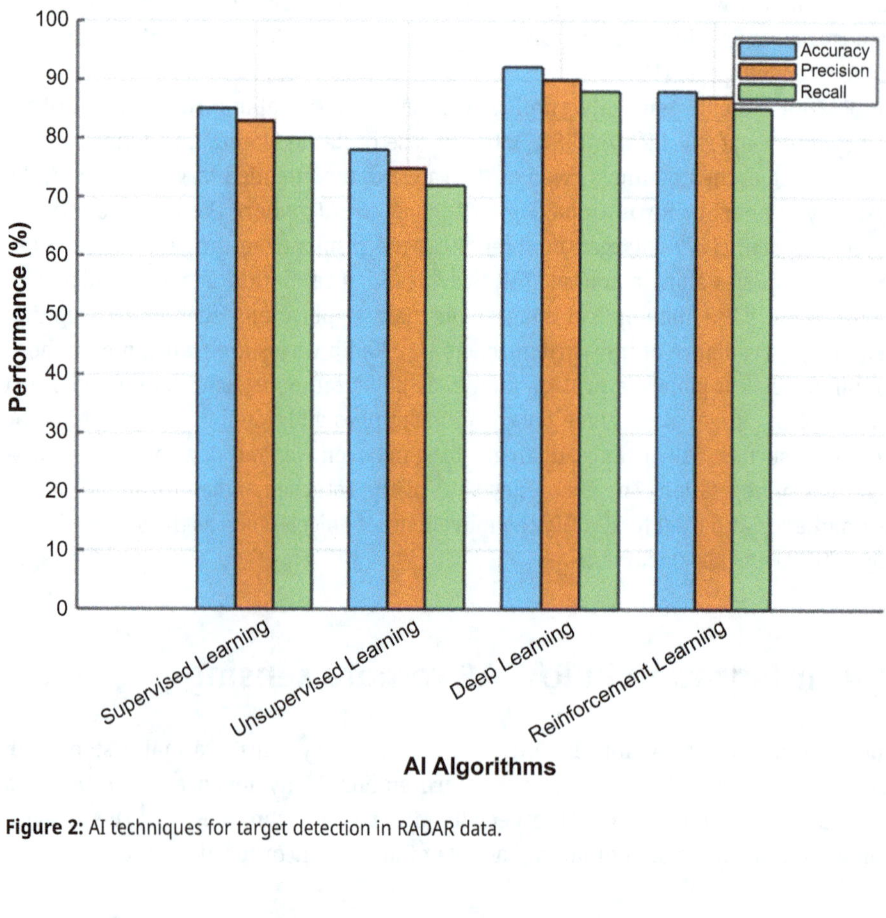

Figure 2: AI techniques for target detection in RADAR data.

However, problems such as noise and interference are major considerations in remote sensing under RADAR technology since they affect data quality and subsequent analysis. Several advanced noise reduction capabilities supported by AI have been developed to enhance the quality and comprehensibility of RADAR data. Using denoising autoencoders, it is possible to automatically predict which parts of the RADAR signals contain noise to improve the resolution and accuracy of the data [17]. These algorithms can detect patterns of noise and interference, which are extremely hard to identify using conventional methods, and effectively reject them without distorting important features. Aside from noise reduction, AI has also enhanced the methods used in data fusion, where data from different sources or at different degrees of sensor information, either optical, Light Detection and Ranging (LiDAR), or RADAR, is integrated and used to form a single perception of the observed scene. In point cloud fusion, such features can be aligned spatially and temporally; computation can show which elements complement each other well to achieve the highest accuracy. AI-derived data fusion strengthens RADAR systems, especially those applied in auto navigation, for greater environmental perception, which is essential. In this regard, AI enhances noise reduction and data fusion to enable RADAR systems to develop better high-resolution data for various applications [18].

4 Literature survey

Most pioneering cases of AI applications in remote sensing were primarily exploratory, emphasizing the enhancement of image classification, feature extraction, and object recognition [19]. Recent advances in big-data technology and AI have triggered the popularity of large labeled datasets, making AI applications significant in the field. Most current research is dedicated to how DL methods, including convolutional neural networks (CNNs) and recurrent neural networks (RNNs), have impacted the analysis of data forms such as SAR and LiDAR. This literature review focuses on the evolution of AI in remote sensing over the years, the significant milestones that have taken place, a comparison of present-day approaches to AI, and the existing and ongoing issues that scholars are still working to overcome [20].

AI has been incorporated into remote sensing since the late 1980s, utilizing simple ML methodologies for identifying and classifying features in satellite images. In the early 2000s, with the advent of ML, techniques for remote sensing became much more automated, primarily through the use of support vector machines (SVM) and decision trees, especially in identifying land use and land cover classes [21]. DL, which emerged in the mid-2010s, brought a new twist: AI can now perform much more complex functions such as feature extraction, real-time object detection, and data processing. Neural networks, specifically CNNs, became widely used for image recognition, including high-resolution remote sensing data, achieving better accuracy and higher efficiency. Recent advancements in cloud computing, edge computing, and big data analytics have further enhanced remote sensing, enabling real-time applications and larger-scale studies [22]. AI continues to evolve, transitioning from rule-based systems to ML and DL-based models.

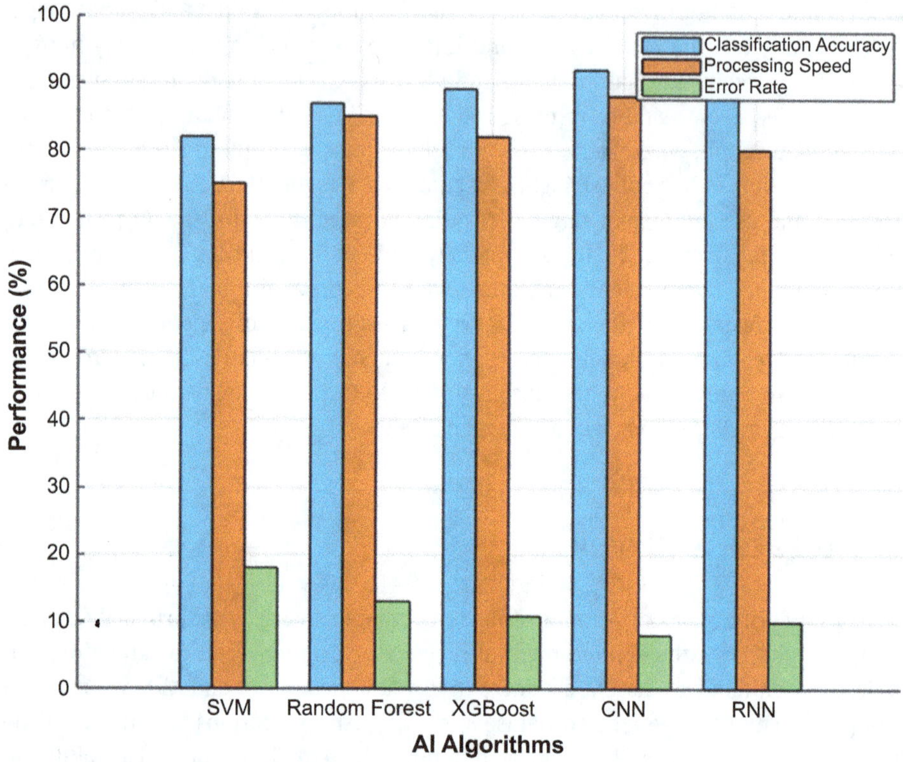

Figure 3: Comparative analysis of AI algorithms in RADAR remote sensing.

Figure 3 compares five algorithms, SVM, random forest, XGBoost, CNN, and RNN, regarding classification accuracy, processing speed, and error rate in RADAR remote sensing applications. The results indicate that CNN has the highest accuracy of 92% and is thus the most appropriate for accurate target identification. XGBoost demonstrated an approximate balance across all characteristics, with high accuracy and moderate computation speed. The accuracy of random forest is somewhat lower than that of CNN and XGBoost, but it operates relatively faster than both. The error rate is lowest with CNN, highlighting its resilience in avoiding the misclassification of incorrect classes. This comparison illustrates how fast and accurate an AI algorithm can be while also showing the ratio of false results in RADAR applications.

There are several major contributions and milestones in advancing AI in remote sensing. The early achievements included the successful use of SVM and K-nearest neighbor (K-NN) algorithms to classify remote sensing imagery for AI image analysis. The advances in CNNs emerged as a global revolution since they allow AI systems to learn spatial hierarchies from satellite images independently and accurately [23]. A major advancement was made by incorporating DL in the computation of SAR and LiDAR, which provided more detailed topographical and environmental analyses [24]. One of the important developments in AI for data fusion is the integration of multiple data sources like optical images, radar, and LiDAR to form comprehensive and precise models. Reinforcement learning has also been applied in real-time settings, especially in autonomous systems where AI operates and evolves in dynamic environments. These innovations have revolutionized fields like disaster response, precision farming, and climate studies, and thus demonstrate the potential of AI to transform the use of remote sensing data across various industries.

5 Emerging AI techniques in RADAR applications

The use of AI in RADAR systems is increasing due to its ability to enhance data collection and analysis speed and efficiency. New approaches, such as DL, transfer learning, and reinforcement learning, enable radar systems to solve more demanding tasks, such as high-resolution imaging, object detection, and environmental surveillance [25]. Transfer learning is also gaining popularity, where trained recognition models are fine-tuned to new RADAR datasets to shorten training time [26]. Another important achievement is the use of generative adversarial networks for data enhancement, particularly in RADAR systems based on satellite images. Reinforcement learning further enables automation, allowing RADAR systems to make informed decisions in complex scenarios, such as selecting signal processing methods in real-time workflows. These new and developing AI techniques are not only improving the performance of RADAR systems in terms of accuracy and speed but are also opening the door to far more independent and, thus, more scalable applications [27].

Supervised learning algorithms, such as SVM and CNN, are commonly used in RADAR imagery to recognize objects, such as vehicles, terrains, and others. In contrast, unsupervised learning is employed on the data to identify patterns or points of anomaly without requiring prior training on such data [28]. Unknown objects or environmental changes can be detected through clustering methods, such as k-means or self-organizing maps. Reinforcement learning enables RADAR systems to learn from their interactions with the environment and, consequently, operate under ever-changing conditions. This is especially true in the military, where RADAR systems must train and make decisions in real-time, for instance, on the optimal plan of operation in environments filled with clutter or hostile conditions. All the aforementioned learning approaches independently and effectively enhance the efficiency, accuracy, and autonomy of existing RADAR systems [29].

The classification of target detection using AI in the RADAR system is another factor where a CNN can be utilized. The CNN convolves filters to the input to extract useful and meaningful features from the RADAR data. The convolution operation is mathematically expressed as

$$y[i,j] = \sum_m \sum_n x[i+m, j+n] \cdot w[m,n]$$

where $x[i,j]$ is the input RADAR image, $w[m,n]$ is the convolutional kernel or filter, and $y[i,j]$ is the output feature map after applying the convolution.

The convolution operation is very helpful for the AI model in recognizing certain details, such as edges or shapes, which are very important for object detection in RADAR data. The data is fed through activation functions such as ReLU, followed by fully connected layers to produce a classification output. Denoising autoencoders or DL techniques are commonly used for noise reduction. The goal is to reconstruct a clean signal $\hat{x}$ from a noisy input x. The objective function of a denoising autoencoder is to minimize the reconstruction error:

$$L(x, \hat{x}) = \frac{1}{2} \sum_i (x_i - \hat{x}_i)^2$$

where x_i is the original noisy signal and $\hat{x}_i$ or is the reconstructed (denoised) signal.

This equation quantifies the dissimilarity between the input and the reconstructed signal. It aims to minimize this error with the help of the AI model. For instance, to emulate the enhancement of real-time speed through the implementation of AI, the speed metric $F(t)$ widely used is the number of frames per second. AI models improve the processing speed $F(t)$ over time by optimizing the number of operations required for each frame:

$$F(t) = F0 + \alpha t$$

where $F0$ is the initial frame rate, α is the rate of improvement in frame rate, and t is time.

This linear model illustrates how AI enhances real-time processing for RADAR applications, as it is utilized in real-time auto-navigation or military RADAR. For AI models such as SVM or CNN applied to RADAR data, the classification accuracy, A, is calculated as:

$$A = \frac{\text{TP} + \text{TN}}{\text{TP} + \text{TN} + \text{FP} + \text{FN}}$$

where TP (true positives) represent correctly identified objects, TN (true negatives) represent correctly identified non-objects, FP (false positives) represent incorrect identification of objects, and FN (false negatives) represent missed objects.

This equation is employed to assess the overall accuracy of the AI model in target identification and classification from RADAR data. AI models developed for environmental monitoring, such as deforestation or urban area growth detection, provide an output for each pil in the RADAR data. A common evaluation metric is the *F*1 score, which balances precision and recall:

$$F1 = 2.\frac{\text{Precision.Recall}}{\text{Precision} + \text{Recall}}$$

where

$$\text{Precision} = \frac{\text{TP}}{\text{TP} + \text{FP}}$$

$$\text{Recall} = \frac{\text{TP}}{\text{TP} + \text{FN}}$$

The *F*1 score measures the harmonic mean of precision and recall values. It applies equally strict criteria to determine whether the AI model is performing well enough in detecting environmental changes without generating a high number of false positives (precision) or missing too many changes (recall).

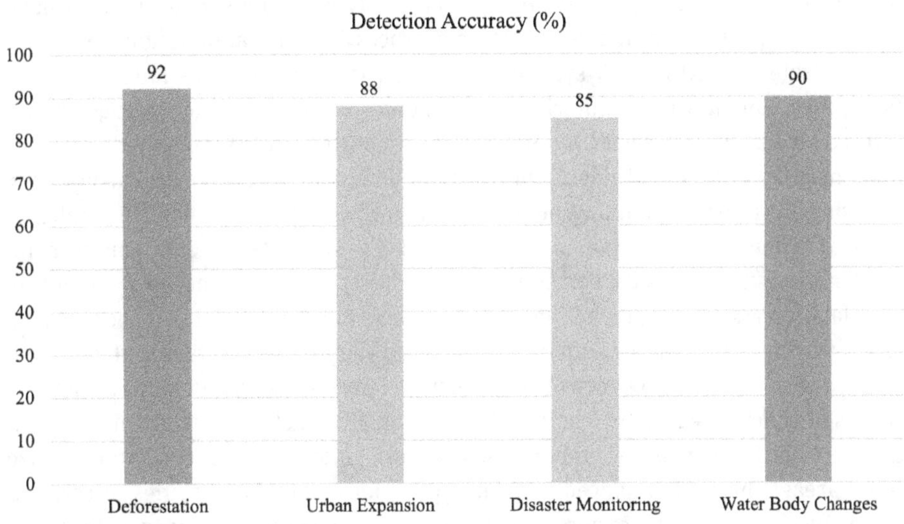

Figure 4: Applications of AI in environmental monitoring using RADAR.

Figure 4 illustrates how AI has contributed to increasing the detection accuracy of all RADAR monitoring environment applications. The applications examined include deforestation, urbanization, disaster management, and water body shifts. The application of AI enhances detection accuracy appreciably, with deforestation achieving the highest accuracy at 92% and water body changes at 90%. Urban expansion and disaster monitoring also demonstrate high detection accuracies, highlighting the potential for successfully utilizing AI-RADAR to monitor environmental changes. This figure underscores how AI has facilitated improvements in environmental monitoring through enhanced data processing.

In SAR and InSAR applications, the salient feature of AI is that it enhances the spatial and radiometric resolution of RADAR images. DL algorithms, such as CNNs, are essential for improving feature extraction and object classification from high-resolution imaging, especially in SAR [30]. These models can identify even small differences in terrain, making them optimal for environmental monitoring, such as deforestation, waterbodies, and urban expansion. AI-based systems also enable the integration of RADAR data with other remote sensing imagery, improving environmental monitoring such as optical or LiDAR. This integration bridges gaps, particularly when combined with AI, in analyzing ground displacement caused by earthquakes or landslides [31].

6 Case studies and applications

In RADAR remote sensing, AI has proven useful across various fields and has been shown to improve data analysis, real-time processing, and automation. Examples demonstrate how AI-RADAR systems assist decision-making in various important fields, including disaster monitoring and response, as well as climate change studies [19]. For instance, in disaster monitoring, AI-supported RADAR quickly determines flood heights, detects landslides, and monitors deformations caused by earthquakes. Applying AI in urban planning helps monitor infrastructure by analyzing stability, changes in land usage, and potential dangers. AI-driven RADAR systems monitor natural disasters such as floods, earthquakes, landslides, and hurricanes, providing precise data for assessing current conditions and coordinating effective responses [32]. SAR, with the help of AI algorithms, has received significant attention in flood monitoring due to its ability to penetrate cloud layers, offering high-quality interferometric results of water spread over relatively large areas. AI models can rapidly process SAR data to identify the most severely flooded regions, guiding rescue teams to prioritize those areas. These AI-enhanced RADAR applications enable authorities to respond more quickly to natural disasters, minimizing losses and casualties by providing critical information that is readily available [33].

AI integration in RADAR remote sensing for infrastructure is transforming urban design and assessment through automated methods within structures, such as health checks, land use, and change detection [34]. Both SAR and InSAR data, combined with AI processing, are utilized to detect subsidence, stability conditions of buildings, and shifts in the surface infrastructure of urban territories. For instance, systems known as RADARs, powered by AI, can identify variations such as cracks or deformations in buildings and bridges and indicate the likelihood of failure. This data is valuable because AI can predict which areas require maintenance and rehabilitation the most, providing that information to urban planners [35]. AI is also employed to track the geographical spread of built-up areas, land cover changes and conversions, zoning infringements, and the overall effects of urbanization. In rapidly developing urban corridors, advanced RADAR systems driven by AI assist in monitoring construction projects to ensure infrastructural development is eco-friendly and code-compliant [36].

7 Conclusion

AI integration in RADAR remote sensing has significantly advanced data processing, analysis, and automation, making real-time applications more efficient and accurate. AI-driven techniques such as DL, reinforcement learning, and transfer learning have improved object detection, classification, noise reduction, and data fusion, enhancing RADAR capabilities across diverse applications. AI-powered SAR and InSAR imaging provide high-resolution insights into environmental monitoring, disaster management, military surveillance, and urban planning. Comparative analyses highlight DL's superiority in classification accuracy, speed, and precision, proving its effectiveness in RADAR applications. Despite challenges like noise interference and high computational demands, AI continues to revolutionize RADAR systems by enabling autonomous decision-making, improved situational awareness, and enhanced disaster response. Future advancements in AI-driven RADAR will further refine data interpretation, support multisensor fusion, and drive more intelligent, adaptive applications. AI's role in RADAR remote sensing will remain pivotal in transforming modern geospatial analysis and remote sensing technology.

References

[1] Dileep, R., Jayanth, J., Ravikira, Vedha, A.S., Shyamala, C., Yuvaraju, T. 2024. Enhancing image fusion via optimized BAT algorithm in brovey transform for remote sensing images. In: 2024 International Conference on Knowledge Engineering and Communication Systems (ICKECS). Presented at the 2024 International Conference on Knowledge Engineering and Communication Systems (ICKECS), 1–6. https://doi.org/10.1109/ICKECS61492.2024.10617149

[2] Ebrahimi, S., Kumar, S. 2025. What helps to detect what? Explainable AI and multisensor fusion for semantic segmentation of simultaneous crop and land cover land use delineation. IEEE Journal of Selected Topics in Applied Earth Observations and Remote Sensing 18, 5423–5444. https://doi.org/10.1109/JSTARS.2025.3532829

[3] Günther, A., Najjar, H., Dengel, A. 2024. Explainable multimodal learning in remote sensing: Challenges and future directions. IEEE Geoscience and Remote Sensing Letters 21, 1–5. https://doi.org/10.1109/LGRS.2024.3404596

[4] Guo, C., Ai, W., Liu, Z., Yang, H., Zhao, X., Liu, G. 2024. A Sentinel-1 synthetic aperture radar image of heavy rainfall process compared with GPM DPR data. In: IGARSS 2024 – 2024 IEEE International Geoscience and Remote Sensing Symposium. Presented at the IGARSS 2024 – 2024 IEEE

International Geoscience and Remote Sensing Symposium, 5674–5678. https://doi.org/10.1109/IGARSS53475.2024.10641779

[5] Han, B., Zhang, S., Shi, X., Reichstein, M. 2024. Bridging remote sensors with multisensor geospatial foundation models. In: 2024 IEEE/CVF Conference on Computer Vision and Pattern Recognition (CVPR). Presented at the 2024 IEEE/CVF Conference on Computer Vision and Pattern Recognition (CVPR), 27852–27862. https://doi.org/10.1109/CVPR52733.2024.02631

[6] Vyas, N., Sethi, G.K., Singh, S. 2024. Comparative analysis of different classifiers on fusion of sentinel datasets for agriculture land. In: 2024 4th International Conference on Technological Advancements in Computational Sciences (ICTACS). Presented at the 2024 4th International Conference on Technological Advancements in Computational Sciences (ICTACS), 1173–1177. https://doi.org/10.1109/ICTACS62700.2024.10840995

[7] Saranya, A., Subhashini, R. 2023. A systematic review of Explainable Artificial Intelligence models and applications: Recent developments and future trends. Decision Analytics Journal 7, 100230. https://doi.org/10.1016/j.dajour.2023.100230

[8] Ji, Y., Liu, A., Shao, S., Yu, C., Chen, X. 2025. Intelligent target detection method for HFSWR based on dual-scale branch fusion network and adaptive threshold control. IEEE Transactions on Radar Systems 3, 379–391. https://doi.org/10.1109/TRS.2025.3540016

[9] Khan, M.U., Kamran, M.A., Khan, W.R., Ibrahim, M.M., Ali, M.U., Lee, S.W. 2024. Multi-sensor fusion for remote sensing of metallic and non-metallic object classification in complex soil environments and at different depths. IEEE Transactions on Geoscience and Remote Sensing 62, 1–13. https://doi.org/10.1109/TGRS.2024.3410530

[10] Li, W., Yang, W., Hou, Y., Liu, L., Liu, Y., Li, X. 2025. SARATR-X: Toward building a foundation model for SAR target recognition. IEEE Transactions on Image Processing 34, 869–884. https://doi.org/10.1109/TIP.2025.3531988

[11] Liu, Q. 2020. Sharpening the pan-multispectral GF-1 camera imagery using the gram-schmidt approach: The different select methods for low resolution pan in comparison. In: Liu, Y., Wang, L., Zhao, L., Yu, Z. (Eds.) Advances in Natural Computation, Fuzzy Systems and Knowledge Discovery, Cham: Springer International Publishing, 417–424. https://doi.org/10.1007/978-3-030-32456-8_45

[12] Oveis, A.H., Meucci, G., Mancuso, F., Berizzi, F., Cantelli-Forti, A. 2024. Generative AI threats to maritime navigation using deceptive ISAR images. IEEE Access 12, 173800–173809. https://doi.org/10.1109/ACCESS.2024.3500774

[13] Pihrt, J., Šimánek, P., Kovalenko, A., Kvapil, J., Charvát, K. 2024. AI-based spatiotemporal crop monitoring by cloud removal in satellite images. In: Annals of Computer Science and Information Systems. Presented at the Proceedings of the 19th Conference on Computer Science and Intelligence Systems (FedCSIS), 485–492.

[14] Peng, X., Zhong, R., Li, Z., Li, Q. 2021. Optical remote sensing image change detection based on attention mechanism and image difference. IEEE Transactions on Geoscience and Remote Sensing 59, 7296–7307. https://doi.org/10.1109/TGRS.2020.3033009

[15] Pirbasti, M.A., McArdle, G., Akbari, V. 2024. Hedgerows monitoring in remote sensing: A comprehensive review. IEEE Access 12, 156184–156207. https://doi.org/10.1109/ACCESS.2024.3485512

[16] Zuo, T., Liu, Y., Liu, H., Lei, Q., Chai, C. 2024. Remote sensing AI interpretation technology based on deep learning analyzes the damaged buildings in Gaza during the Palestinian-Israeli Conflict. In: 2024 5th International Conference on Geology, Mapping and Remote Sensing (ICGMRS). Presented at the 2024 5th International Conference on Geology, Mapping and Remote Sensing (ICGMRS), 7–14. https://doi.org/10.1109/ICGMRS62107.2024.10581371

[17] Zhou, -X.-X., Li, -Y.-Y., Luo, Y.-K., Sun, Y.-W., Su, Y.-J., Tan, C.-W., Liu, Y.-J. 2022. Research on remote sensing classification of fruit trees based on Sentinel-2 multi-temporal imageries. Scientific Reports 12, 11549. https://doi.org/10.1038/s41598-022-15414-0

[18] Yeong, D.J., Panduru, K., Walsh, J. 2025. Exploring the unseen: A survey of multi-sensor fusion and the role of explainable AI (XAI) in autonomous vehicles. Sensors 25, 856. https://doi.org/10.3390/s25030856

[19] Janga, B., Asamani, G.P., Sun, Z., Cristea, N. 2023. A review of practical ai for remote sensing in earth sciences. Remote Sensing 15, 4112. https://doi.org/10.3390/rs15164112

[20] Chakraborty, C., Bhattacharya, M., Pal, S., Lee, -S.-S. 2024. From machine learning to deep learning: Advances of the recent data-driven paradigm shift in medicine and healthcare. Current Research in Biotechnology 7, 100164. https://doi.org/10.1016/j.crbiot.2023.100164

[21] Estes, J.E., Sailer, C., Tinney, L.R. 1986. Applications of artificial in[TEL]ligence techniques to remote sensing*. The Professional Geographer 38, 133–141. https://doi.org/10.1111/j.0033-0124.1986.00133.x

[22] Sarker, I.H. 2021. Deep learning: A comprehensive overview on techniques, taxonomy. Applications and Research Directions. SN COMPUT. SCI 2, 420. https://doi.org/10.1007/s42979-021-00815-1

[23] Sun, Z., Sandoval, L., Crystal-Ornelas, R., Mousavi, S.M., Wang, J., Lin, C., Cristea, N., Tong, D., Carande, W.H., Ma, X., Rao, Y., Bednar, J.A., Tan, A., Wang, J., Purushotham, S., Gill, T.E., Chastang, J., Howard, D., Holt, B., Gangodagamage, C., Zhao, P., Rivas, P., Chester, Z., Orduz, J., John, A. 2022. A review of earth artificial intelligence. Computers & Geosciences 159, 105034. https://doi.org/10.1016/j.cageo.2022.105034

[24] Mashala, M.J., Dube, T., Mudereri, B.T., Ayisi, K.K., Ramudzuli, M.R. 2023. A systematic review on advancements in remote sensing for assessing and monitoring land use and land cover changes impacts on surface water resources in semi-arid tropical environments. Remote Sensing 15, 3926. https://doi.org/10.3390/rs15163926

[25] Garikapati, D., Shetiya, S.S. 2024. Autonomous vehicles: Evolution of artificial intelligence and the current industry landscape. Big Data and Cognitive Computing 8, 42. https://doi.org/10.3390/bdcc8040042

[26] Sultana, F., Sufian, A., Dutta, P. 2020. A review of object detection models based on convolutional neural network. In: Mandal, J.K., Banerjee, S. (Eds.) Intelligent Computing: Image Processing Based Applications, Singapore: Springer, 1–16. https://doi.org/10.1007/978-981-15-4288-6_1

[27] Ma, Z., Mei, G., Xu, N. 2024. Generative deep learning for data generation in natural hazard analysis: Motivations, advances, challenges, and opportunities. Artificial Intelligence Review 57, 160. https://doi.org/10.1007/s10462-024-10764-9

[28] Jiang, W., Ren, Y., Liu, Y., Leng, J. 2022. Artificial neural networks and deep learning techniques applied to radar target detection: A review. Electronics 11, 156. https://doi.org/10.3390/electronics11010156

[29] Chan, J.H., Liu, K., Chen, Y., Sagar, A.S.M.S., Kim, Y.-G. 2024. Reinforcement learning-based drone simulators: Survey, practice, and challenge. Artificial Intelligence Review 57, 281. https://doi.org/10.1007/s10462-024-10933-w

[30] Sun, Y., Montazeri, S., Wang, Y., Zhu, X.X. 2020. Automatic registration of a single SAR image and GIS building footprints in a large-scale urban area. ISPRS Journal of Photogrammetry and Remote Sensing 170, 1–14. https://doi.org/10.1016/j.isprsjprs.2020.09.016

[31] Zhao, T., Wang, S., Ouyang, C., Chen, M., Liu, C., Zhang, J., Yu, L., Wang, F., Xie, Y., Li, J., Wang, F., Grunwald, S., Wong, B.M., Zhang, F., Qian, Z., Xu, Y., Yu, C., Han, W., Sun, T., Shao, Z., Qian, T., Chen, Z., Zeng, J., Zhang, H., Letu, H., Zhang, B., Wang, L., Luo, L., Shi, C., Su, H., Zhang, H., Yin, S., Huang, N., Zhao, W., Li, N., Zheng, C., Zhou, Y., Huang, C., Feng, D., Xu, Q., Wu, Y., Hong, D., Wang, Z., Lin, Y., Zhang, T., Kumar, P., Plaza, A., Chanussot, J., Zhang, J., Shi, J., Wang, L. 2024. Artificial intelligence for geoscience: Progress, challenges, and perspectives. The Innovation 5, 100691. https://doi.org/10.1016/j.xinn.2024.100691

[32] Albahri, A.S., Khaleel, Y.L., Habeeb, M.A., Ismael, R.D., Hameed, Q.A., Deveci, M., Homod, R.Z., Albahri, O.S., Alamoodi, A.H., Alzubaidi, L. 2024. A systematic review of trustworthy artificial

intelligence applications in natural disasters. Computers and Electrical Engineering 118, 109409. https://doi.org/10.1016/j.compeleceng.2024.109409
[33] Amitrano, D., Di Martino, G., Di Simone, A., Imperatore, P. 2024. Flood detection with SAR: A review of techniques and datasets. Remote Sensing 16, 656. https://doi.org/10.3390/rs16040656
[34] Shi, W., Zhang, M., Zhang, R., Chen, S., Zhan, Z. 2020. Change detection based on artificial intelligence: State-of-the-art and challenges. Remote Sensing 12, 1688. https://doi.org/10.3390/rs12101688
[35] Lu, J. 2023. Application of artificial intelligence technology in bridge construction and maintenance. Highlights in Science, Engineering and Technology 75, 330–337. https://doi.org/10.54097/cbm3py13
[36] Mohsen, B.M. 2024. AI-driven optimization of urban logistics in smart cities: Integrating autonomous vehicles and iot for efficient delivery systems. Sustainability 16, 11265. https://doi.org/10.3390/su162411265

Ashutosh Pagrotra

Revolutionizing precision agriculture: the synergy of RADAR, Internet of things (IoT), and satellite technology

Abstract: This chapter explores the opportunity to use radio detection and ranging (RADAR) technology in combination with the Internet of things (IoT) and satellite images to improve the efficiency of precision agriculture. It begins by explaining RADAR systems' historical background and importance in monitoring, especially farming, where they can collect data even in cloudy weather conditions. The chapter also examines how RADAR and IoT are intertwined. IoT provides real-time data on soil moisture, weather conditions, and crop status, which, when combined with RADAR's large-scale monitoring capabilities, offers a holistic picture of agricultural conditions. High-resolution satellite imagery benefits crop monitoring by capturing more spatial detail, enabling precise assessments of vegetation health and soil quality. These integrated technologies are illustrated through several case studies and examples that demonstrate their implementation and the positive outcomes in areas such as irrigation success rates, crop yield prediction, and early diagnosis of crop diseases, thereby conserving resources and improving yields. The chapter also addresses challenges such as data integration and high-resolution monitoring.

Keywords: Precision agriculture, IoT integration, RADAR systems, satellite imagery, crop yield prediction, soil monitoring

1 Introduction

1.1 Background on RADAR technology

RADAR, a crucial technology invented during World War II, has become even more influential in military and civilian activities. At its core, RADAR typically transmits electromagnetic waves and detects returning echoes for precise distance determinations, including velocity and composition [1]. Due to RADAR's capability to penetrate clouds and generate real-time data, it has proven useful for various applications, including soil moisture borehole monitoring, crop health assessment, and disaster response. Integrating IoT technologies allows the spatial resolution and real-time data

Ashutosh Pagrotra, Department of Biomechatronics, National Taiwan University, Taipei, Taiwan, e-mail: ashutoshpagrotra@gmail.com

https://doi.org/10.1515/9783111572970-010

processing issues of traditional RADAR systems to be overcome through a combination of high-resolution, localized data, and RADAR's broad coverage.

1.2 Emergence of IoT in RADAR systems

The synergy between radar technologies and the IoT has now noticeably expanded the capabilities of monitoring systems, especially for farming [2]. IoT instruments like soil moisture sensors, weather stations, and drones, working together with radar arrays, greatly improve precision agriculture. As shown in Figure 1, the satellite sends an electromagnetic signal toward the Earth's surface, and land features bounce this signal back to the satellite. Advanced IoT technology is utilized on servers that analyze the signal data to produce a final processed image of the land. By integrating IoT data with RADAR systems, land cover classification can be enhanced with additional ground truth information and more efficient data processing, resulting in improved accuracy.

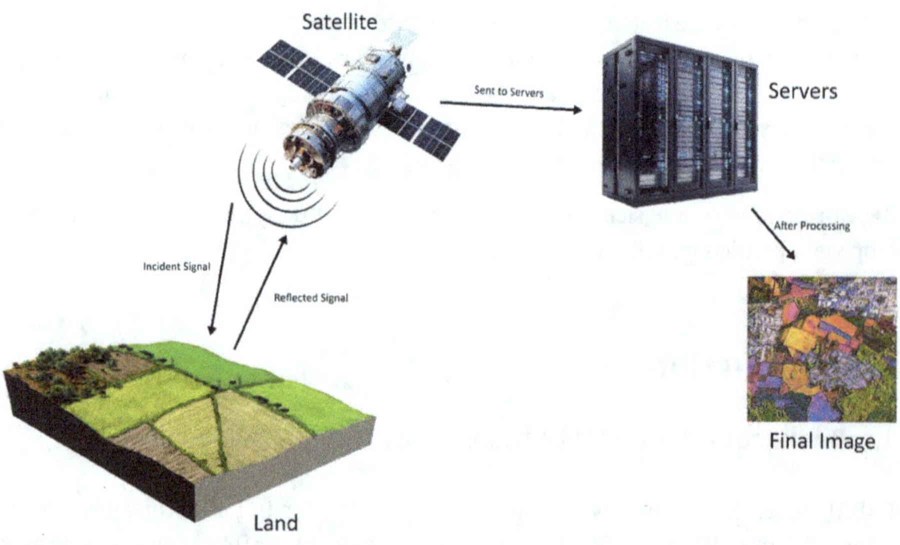

Figure 1: The transmission and receiving of the signals are sent to servers for processing and obtaining the final image for visualization.

2 Fundamentals of RADAR technology

2.1 Basic principles of RADAR

RADAR works by emitting electromagnetic waves and studying the signals reflected (or echoes) off objects. The basic functioning of RADAR can be summarized as follows:

1. **Transmission:** A transmitter sends electromagnetic radiation in a given direction, often in the radio or microwave frequency range [3].
2. **Propagation:** These waves propagate through space and bounce back – from buildings, airplanes, vehicles, or any other structure, or even terrain and foliage [4].
3. **Reflection (echo):** The reflected waves, or echoes as they are called, are captured back by the RADAR receiver [5].
4. **Detection:** Using the given time gap between the transmission and reception of the signal, RADAR determines the object's distance. It can also measure the object's velocity, direction, and size through the Doppler shift of the transmitted signal and its strength [6].

This process enables the RADAR systems to see beyond the visible range and through clouds and darkness; hence, it has extensive applications in areas such as air traffic control, weather forecasting, and various military uses. The basic elements of a RADAR system are the transmitter, receiver, antenna, signal processor, and display [7]. RADAR's cloud-penetrating capability in agriculture makes it ideal for large-scale monitoring exercises, such as crop health and irrigation. Table 1 presents a comparison of several technologies used in precision agriculture.

Table 1: Comparison of technologies used in precision agriculture.

Technology	Functionality	Benefits	Limitations	Source
Radar	Measures distance and object characteristics using electromagnetic waves	All-weather capability, large-scale monitoring, and soil moisture detection	Lower resolution compared to optical sensors and high data processing requirements	[8]
IoT sensors	Collects localized, real-time data on soil moisture, temperature, humidity, etc.	Enables precision farming, resource efficiency, and real-time alerts	High initial costs and data integration challenges	[9]
Satellite imagery	Provides high-resolution images for crop health and environmental monitoring	Large-scale data collection with high spatial and temporal resolution	Limited by weather conditions and cloud cover	[10]

2.2 Despite these valuable applications, RADAR systems have several limitations

- **Resolution limitations:** Typically, traditional RADARs have lower spatial resolution compared to optical systems, such as cameras or LiDAR. Thus, detecting small or closely spaced objects is difficult [11].
- **Complex data processing:** RADAR systems rapidly collect large volumes of data, especially for weather or environmental monitoring, which can be complicated and time-consuming to interpret [4].
- **Interference from other sources:** The signal-to-noise ratio for the measurement may be reduced by electromagnetic sources, such as cell towers [12].
- **Dependence on direct line-of-sight:** RADAR systems operate based on a direct line of sight to the object being monitored. A dense built environment or terrain with obstacles complicating the line of sight along the path will be less effective, as the signal may be blocked or distorted [5].

2.3 Specific challenges in agriculture monitoring

While RADAR technology offers several advantages for agriculture, its application in this field also faces unique challenges [1]:

1. **Vegetation and soil moisture monitoring:** In particular, soils and vegetation are very complex, and crop fields may contain many different types of soils and moisture levels, as well as differing vegetation structures, making it difficult to interpret data accurately. Scattering from rough terrain or dense canopies can reduce soil moisture retrieval or crop classification [13].
2. **Resolution and scale:** Traditional RADAR systems rarely have sufficient resolution required for precision farming, where details at the plant level are important. Although RADAR is effective for large-scale monitoring, it may not capture the details needed for small-scale or localized crop management [14].
3. **Data integration with other technologies:** RADAR is increasingly integrated with other sensing technologies, including IoT-based soil sensors and optical satellite data for agricultural monitoring. However, the real challenge is to process and integrate these diverse data sources in real-time and efficiently to enable actionable insights for farmers [15].
4. **Interference and signal distortion:** RADAR signals generally interfere in areas such as agricultural regions with a high amount of infrastructure or electrical installations, where there is data noise. Terrain variability also causes signal distortion and, therefore, creates inconsistencies and inaccuracies in the readings for large plots of land; this becomes harder to mitigate [16].
5. **Cost and accessibility:** Ground-based RADAR systems are limited due to the high deployment and maintenance costs in large agricultural areas [17].

6. **Adaptability to varying conditions:** The environment for agriculture is dynamic and ever-changing. RADAR data is influenced by weather conditions, seasonal variations, and varying crop growth stages. Therefore, the RADAR system must be continuously adapted [18].

3 The Importance of satellite imagery in agriculture

3.1 Types of satellite data (multispectral and hyperspectral)

Satellite data comes in many forms, each with a unique perspective on remote agricultural conditions. Two critical types, multispectral and hyperspectral imaging, are used to track crops, soils, and other environmental indices:

- **Multispectral data:** Multispectral satellite images contain data about a small set of wide electromagnetic spectrum bands. This usually includes the visible (red, green, and blue) and near-infrared (NIR) bands. For farming, multispectral photography is very useful for computing indices such as the normalized difference vegetation index (NDVI), a frequently used indicator of the health of plants. The NDVI measures the density and health of crops by comparing the visible reflective light with NIR light from the plants. For instance, the Sentinel-2 satellite of the Copernicus program monitors soil and vegetation in depth using its 13 spectral bands [19].
- **Hyperspectral data:** While standard multispectral sensors gather information over several large spectral bands, often only a few, hyperspectral imagery provides virtually hundreds of small spectral bands containing much more detailed information about the object under observation. Remote sensing data is important in crop health assessment; it provides detailed information about the status of crops, soil, moisture content, and even diseases that might be hard to identify early. Multispectral and hyperspectral sensors are different because the latter can distinguish the finest changes in crop physiology that are otherwise imperceptible to the human eye [20].

3.2 Case studies of IoT and satellite data integration in agriculture

The image shown in Figure 2 illustrates several techniques used for monitoring land and water bodies to predict yield. Three panels are shown: (a) moisture index mapping (water availability during different seasons for different regions), (b) yield prediction (crop yield estimation based on environmental factors using imagery), and (c) soil monitoring (identification of soil conditions that are important for productivity in

Figure 2: Representation of land cover classes: (a) moisture index, (b) yield prediction, and (c) soil monitoring.

agriculture). Together, these techniques improve agricultural management precision and enable data-driven yield forecasting.

3.2.1 Crop monitoring

Unlike conventional farming, precision agriculture requires frequent observation of plant status to determine the best production parameters. Combining satellite imagery with IoT sensors provides farmers with access to the state of their crops at any point during the entire growing season:

- **Satellite imagery:** Sentinel-2 satellite multispectral data allows the observation of vegetation using NDVI to monitor its health status. Such data assist in determining the parts of the field where crops may be under water stress, attacked by pests, or suffering from inadequate nutrients [21].
- **IoT sensors:** Another form of IoT that works at the surface level provides real-time data on moisture, temperature, and even nutrient content in the ground, thus complementing satellite imagery [22].

3.2.2 Soil moisture analysis

It was clear that soil moisture is a vital element in determining crop yield, and satellite imagery data and RADAR are essential in estimating the extent of soil moisture:

- **RADAR and IoT:** RADAR, as in Sentinel-1 within the Copernicus program, is highly effective in estimating soil moisture. It can measure the moisture of the upper layers of the soil and, thus, provide valuable insights into field conditions. Conventional drip irrigation systems rely on a few points for moisture input into the soil, making localized measurements using IoT sensors possible, especially those installed at different depths. This integration is crucial in providing farmers with a bird's-eye view of WRaS for a large region and a detailed view of a specific area [23].
- **Satellite imagery:** There are limits to what can be gathered from RADAR, and satellite images can supplement this information by revealing the impact of moisture content on crops and soil. Using NDVI and other indices analysis, farmers can determine whether irrigation changes positively affect crop status over a given time [21].

3.2.3 Yield prediction

Yield prediction is crucial to maintaining food supplies and ensuring the efficient distribution of agricultural products. When IoT data is combined with satellite imagery, farmers can predict output more precisely, aiding in decisions related to resource distribution:

- **Satellite data:** Through remote sensing, satellite images depict the crop status and development during the growing period. For example, a comparative assessment of historical and current conditions provides farmers with evidence to forecast the probable crop production volume toward the end of the cropping season [24].
- **IoT sensors:** Real-time data from IoT sensors concerning soil humidity, temperature, and plant growth can complement yield prediction models. Year-round monitoring allows farmers to adjust their management methods according to yield data received from IoT during a planting cycle [25].

Example: In Argentina, the authors integrated Sentinel-2-acquired imaging data with IoT devices containing soil moisture and weather sensors to develop a yield prediction model for maize. It successfully simulated yields with an error of less than 5% and enabled those involved in farming to decide on resource use and harvesting time.

3.2.3.1 Key benefits

- **Increased precision:** IoT sensors provide real-time data to farmers, enabling them to tailor their inputs (water, fertilizer, pesticides, among others) based on smart insights.
- **Environmental sustainability:** Optimized irrigation increases efficiency, reduces costs, and conserves water, especially in water-scarce areas.
- **Cost savings:** Comparing RADAR with other IoT sensors, RADAR takes fewer measurements and supports fewer materials, thereby reducing manual labor and the frequency of field inspections, ultimately saving time and money [26].

4 Machine learning and AI in processing RADAR and satellite data

RADAR systems and satellite imagery are just two data sources that rely on machine learning (ML) and artificial intelligence (AI) to process massive amounts of data. Some relatively new tools and techniques that enhance RADAR technology in agriculture are presented in Table 2.

Table 2: New tools and technologies enhancing RADAR in agriculture.

Tool	Description	Role in enhancing RADAR capabilities	Source
IoT-based soil moisture sensors	Sensors that measure soil moisture levels in real time	Provide localized, high-resolution data to complement Radar's large-scale monitoring for optimized irrigation	[27]
Automated irrigation systems	System that automatically manages water usage based on sensor data	Utilize radar and IoT data to ensure precise and efficient water distribution	[28]
Edge computing	On-site data processing for real-time decision-making	Reduces latency, enabling immediate responses to radar and IoT sensor data	[29]
AI and machine learning models	Algorithm that analyzes and interprets complex datasets	Enhance predictive analytics using combined radar, IoT, and satellite data for smarter agricultural decisions	[30]
Drones and radar capabilities	UAVs equipped with radar for aerial crop monitoring	Provide detailed and flexible field assessments, complementing ground-based radar systems	[31]

Farmers can extract actionable insights from complex datasets through these technologies, consequently making smarter decisions and gaining predictive capabilities.

1. **Data fusion**:
   - RADAR and satellite imagery capture large-scale environmental data, whereas IoT sensors supply localized real-time information. Machine learning algorithms can integrate these datasets to generate comprehensive models that provide an in-depth view of soil conditions, crop health, and environmental factors. This process, known as data fusion, helps create predictive models that account for multiple variables, delivering improved results for agricultural monitoring.

Example: Machine learning algorithms can combine RADAR data on soil moisture with satellite imagery of crop health (such as NDVI) and IoT sensor data on temperature, nutrients, and forecasts to help predict risky areas in the field due to drought or nutrient deficiency [32].

5 Precision agriculture: role of advanced computing

Closely related to this are data analysis technologies, including but not limited to cloud computing, edge computing, and high-performance servers to parse the data generated by radar, IoT sensors, and satellite images. These technologies allow farmers to practice precision agriculture, which is carried out with dexterity at the regional and individual farm levels:

1. **Cloud computing**:
   - Cloud computing allows data from RADAR and IoT devices to satellites to be stored, processed, and analyzed without requiring extensive local hardware resources. This enables farmers to upload information to the cloud, where advanced algorithms process the data to present actionable insights. The cloud also facilitates real-time monitoring, as data from these multiple sensors is aggregated, processed, and quickly sent to the farmers.
2. **Edge computing**:
   - Despite cloud computing being ideal for large-scale processing, edge computing processes data closer to the source through data processing on local devices (e.g., IoT sensors or nearby servers). The big advantage is that once you eliminate the latency, you can make real-time decisions; for instance, if it's automated irrigation, you have to turn it on and off very quickly.
3. **Big data analytics**:
   - Big data analytics is critical in precision agriculture, where data is constantly collected from radar, satellite, and IoT devices. These large datasets can be run through advanced computing systems that process and analyze them for insights to guide farming decisions. Farmers can identify trends and patterns in the data using big data analytics and become more effective at crop management practices.

6 Practical applications of RADAR, IoT, and satellite imagery in agriculture

6.1 Use of satellite imagery for monitoring vegetation and crops

Monitoring vegetation and crops is important through satellite imagery, in part due to its large-scale, high-resolution data that allows vegetation and crop health, growth, and performance to be continually assessed. Various satellite-based indices – the NDVI being one example – measure the reflection of light in red and NIR wavelengths to inform farmers about how crops are thriving.

- **NDVI:** One of the most commonly used indices to evaluate plant health is NDVI. Higher NIR and lower visible reflectance are characteristic of healthy vegetation, and vice versa. NDVI compares areas with thriving crops to those suffering from stress caused by drought, nutrient depletion, or diseases [11].
- **Enhanced vegetation index (EVI):** Like NDVI, the EVI enhances sensitivity to vegetation and reduces background noise from soil and atmospheric effects.

When incorporated, it has a special utility in monitoring forests or dense crop canopies [33].
- **Soil-adjusted vegetation index (SAVI):** The SAVI is designed for environments where soil brightness plays a significant role in characterizing an area's spectral signature, such as semi-arid or sparsely vegetated regions. It substantially contributes to this signature, aiding farmers in better-separating vegetation from bare soil [34].

6.2 Practical use in agriculture

- **Growth monitoring:** Time-series satellite images allow farmers to track the development of crops throughout a growing season. A sudden drop can indicate areas of crop stress; thus, early intervention may be possible [35].
- **Disease detection:** Satellites locate areas where crop output is not performing well. They may also respond by detecting changes in the spectral signature, signaling the presence of disease outbreaks or pest infestations [36].
- **Water stress analysis:** Multispectral imagery enables farmers to identify areas where water stress occurs, allowing them to optimize irrigation practices [37].

Example: Satellite imagery and ground-based sensors were used to monitor maize and wheat fields in Kenya. The farmers tracked changes in NDVI values, optimizing water usage and detecting crop diseases early to increase the yield by nearly half while maintaining quality [38].

6.3 Integration of IoT for precision farming

Precision farming uses data-driven technologies, such as IoT devices or satellite imagery, to optimize farm practices at the micro-scale. Real-time data on soil conditions, temperature, humidity, and more can be collected by IoT-based sensors, which can subsequently be integrated with satellite data to manage resources more efficiently and achieve better crop performance:
- **Soil and climate monitoring:** IoT-based soil moisture sensors measure water availability in different parts of the field in real-time. Combined with satellite imagery of broader environmental conditions, this data informs farmers when and where to irrigate [39].
- **Variable rate application (VRA):** This information can help with precision applications of fertilizers, pesticides, and water, decreasing waste and increasing efficiency. For instance, areas with lower NDVI values might require more nutrients, and IoT sensors can relay real-time information about soil conditions to optimize fertilization [40].

- **Automation:** The IoT and connecting devices to irrigation systems can greatly extend their lifespans. This allows for automated irrigation based on real-time data from embedded soil sensors and RADAR systems measuring soil moisture on a macroscale [41].

Example: IoT sensors and satellite imagery were used in vineyards in California for precision irrigation management. Vineyard managers reduced water use by 30% by monitoring soil moisture and plant water uptake while maintaining high-quality grapes [42].

6.4 Case studies of agricultural projects utilizing RADAR, IoT, and satellite data

6.4.1 Sentinel satellites and IoT for crop monitoring in Argentina

- **Overview:** To monitor soybean fields, farmers in Argentina used Sentinel-2 satellite data in combination with IoT sensors. The satellite provided multispectral data on crop health, while IoT sensors provided real-time data on soil moisture and temperature [43].
- **Outcome:** Farmers reduced their water usage by 20% by better-utilizing satellite and IoT data. They also discovered problems with nutrient deficiencies earlier, which they resolved with timely fertilization. The yield increased by up to 15% compared to the previous season.

6.4.2 Indore soil moisture monitoring in India using Sentinel-1 and IoT sensors

- **Overview:** Sentinel-1 RADAR data for soil moisture, in conjunction with IoT-based soil sensors, were used to monitor rice fields in southern India. This project aimed to optimize irrigation and water conservation in water-scarce regions [44].
- **Outcome:** RADAR and IoT were integrated for precisely controlled soil moisture systems. As a result, farmers saved 25% of their water usage while maintaining the same crop yields. The project also decreased water-pumping energy consumption and operational costs [45].

7 Conclusion

By integrating RADAR, IoT, and satellite imagery into modern agriculture, RADAR technology is supplemented by real-time localized data on crop health, soil moisture, and temperature collected by IoT sensors. Adding these sensors to RADAR has improved precision and reliability in agricultural monitoring. As far as the future of agriculture is concerned, several technological trends are of great importance. First, the analyzed trends suggest that AI and machine learning will become the primary drivers of change in data interpretation. It will help AI extrapolate findings from RADAR, IoT, and satellite data, providing much deeper predictive capabilities. This advancement will allow farmers to improve their adaptation to environmental conditions and optimize their farming resources, which will greatly enhance the productivity of agriculture. Finally, more prominence will be given to global collaboration for food security. When countries collaborate and address global agricultural challenges with the help of modern technologies, they can develop more sustainable food systems to feed the world's constantly growing population.

References

[1] Skolnik, M.I. 2007. Introduction to radar systems, 3. ed., internat. ed., [Nachdr.]. ed, McGraw-Hill electrical engineering series, Boston: McGraw-Hill.

[2] Stimson, G.W. 1998. Introduction to Airborne Radar, 2nd ed. Mendham, N.J: SciTech Pub.

[3] Skolnik, M.I. (Ed.) 2008. Radar Handbook, 3rd ed. New York: McGraw-Hill.

[4] Richards, M.A. 2014. Fundamentals of Radar Signal Processing, 2nd ed. New York: McGraw-Hill Education.

[5] Nathanson, F.E., Reilly, J.P., Cohen, M. 1991. Radar Design Principles: Signal Processing and The Environment, 2nd ed. New York: McGraw-Hill.

[6] Mahafza, B.R. 2013. Radar Systems Analysis and Design using MATLAB, 3rd ed. Boca Raton ; London: CRC/Taylor & Francis.

[7] Weiss, M., Jacob, F., Duveiller, G. 2020. Remote sensing for agricultural applications: A meta-review. Remote Sensing of Environment 236, 111402. https://doi.org/10.1016/j.rse.2019.111402

[8] Wangfei, Z., Erxue, C., Zengyuan, L.I., Hao, Y., Lei, Z. 2020. Review of applications of radar remote sensing in agriculture (in English). Ldxb 9, 444–461. https://doi.org/10.12000/JR20051

[9] Sondhiya, R.R., Singh, V.K. 2024. Smart sensing technologies for real-time monitoring of soil health in precision agriculture. Journal of Applied Optics, 295–301.

[10] Segarra, J., Buchaillot, M.L., Araus, J.L., Kefauver, S.C. 2020. Remote sensing for precision agriculture: Sentinel-2 improved features and applications. Agronomy 10, 641. https://doi.org/10.3390/agronomy10050641

[11] Rouse, J.W., Haas, R.H., Deering, D.W., Schell, J.A., Harlan, J.C. 1974. Monitoring the Vernal Advancement and Retrogradation (Green Wave Effect) of Natural Vegetation, No. E75-10354.

[12] Rajak, P., Ganguly, A., Adhikary, S., Bhattacharya, S. 2023. Internet of Things and smart sensors in agriculture: Scopes and challenges. Journal of Agriculture and Food Research 14, 100776. https://doi.org/10.1016/j.jafr.2023.100776

[13] Hashemi, M.G.Z., Jalilvand, E., Alemohammad, H., Tan, P.-N., Das, N.N. 2024. Review of synthetic aperture radar with deep learning in agricultural applications. ISPRS Journal of Photogrammetry and Remote Sensing 218, 20–49. https://doi.org/10.1016/j.isprsjprs.2024.08.018

[14] Jain, D.R. 2024. Advances and challenges in remote sensing-based crop monitoring: Integrating data for enhanced agricultural decision-making. IJIRMPS – International Journal of Innovative Research in Engineering & Multidisciplinary Physical Sciences 12.

[15] Richards, M.A., Scheer, J., Holm, W.A., Melvin, W.L. (Eds.) 2010. Principles of Modern Radar, Raleigh, NC: SciTech Pub.

[16] Anastasiou, E., Fountas, S., Voulgaraki, M., Psiroukis, V., Koutsiaras, M., Kriezi, O., Lazarou, E., Vatsanidou, A., Fu, L., Bartolo, F.D., Barreiro-Hurle, J., Gómez-Barbero, M. 2023. Precision farming technologies for crop protection: A meta-analysis. Smart Agricultural Technology 5, 100323. https://doi.org/10.1016/j.atech.2023.100323

[17] Sishodia, R.P., Ray, R.L., Singh, S.K. 2020. Applications of remote sensing in precision agriculture: A review. Remote Sensing 12, 3136. https://doi.org/10.3390/rs12193136

[18] Mani, P.K., Mandal, A., Biswas, S., Sarkar, B., Mitran, T., Meena, R.S. 2021. Remote sensing and geographic information system: A tool for precision farming. In: Mitran, T., Meena, R.S., Chakraborty, A. (Eds.) Geospatial Technologies for Crops and Soils. Singapore: Springer Singapore, 49–111. https://doi.org/10.1007/978-981-15-6864-0_2

[19] Sethy, P.K., Pandey, C., Sahu, Y.K., Behera, S.K. 2022. Hyperspectral imagery applications for precision agriculture – A systemic survey. Multimedia Tools and Applications 81, 3005–3038. https://doi.org/10.1007/s11042-021-11729-8

[20] Lu, B., Dao, P.D., Liu, J., He, Y., Shang, J. 2020. Recent advances of hyperspectral imaging technology and applications in agriculture. Remote Sensing 12, 2659. https://doi.org/10.3390/rs12162659

[21] Chicaiza, K., Paredes, R.X., Sarzosa, I.M., Yoo, S.G., Zang, N. 2024. Smart farming technologies: A methodological overview and analysis. IEEE Access 12, 164922–164941. https://doi.org/10.1109/ACCESS.2024.3487497

[22] Mahapatra, J., Sahni, R.K., Sahoo, P.K., Shrinivasa, D.J. 2024. IoT-based real-time farm management system for smart agriculture. In: Chouhan, S.S., Saxena, A., Singh, U.P., Jain, S. (Eds.) Artificial Intelligence Techniques in Smart Agriculture. Singapore: Springer Nature Singapore, 267–287. https://doi.org/10.1007/978-981-97-5878-4_16

[23] Han, Y., Bai, X., Shao, W., Wang, J. 2020. Retrieval of soil moisture by integrating sentinel-1A and MODIS data over agricultural fields. Water 12, 1726. https://doi.org/10.3390/w12061726

[24] Zhuo, W., Huang, J., Li, L., Zhang, X., Ma, H., Gao, X., Huang, H., Xu, B., Xiao, X. 2019. Assimilating soil moisture retrieved from Sentinel-1 and Sentinel-2 Data into WOFOST model to improve winter wheat yield estimation. Remote Sensing 11, 1618. https://doi.org/10.3390/rs11131618

[25] Ahmed, T., Javed, N., Faisal, M., Sadia, H. 2023. A Framework for smart agriculture system to monitor the crop stress and drought stress using Sentinel-2 Satellite image. In: Mathur, G., Bundele, M., Tripathi, A., Paprzycki, M. (Eds.) Proceedings of 3rd International Conference on Artificial Intelligence: Advances and Applications, Algorithms for Intelligent Systems. Singapore: Springer Nature Singapore, 345–361. https://doi.org/10.1007/978-981-19-7041-2_27

[26] Laha, S.R., Pattanayak, B.K., Pattnaik, S., Mishra, D., Kumar Nayak, D.S., Dash, B.B. 2023. An IOT-Based soil moisture management system for precision agriculture: Real-Time monitoring and automated irrigation control. In: 2023 4th International Conference on Smart Electronics and Communication (ICOSEC). Presented at the 2023 4th International Conference on Smart Electronics and Communication (ICOSEC). Trichy, India: IEEE, 451–455. https://doi.org/10.1109/ICOSEC58147.2023.10276266

[27] Qamar, N., Ali, M.S., Siddique, A.M., Qureshi, H.U., Ali, U., Khurram, A.A. 2024. IoT-based soil and weather sensors for crop monitoring: A step towards smart agriculture. In: 2024 Global Conference on Wireless and Optical Technologies (GCWOT). Presented at the 2024 Global Conference on

Wireless and Optical Technologies (GCWOT). Malaga, Spain: IEEE, 1–7. https://doi.org/10.1109/GCWOT63882.2024.10805658
[28] Garg, S., Pundir, P., Jindal, H., Saini, H., Garg, S. 2021. Towards a Multimodal System for Precision Agriculture using IoT and Machine Learning, https://doi.org/10.48550/ARXIV.2107.04895
[29] Risheh, A., Jalili, A., Nazerfard, E. 2020. Smart Irrigation IoT Solution using Transfer Learning for Neural Networks, https://doi.org/10.48550/ARXIV.2009.12747
[30] Polic, M., Car, M., Tabak, J., Orsag, M. 2022. Robotic irrigation water management: Estimating soil moisture content by feel and appearance. https://doi.org/10.48550/ARXIV.2201.07653
[31] Raj, M., Harshini, N.B., Gupta, S., Atiquzzaman, M., Rawlley, O., Goel, L. 2024. Leveraging precision agriculture techniques using UAVs and emerging disruptive technologies. Energy Nexus 14, 100300. https://doi.org/10.1016/j.nexus.2024.100300
[32] Shojaeezadeh, S.A., Elnashar, A., Weber, T.K.D. 2024. A Novel Fusion of Optical and Radar Satellite Data for Crop Phenology Estimation using Machine Learning and Cloud Computing, https://doi.org/10.48550/arXiv.2409.00020
[33] Huete, A., Didan, K., Miura, T., Rodriguez, E.P., Gao, X., Ferreira, L.G. 2002. Overview of the radiometric and biophysical performance of the MODIS vegetation indices. Remote Sensing of Environment 83, 195–213. https://doi.org/10.1016/S0034-4257(02)00096-2
[34] Huete, A.R. 1988. A soil-adjusted vegetation index (SAVI). Remote Sensing of Environment 25, 295–309. https://doi.org/10.1016/0034-4257(88)90106-X
[35] Mulla, D.J. 2013. Twenty five years of remote sensing in precision agriculture: Key advances and remaining knowledge gaps. Biosystems Engineering, Special Issue: Sensing Technologies for Sustainable Agriculture 114, 358–371. https://doi.org/10.1016/j.biosystemseng.2012.08.009
[36] Zhang, N., Wang, M., Wang, N. 2002. Precision agriculture – A worldwide overview. Computers & Electronics in Agriculture.
[37] Gao, B. 1996. NDWI – A normalized difference water index for remote sensing of vegetation liquid water from space. Remote Sensing of Environment 58, 257–266. https://doi.org/10.1016/S0034-4257(96)00067-3
[38] Dengia, A., Dechassa, N., Wogi, L., Amsalu, B. 2023. A simplified approach to satellite-based monitoring system of sugarcane plantation to manage yield decline at Wonji-Shoa Sugar Estate, central Ethiopia. Heliyon vol. 9, e18982. https://doi.org/10.1016/j.heliyon.2023.e18982
[39] Bogena, H.R., Herbst, M., Huisman, J.A., Rosenbaum, U., Weuthen, A., Vereecken, H. 2010. Potential of wireless sensor networks for measuring soil water content variability. Vadose Zone Journal 9, 1002–1013. https://doi.org/10.2136/vzj2009.0173
[40] Strock, J.S., Johnson, J.M.F., Tollefson, D., Ranaivoson, A. 2022. Rapid change in soil properties after converting grasslands to crop production. Agronomy Journal 114, 1642–1654. https://doi.org/10.1002/agj2.21045
[41] Kim, W.-S., Lee, W.-S., Kim, Y.-J. 2020. A review of the applications of the internet of things (IoT) for agricultural automation. Journal of Biosystems Engineering 45, 385–400. https://doi.org/10.1007/s42853-020-00078-3
[42] Pascoal, D., Silva, N., Adão, T., Lopes, R.D., Peres, E., Morais, R. 2024. A technical survey on practical applications and guidelines for IoT sensors in precision agriculture and viticulture. Scientific Reports 14, 29793. https://doi.org/10.1038/s41598-024-80924-y
[43] Berveglieri, A., Imai, N.N., Watanabe, F.S.Y., Tommaselli, A.M.G., Ederli, G.M.P., De Araújo, F.F., Lupatini, G.C., Honkavaara, E. 2024. Remote prediction of soybean yield using UAV-based hyperspectral imaging and machine learning models. Agricultural Engineering 6, 3242–3260. https://doi.org/10.3390/agriengineering6030185

[44] Liu, Y., Rao, P., Zhou, W., Singh, B., Srivastava, A.K., Poonia, S.P., Van Berkel, D., Jain, M. 2022. Using Sentinel-1, Sentinel-2, and Planet satellite data to map field-level tillage practices in smallholder systems. PLoS ONE vol. 17, e0277425. https://doi.org/10.1371/journal.pone.0277425
[45] Vyas, N., Singh, S., Sethi, G.K. 2025. A novel image fusion-based post classification framework for agricultural variations detection using Sentinel-1 and Sentinel-2 data. Earth Science Informatics 18, 40. https://doi.org/10.1007/s12145-024-01506-0

Hardik Dhiman* and Syna

Integrating AI with RADAR remote sensing: applications in disaster mitigation, defense, and climate change

Abstract: This chapter delves into advanced RADAR remote sensing applications powered by artificial intelligence (AI). As AI techniques advance, RADAR data is increasingly utilized to address complex global challenges such as disaster response, military intelligence, and climate change adaptation. The chapter discusses advanced AI methodologies that enhance RADAR's predictive capabilities in detecting earthquakes, landslides, and floods, as well as monitoring and managing wildfires. Additionally, the chapter explores the integration of RADAR with other remote-sensing technologies to improve situational awareness in military operations and environmental conservation efforts. It also examines challenges such as data fusion, large-scale RADAR processing, and the demand for computational efficiency. The chapter highlights emerging AI-driven innovations that are set to revolutionize RADAR applications in remote sensing, paving the way for more precise and autonomous decision-making systems.

Keywords: RADAR remote sensing, disaster management, climate change monitoring, military applications, data fusion, computational challenges

1 Introduction

1.1 Disaster management and mitigation

RADAR remote sensing and AI applications have been effective in disaster management. Earthquakes, floods, landslides, hurricanes, and wildfires continue to devastate lives, property, and ecosystems [1]. Prevention and early monitoring are necessary to reduce the impact of these events. When paired with AI and data processing, RADAR's capabilities – penetrating clouds, detecting surface changes, and operating in all weather – enhance disaster management in specific areas like early warning and response [2].

*__Corresponding author: Hardik Dhiman,__ Department of Electrical and Control Engineering, National Yang Ming Chiao Tung University Hsinchu, Taiwan, e-mail: hardik.dhiman29@gmail.com
Syna, Department of Mechanical Engineering, National Chung Cheng University, Taiwan, e-mail: syna200502@gmail.com

https://doi.org/10.1515/9783111572970-011

1.2 Earthquake monitoring and damage assessment

Earthquakes are among the most devastating natural calamities, causing widespread destruction of buildings and often resulting in loss of life. RADAR remote sensing, especially synthetic aperture radar (SAR), significantly contributes to post-earthquake initiatives by responding to ground deformation, tectonic plate movements, and stress on fault lines [3]. SAR measures earthquake-induced ground deformation through image comparisons taken before and after seismic events. Interferometric SAR (InSAR) combines two SAR images, with phase differences between these images indicating ground displacement accurate to the millimeter level. InSAR creates interferograms that depict uplift, subsidence, or shifts within fault zones. According to SAR, radar backscatter from SAR traces the effects of seismic activities on soil and rock formations. SAR data is integrated with AI to efficiently detect deformation patterns, classify damaged zones, and assess risk. Remote sensing imagery acquired at any time of the day and under varying climatic conditions is critical for rapid earthquake response and damage assessment, making SAR necessary [4].

The images acquired by SAR can easily detect slight changes in the ground surface that are often a result of an earthquake. Machine learning and deep reinforcement learning systems are proficient in analyzing massive volumes of SAR data to locate the zones that depict relative shifts on the Earth's surface due to an earthquake shock [5]. AI models using pre- and post-event RADAR images support operational response teams and improve damage assessment accuracy. Structural damages can be identified, and areas considered for rescue and recovery operations can be determined from RADAR data using AI models. These models can also alert the authorities about the chances of future aftershocks or subsequent ground modifications, for which preventive measures can be taken to minimize damage [6].

Beyond post-disaster assessment, AI-driven RADAR data analysis can effectively monitor post-earthquake conditions [7]. AI methods analyzing ground displacements over time can predict tectonically active, earthquake-prone areas. Such information is vital in disaster management planning; governments, organizations, and others can establish early warning mechanisms, regulate construction to ensure that structures meet disaster standards, and improve the resilience of facilities in disaster-prone areas [8].

1.3 Flood detection and response

Floods are the most common and deadly natural disasters; millions experience flooding yearly. RADAR remote sensing, particularly SAR systems, is regularly employed in flood identification and mapping due to its independence from prevailing weather conditions, such as rain, which characterize flood-creating conditions [9]. AI provides three key benefits: streamlining RADAR data processing, enhancing flood detection efficiency, and improving monitoring and response coordination. Flood mapping of a region using RADAR entails the identification of variations in surface reflectivity, particularly when the terrain transforms from dry to flooded.

To increase the accuracy and precision of flood boundary detection, a more complex analysis can be used, for instance, based on deep learning models, including convolutional neural networks (CNNs) [10]. Real-time detection of floods is an important aspect of disaster management. RADAR data can be input into various AI models so that, relative to the degree of flooding, authorities can issue timely notifications for evacuation and deploy useful resources to the affected area. AI models can use RADAR data and various parameters, including rainfall and elevation, to determine the probabilities of future flooding in specific areas. These plans enable agencies to reinforce flood barriers, protect structures, and prioritize resources in threatened regions. However, predicting flood damage and applying AI techniques to RADAR data requires object recognition [11]. For example, AI models can help determine the extent of infrastructure, agricultural land, and houses destroyed following a flood by comparing RADAR images taken before and after the disaster. Such information is crucial when discussing the organization of the search and rescue operations, delivering assistance, and planning the rebuilding process [12].

1.4 Landslide prediction and monitoring

Due to the ability of InSAR technology to detect ground displacement in the millimeter range, it can be used effectively to monitor landslides [13]. AI algorithms can process InSAR data to map surface deformation patterns that could lead to the potential occurrence of a landslide. Current risk models include decision trees and neural networks, which can be employed to train models using previous RADAR data and other geographic information, including rainfall, soil type, and vegetation cover, to identify areas predisposed to landslides [14]. AI-enhanced RADAR data enables continuous monitoring of landslide-prone slopes, early detection of ground movement, and timely evacuation of at-risk communities [15]. Besides its use in landslide prediction and monitoring, AI is also useful during damage assessment in the event of a landslide. In particular, AI models can learn to interpret data from RADAR imagery, identifying the extent of the landslide, the infrastructure items impacted, and the areas where human search and rescue operations should be concentrated [16].

1.5 Wildfire detection and suppression

Early detection and rapid suppression are important for minimizing damage to ecosystems and property, as well as preventing the loss of human life. AI and RADAR remote sensing provide effective tools for monitoring wildfire-prone areas, in addition to detecting fires at their nascent stage to guide suppression efforts. Vegetation burning or fire-induced structural changes in the landscape can result in alterations to surface reflectivity that RADAR sensors are capable of detecting [17]. AI algorithms can analyze these RADAR data alongside thermal and optical remote sensing data to detect wildfires at an early stage. In addition to RNNs, deep learning models can be trained to recognize temporal patterns related to fire outbreaks and predict their spread based on environmental conditions, such as wind speed, temperature, and humidity [18].

Besides active fires, AI-enhanced RADAR data can be utilized to detect the risk of future wildfires. By analyzing historical data concerning fires, vegetation cover, and climate conditions, AI models can identify regions with a very-high risk of wildfires and support authorities with appropriate preventive measures, such as controlled burns, firebreaks, and improved forest management practices [19]. AI-enhanced RADAR data also plays a key role in coordinating wildfire suppression efforts. These models utilize real-time updates on fire progression to enable firefighting teams to allocate resources more effectively and work to protect critical infrastructure while prioritizing the safe evacuation of at-risk communities. Integrating RADAR remote sensing into AI has greatly improved disaster management and mitigation. This includes applications such as earthquake monitoring, flood detection, landslide prediction, and wildfire suppression, providing crucial information for better handling natural disasters. Improved RADAR data allows for real-time monitoring, early warnings through AI systems, and damage assessment, thus helping to limit the impacts of disasters on human life and infrastructure [20]. The further development of AI and RADAR technologies will be fundamental to protecting communities from natural disasters that are becoming stronger and more frequent due to climate change [21].

2 Military and defense applications of RADAR remote sensing with artificial intelligence

2.1 Introduction to RADAR in defense

Various military and defense operations have been possible for decades using RADAR technology. RADAR systems are important for aircraft, ships, vehicles, and other objects buried within complex terrains. Integrating AI with RADAR further enables higher levels of data processing, automation of target recognition, and predictive analytics that make quick decision-making seamless, even in real-time combat situations. This section explores various dimensions of AI-integrated RADAR in defense applications based on efficiency, accuracy, and operational safety enhancements [22].

2.2 Automated target detection and classification

One of the key defense applications of integrating RADAR with AI is automatic target detection and classification [23]. Traditional RADAR systems only provide data in raw form that requires human analysis, which often results in delays in spotting threats. AI algorithms can be trained on vast datasets to classify target types according to their unique signatures. A typical example is that CNNs can analyze RADAR signals to classify objects as friendly or hostile, reducing the probability of misidentification. In particular, this becomes relevant in dense operational areas where civilian and military assets coexist. Advanced AI systems can identify subtle features that distinguish objects, such as differentiating combat vehicles from civilian transport in low-visibility conditions. AI-driven systems can adapt to identify new threat variations, thus extending the flexibility and effectiveness of RADAR in real-world applications. [24]. Figure 1 illustrates the use of RADAR in missile interception.

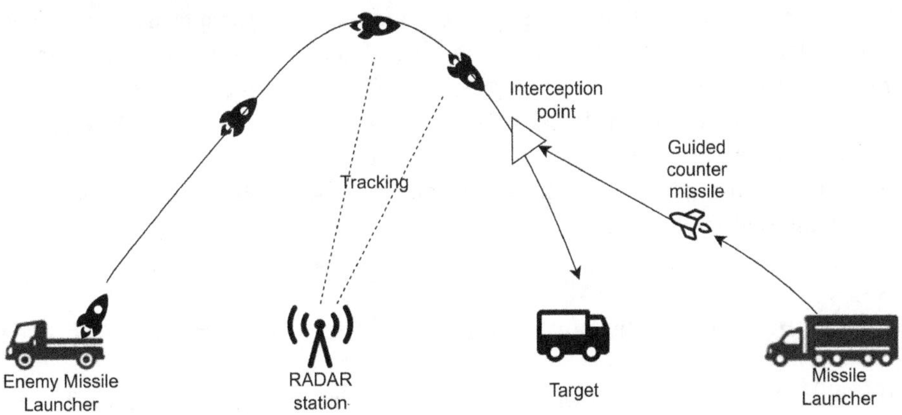

Figure 1: Missile interception using RADAR.

2.3 Surveillance and reconnaissance

The intelligence collection and the dimension of information are two crucial aspects of modern-day warfare strategy. Surveillance radar systems are installed along land borders, sea, and air [25]. For example, an AI-based vertical tracking system can follow multiple images and their motion, predict the course of these images, and warn the defense forces about targeted threats [26]. Thus, machine learning algorithms filter data, dismissing non-threatening objects such as birds and commercial jets. In this way, the military can concentrate on real threats. This capability is particularly important within intricate settings, such as the expanse of water where the activities of military vessels intersect with those of civilian vessels. In addition, AI-RADAR systems can adjust algorithms for processing information depending on the mission's goals [27]. For instance, when the combat readiness status is elevated for a prolonged time, the system may be set to a mode that focuses on even the slightest target behavioral changes for enemy detection and penetration.

2.4 Navigation and guidance systems

Navigation and guidance are major issues in missile systems, UAVs, and all other autonomous platforms. RADAR sensors provide essential data on distance, direction, and speed necessary to navigate these systems more accurately in hostile environments [28]. For example, a radar navigation system using AI can alter the flight path of guided munitions based on the target's location if it has moved. This enables engagement with targets with greater precision than before. In UAVs, AI-enhanced RADAR systems facilitate autonomous flights over complicated terrains, including mountainous regions and densely populated cities. The AI system analyzes real-time RADAR data to adjust flight paths around detected obstacles or identify potential threats. Such autonomous adaptability is most effectively utilized in reconnaissance missions where direct control cannot be exercised or is minimal. AI-based navigation systems continuously learn from experience and become more effective over time, emerging as a formidable force in combat zones, which are almost always characterized by unpredictability.

2.5 Counter-drone technology

The addition of low-cost, lightweight unmanned aerial vehicles has introduced more challenges for defense agencies. Drones can be deployed by an opposing force for spying, payload delivery, and even attacks, complicating conventional defensive strategies. Permanent eradication of drone threats will rely on RADAR systems enhanced with AI [29]. AI models that analyze RADAR signals are already available and can be used to detect small drones flying close to the ground, which would be difficult to identify using traditional methods. AI can also distinguish between drones and other harmless objects, such as birds, thereby effectively minimizing false alerts. Since countering drone threats in airspace is time-intensive, RADAR-enhanced AI systems can predict and track hostile drones, enabling their neutralization before they reach critical targets. These systems are capable of eliminating threats without requiring user involvement. Augmenting traditional RADAR systems with AI in counter-drone strategies provides a holistic and effective solution to a problem that continues to grow, particularly in urban areas or complex scenarios where aerial systems may be deployed discreetly.

2.6 Challenges and ethical considerations

It is important to ensure that AI-driven RADAR systems do not violate international laws of armed conflict or the rules of engagement [30]. Since enemy forces may use similar AI-enhanced RADAR systems, the rise of automated warfare underscores the need to counter AI advancements. Technological constraints are still in place, including the requirement for high processing capabilities and encrypted data storage. Solutions to these problems are imperative to safely and efficiently implement upgraded RADAR systems with AI technology. The application of AI in military RADAR systems offers certain advantages in conducting military operations. On the other hand, it is equally important to mitigate the ethical and technical constraints that may hinder the implementation of such technologies. By doing so, the defense entities exploring AI-RADAR warfare can achieve greater success in terms of speed, flexibility, and effectiveness, thus transforming the way wars are fought and strategies are developed.

3 Climate change studies

3.1 Introduction

Climate change has emerged as the most challenging issue of the twenty-first century, as its effects cut across various aspects: the environment, society, and the economy. Due to the dynamic nature of the environment, monitoring and evaluation of biophysical features can be very data-intensive. In most cases, such data need to be collected from remote or inaccessible zones. A data-driven approach using the long wavelengths of RF RADAR is essential for applications requiring consistency and temporal coverage [31].

3.2 Monitoring ice sheets and glaciers

The increasing global temperature trend causes ice sheets and glaciers to melt, mainly in polar areas and high mountainous ranges. Features of RADAR remote sensing technology allow the capture of these surface changes because it can see through clouds and systematically scan vast territories covered with ice. SAR makes it possible to take highly detailed images showing the movement of ice, changes in its thickness, and processes of melting or freezing [32]. AI's value lies in its ability to process complex RADAR data efficiently. For example, RADAR images showing changes within the ice cover can be analyzed using CNNs, while time series analysis methods monitor changes over a period. AI-powered segmentation of RADAR glacier images enables area estimation, revealing correlations between rising temperatures and glacier melt.

Such forecasts have helped in understanding the impact of climate change on populations already at risk, particularly in their case, the rise in sea levels.

3.3 Sea-level rise detection

Uplifting trends in sea levels, attributed to the melting of glaciers and enhanced heat absorption of water, emphasize the dangers that climate change brings to areas at sea level and marshes. Such measurements would be hard to take worldwide, but there is an alternative: using RADAR satellite remote sensing coupled with altimetry. A RADAR altimeter fitted to a satellite enables its user to measure the distance between the satellite and the surface of the Earth for effective sea-level measurement of large water bodies, such as oceans [33]. The role of AI at this point is paramount, as it involves managing thousands of pieces of information in real-time and making forecasts, which are necessary for intervention in the regions at risk.

3.4 Vegetation and carbon cycle monitoring

The condition of vegetation is an important parameter of the carbon cycle because plants consume carbon dioxide during the process of photosynthesis. RADAR is beneficial in evaluating biomass and vegetation cover in most aspects due to the limitations of optical sensors in dense forest canopies or under cloudy conditions [34]. Advanced RADAR techniques, such as Polarimetric SAR (PolSAR) and Interferometric SAR (InSAR) can resolve various vegetation types and monitor the dynamics of vegetation biomass with a high degree of precision. AI-driven models assist in managing RADAR data to assess land use changes, carbon stocks, and emissions, for instance, in tropical forests, which are key areas of carbon sequestration. Such information is crucial for carbon accounting status and policies concerning reducing emissions from deforestation and forest degradation (REDD+) projects. RADAR and AI enable real-time carbon source/sink assessments, advancing our understanding of global carbon budgets and climate change mitigation.

3.5 Soil moisture and agricultural impacts

Soil moisture is a similarly an important factor affecting crop production, water or hydrological cycles, and the proper functioning of ecosystems. The active satellite remote sensing method, especially SAR, has made it possible to estimate soil moisture through surface roughness and dielectric property analysis. Soil moisture estimations from RADAR data are achieved using AI algorithms, which provide valuable information for understanding the impact of climate change on agricultural practices [35].

3.6 Challenges and future directions

RADAR remote sensing with AI has many advantages for climate change studies. However, some challenges need to be resolved. Processing RADAR data requires significant computational power and often necessitates specific computing technologies, which might slow down usage across the board. Furthermore, the fact that RADAR images differ from non-RADAR images, whether in resolution or file types, makes, for instance, the combination of RADAR images, optical images, and climate models complex [36]. This is one of the reasons driving research on AI. Such data is reliable and consistent across many different environmental variables. RADAR data and its associated applications can range from measuring the polar ice cap to predicting the rise in sea level. As illustrated in Figure 2, its unique properties make RADAR systems a critical tool in the fight against global climate change. The benefits of AI are not limited to simply improving the degree of precision in the analysis of data provided by RADAR; these benefits extend the operations of RADAR to much more efficient and appropriate time frames for the situations faced by policymakers, scientists and the communities under threat from climate change.

4 Challenges and future directions

The current growth trend in the deployment of AI on radar-operated remote sensing devices has created several possibilities and challenges for the future. This segment addresses the existing economic, engineering, and ethical issues in this area. It suggests ways aimed at developing the use of AI in conjunction with radar technology to maximize the full benefits of remote sensing.

4.1 Technical challenges

Processing RADAR data, which is usually collected from different sites and under varying conditions, is one of the main technical challenges. Most RADAR sensors experience various noise interferences and present signals with differing values and frequencies in the range of materials they can penetrate and structures they can detect. Such data is highly non-uniform and thus necessitates advanced preprocessing strategies like noise suppression, regularization, and re-sampling. The complexity of RADAR signals requires sophisticated processing, often relying on advanced AI models to handle noisy data, although these models are costly to develop and maintain. Another significant challenge is data labeling. Specifically, in supervised learning, where AI algorithms are expected to solve problems such as classification, they depend on datasets that have been accurately labeled. Completing the task of labeling RADAR data in-

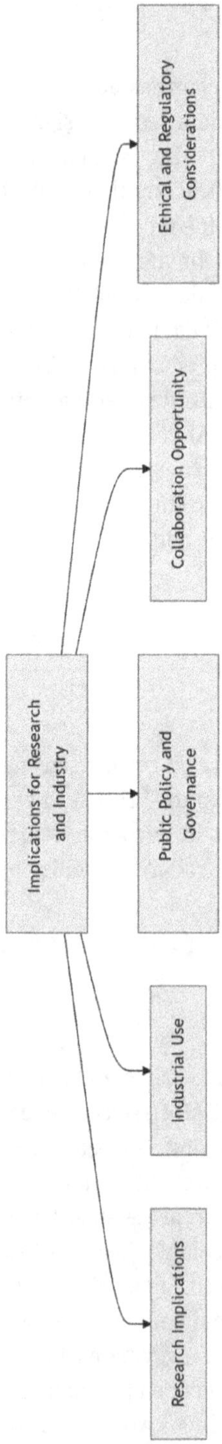

Figure 2: Implications for research and industry.

volves substantial effort, as it requires expertise in both RADAR technology and the application domain. Consequently, the unavailability of labeled datasets stands out as a major bottleneck because many deep learning models, which require large amounts of data, cannot be optimized. Other approaches have been proposed, such as unsupervised, self-supervised, or transfer learning. However, these methods are not without drawbacks and may fail to achieve the required precision in certain cases.

Also, data fusion with other types of sensors, e.g., optical or hyperspectral imaging systems, creates another challenge that is difficult but worth attempting. On the one hand, it is advantageous to incorporate RADAR data with other data types as it enhances the performance of the resulting model. Still, on the other hand, it adds more complexity during facilitated data preparation and model construction. Information from different modalities is difficult to integrate and requires proper settings for each due to the compatibility issues of the different features of the data gathered.

4.2 Computational challenges

The computational demands of processing and analyzing RADAR data with AI techniques are considerable. RADAR remote sensing generates vast amounts of high-dimensional data, and applying deep learning models to analyze this data requires substantial computing resources [37]. In particular, training large neural networks on RADAR data can be time-consuming and resource-intensive, often necessitating high-performance computing (HPC) systems or cloud-based solutions. Model efficiency is also a critical computational challenge. Many RADAR remote sensing applications, such as real-time surveillance or autonomous systems, require low-latency processing to deliver timely insights. However, most deep learning models require significant computation and may not meet real-time latency needs. Moreover, deploying AI models on edge devices presents unique challenges in RADAR remote sensing. Edge computing allows for data processing closer to the source, enabling real-time decision-making. However, RADAR data processing algorithms are often complex and require significant memory and processing power, making it challenging to deploy them on edge devices with limited capacity.

4.3 Ethical and regulatory challenges

As AI further integrates into RADAR remote sensing, many ethical and regulatory challenges significant to society will need to be addressed [38]. The most important of these issues is data privacy in applications related to RADAR's surveillance or traffic monitoring, wherein the locations or behaviors of specific individuals may inadvertently be tracked. Ensuring that such applications comply with data protection regulations, such as the General Data Protection Regulation (GDPR) in Europe, is critical to avoiding privacy violations. Model bias is another major ethical concern in AI models. RADAR data influenced by environmental conditions may lead to model bias if training and ground truth data lack diversity.

Explainability and transparency of models are usually very important in all kinds of RADAR remote-sensing applications, especially when results are used in high-stakes sectors such as defense or disaster management. Many of these models, especially neural networks, are often considered "black boxes" since their internal mechanisms are usually not interpretable. Therefore, developing inherently interpretable models or methods for explaining the decisions of complex AI models is crucial for building trust in these systems and ensuring compliance with emerging regulatory standards.

4.4 Future directions

To tackle these challenges, the research area must focus more on developing robust, efficient, and interpretable AI techniques specific to RADAR remote sensing. Unsupervised and self-supervised learning are some of the most promising areas since, with high volumes of unlabeled RADAR data, there is the potential to overcome barriers resulting from labeled data shortages. Self-supervised techniques can uncover patterns in unlabeled data, enabling the development of robust models without extensive labeling efforts. Another promising direction involves hybrid modeling methods that integrate physics-based models with machine learning. These hybrid models bridge the gap between purely data-driven and physics-driven approaches in truly challenging environments. Federated learning can also accelerate AI for RADAR remote sensing [39]. It may enable the joint training of collaborative models across organizations without sharing sensitive data.

Edge AI could provide a solution for real-time RADAR data processing, for instance, in autonomous vehicles and security-related applications. It could analyze real-time RADAR data directly from its source without much latency by deploying lightweight AI models on edge devices, drones, or satellites. Therefore, efficient research into model architectures, such as pruning and quantization, is vital to making AI models feasible with limited computational resources on edge hardware. Technical, computational, and ethical challenges require significant interdisciplinary efforts to integrate AI with the RADAR remote sensing domain and develop innovative solutions. Further advances in self-supervised learning, hybrid modeling, federated learning, and edge AI will enable further enhancements to the capability and usability of AI-RADAR systems and permit their use in a wide range of applications. Although AI integrated with RADAR remote sensing holds great promise, it also highlights forthcoming developments needed to meet various practical application demands.

5 Case studies: real-world applications and success stories of RADAR remote sensing with AI

The joint application of AI and RADAR remote sensing has brought revolutionary developments to numerous areas, including environmental monitoring and defense. This section contains case studies that capture the practical use of AI-enhanced RADAR remote sensing. By understanding these applications, it is possible to envision the possibilities, challenges, and future perspectives of AI RADAR.

5.1 Case study 1: deforestation monitoring in the amazon

One notable application of RADAR remote sensing with ML tools is in managing the deforestation in the Amazon basin. Cloud cover and the night sky usually hamper conventional optical satellite images in most rain-forested areas, normally resulting in scarce and fragmented data. On the other hand, SAR sensors can penetrate cloud cover and operate during night hours [40]. In 2022, a fusion of governmental and non-governmental organizations applied a CNN-based classification algorithm for RADAR data processing, which enabled the separation of forested and deforested areas. This automated approach effectively mapped deforestation, achieving 95% detection accuracy – far surpassing previous manual methods. AI-driven classification can drastically reduce the time required to process and interpret vast datasets. RADAR's ability to penetrate cloud cover ensures consistent monitoring, while AI algorithms interpret data accurately, minimizing reliance on optical imaging alone.

5.2 Case study 2: flood detection and prediction in Southeast Asia

Flooding is a frequent natural calamity in Southeast Asia, underscoring the need for prompt intervention measures in flood detection and prediction. In 2021, research conducted within the Mekong Delta regions proposed using a recurrent neural network (RNN) model for real-time analysis and forecasting of flood detection based on SAR-based RADAR for agriculture and disaster management [41]. An RNN model trained on historical RADAR imagery and basic hydrology data overcomes limitations, enabling accurate flood predictions for low-lying areas. Additionally, it was possible to incorporate AI techniques with RADAR's spatial-temporal data to predict possible flood events several days in advance. This AI-RADAR model facilitated local administrations in taking early steps toward tackle the threat, thereby reducing the risk of flooding disasters for residents. Techniques such as RNN can successfully forecast and simulate disaster situations if a model is sufficiently trained on high-resolution

RADAR data. Using RADAR data and AI enables prompt action, greatly improving the ability to manage risks in areas vulnerable to catastrophes in a preventive manner.

6 Comparative analysis of AI techniques in RADAR applications

These case studies showcase the multifaceted applicability of AI in RADAR applications [42]. However, each AI methodology serves specific purposes dictated by the nature of the data and the prevailing operational environment. The application of CNNs is recommended for tasks that require recognition of static images and their boundaries, which is particularly relevant in the case of forest monitoring. Object detection algorithms like YOLO, on the other hand, are suitable for environments prone to rapid changes and, therefore, require real-time analysis, such as in military operations.

7 Lessons learned from implemented solutions

Data quality and preprocessing: AI models are only as good as the data they are trained on; thus, data quality and accuracy are essential to their success. Several preprocessing steps, which involve noise reduction, calibration, and feature extraction, are required to enhance data quality so that it becomes suitable for use in applications involving ground-penetrating radar.

Model generalizability: Models trained with data from RADAR should be flexible enough to accommodate a wide range of environmental conditions. Since the variety of training data is extensive, there will be improved generalization across different geographical and climatic conditions.

Model complexity balance: The more complex a model is, the more accurate the prediction will generally be, but it can also be computationally expensive. A solution that best balances model complexity against computational efficiency is crucial, especially when the application needs to run in real time.

Human expertise is indispensable: As much as AI automates tasks, interpreting results, validating model predictions, and making context-sensitive decisions demand human expertise. For instance, disaster management or military applications require human oversight to lend credibility to the many outputs emanating from the AI system.

8 Future prospects for AI-powered RADAR applications

These case studies raise the prospect of an encouraging future with AI-powered RADAR remote sensing and, hence, warrant future research into:

Interpretability of models: The interpretable model plays an important role in developing AI models, especially in ensuring consistency in building transparency and trust.

Cross-disciplinary collaboration: Effective solutions can be achieved through active collaboration among AI researchers, radar engineers, and domain-specific experts such as environmental scientists and military strategists.

Data fusion: Merging radar with LiDAR and hyperspectral imaging further enhances the accuracy and resilience of the AI model.

These case studies highlight AI's transformative potential in RADAR remote sensing, ranging from technical advancements to operational improvements. By addressing challenges such as data quality, model generalization, and computational constraints, these real-world insights pave a pathway for further innovation in a rapidly evolving field.

9 Conclusion

The combination of RADAR remote sensing and AI is well-suited for technology usage in environmental monitoring, agriculture, disaster management, and urban planning, which are critical global concerns. One of the most important areas of focus on the ground is environmental monitoring. RADAR and AI track deforestation, urban sprawl, and water resources, contributing to ecological preservation and policy enforcement. In the case of disaster management, RADAR applications predict floods, landslides, and earthquakes, while the strength of AI lies in early warning systems and improving resource allocation. Urban planning and smart cities can advance by applying RADAR and AI technologies for infrastructure monitoring, traffic management, and sustainable urban growth. The future includes high-resolution RADAR systems for applications based on drones and multidimensional data analyses carried out using AI, which autonomously performs tasks such as crop monitoring, forest fire detection, and remote infrastructure inspection.

This research broadens access to insights into environmental science, agriculture, and disaster preparedness. Industries benefit through precision farming, infrastructure monitoring, and cost efficiency, while policymakers can use RADAR-AI systems for disaster resilience and sustainable urban planning. Joint efforts and ethical frameworks ensure that new technologies advance responsibly and inclusively. There are great prospects when RADAR remote sensing technology is combined with AI due to its advanced capability to monitor, predict, and react to changes in environmental and social dynamics. Nevertheless, with increased investments in research and partnerships with relevant industries for appropriate use, these advancements could help build a future economy that is sustainable, resilient and, most importantly, based on data.

References

[1] Rohling, H. and Moller, C. (2008) "Radar waveform for automotive radar systems and applications," 2008 IEEE Radar Conference. 2008 IEEE Radar Conference (RADAR), IEEE. doi:10.1109/radar.2008.4721121.
[2] Abid, S.K., Sulaiman, N., Chan, S.W., Nazir, U., Abid, M., Han, H., Ariza-montes, A., Vega-muñoz, A. 2021. Toward an integrated disaster management approach: How artificial intelligence can boost disaster management. J. S. 13, 12560.
[3] Elliott, J. 2020. Earth observation for the assessment of earthquake hazard, risk and disaster management. J. S. I. G. 41, 1323–1354.
[4] Dell'acqua, F., Gamba, P. 2012. Remote sensing and earthquake damage assessment: Experiences, limits, and perspectives. J. P. O. T. I. 100, 2876–2890.
[5] Menderes, A., Erener, A., Sarp, G. 2015. Automatic detection of damaged buildings after earthquake hazard by using remote sensing and information technologies. J. P. E. & Science, P. 15, 257–262.
[6] Tomiyasu, K. 1978. Tutorial review of synthetic-aperture radar (SAR) with applications to imaging of the ocean surface. J. P. O. T. I. 66, 563–583.
[7] Headrick, J., Thomason, J. 1998. Applications of high-frequency radar. J. R. S. 33, 1045–1054.
[8] Yamazaki, F., Liu, W. 2016. Remote sensing technologies for post-earthquake damage assessment: A case study on the 2016 Kumamoto earthquake. In: 6th Asia Conf. on Earthquake Engg.
[9] Gebremichael, E., Molthan, A.L., Bell, J.R., Schultz, L.A., Hain, C. 2020. Flood hazard and risk assessment of extreme weather events using synthetic aperture radar and auxiliary data: A case study. J. R. S. 12, 3588.
[10] Munawar, H.S., Hammad, A.W., Waller, S.T. 2022. Remote sensing methods for flood prediction: A review. J. S. 22, 960.
[11] Mellett, J.S. 1995. Ground penetrating radar applications in engineering, environmental management, and geology. J. J. O. A. G. 33, 157–166.
[12] Klemas, V. 2015. Remote sensing of floods and flood-prone areas: An overview. J. J. O. C. R. 31, 1005–1013.
[13] Zhang, Y., Meng, X., Dijkstra, T., Jordan, C., Chen, G., Zeng, R., Novellino, A. 2020. Forecasting the magnitude of potential landslides based on InSAR techniques. J. R. S. O. E. 241, 111738.
[14] Casagli, N., Intrieri, E., Tofani, V., Gigli, G., Raspini, F. 2023. Landslide detection, monitoring and prediction with remote-sensing techniques. J. N. R. E. & Environment 4, 51–64.
[15] Akosah, S., Gratchev, I., Kim, D.-H., Ohn, S.-Y. 2024. Application of artificial intelligence and remote sensing for landslide detection and prediction: Systematic review. J. R. S. 16, 2947.
[16] Zhong, C., Liu, Y., Gao, P., Chen, W., Li, H., Hou, Y., Nuremanguli, T., MA, H. 2020. Landslide mapping with remote sensing: Challenges and opportunities. J. I. J. O. R. S. 41, 1555–1581.
[17] Anghelescu, L., Diaconu, B.M. 2024. Advances in detection and monitoring of coal spontaneous combustion: Techniques, challenges, and future directions. J. F. 7, 354.
[18] Allison, R.S., Johnston, J.M., Craig, G., Jennings, S. 2016. Airborne optical and thermal remote sensing for wildfire detection and monitoring. J. S. 16, 1310.

[19] Leblon, B., Bourgeau-Chavez, L. and San-Miguel-Ayanz, J. (2012) "Use of Remote Sensing in Wildfire Management," Sustainable Development - Authoritative and Leading Edge Content for Environmental Management. InTech. doi:10.5772/45829.
[20] Govil, K., Welch, M.L., Ball, J.T., Pennypacker, C.R. 2020. Preliminary results from a wildfire detection system using deep learning on remote camera images. J. R. S. 12, 166.
[21] San-miguel-ayanz, J., Ravail, N. 2005. Active fire detection for fire emergency management: Potential and limitations for the operational use of remote sensing. J. N. H. 35, 361–376.
[22] Ali, A., Shehzad, K., Farid, Z., Farooq, M.U. 2021. Artificial intelligence potential trends in military. J. F. U. J. O. E. & SCIENCES, A. 2, 1–11.
[23] Wrabel, A., Graef, R., Brosch, T. 2021. A survey of artificial intelligence approaches for target surveillance with radar sensors. J. I. A. & MAGAZINE, E. S. 36, 26–43.
[24] Baeza, V.M. et al. (2025) "AI-Driven Tactical Communications and Networking for Defense: A Survey and Emerging Trends." arXiv. doi:10.48550/ARXIV.2504.05071.
[25] Suo, J. et al. (2023) "Computational Imaging and Artificial Intelligence: The Next Revolution of Mobile Vision," Proceedings of the IEEE. Institute of Electrical and Electronics Engineers (IEEE). doi:10.1109/jproc.2023.3338272.
[26] Kumar, G. and Altalbe, A. (2024) "Artificial intelligence (AI) advancements for transportation security: in-depth insights into electric and aerial vehicle systems," Environment, Development and Sustainability. Springer Science and Business Media LLC. doi:10.1007/s10668-024-04790-4.
[27] Srinivas, K.K., Peddi, A., Ramakuri, S.K., Vardhini, P.H., Avinash, P.S., Sirimalla, R. 2022. Artificial intelligence-driven techniques to advanced signals and communication systems. In: 2022 International Mobile and Embedded Technology Conference (MECON), IEEE, 307–310.
[28] Khalil, R.A., Haris, M. and Saeed, N. (2023) "Beyond Line of Sight Defense Communication Systems: Recent Advances and Future Challenges." arXiv. doi:10.48550/ARXIV.2312.06491.
[29] Johnson, J. 2020. Artificial intelligence, drone swarming and escalation risks in future warfare. J. T. R. J. 165, 26–36.
[30] Kraska, J. 2021. Command accountability for AI weapon systems in the law of armed conflict. J. I. L. S. 97, 22.
[31] Zhao, J., Xie, H., Ma, J., Wang, K. 2021. Integrated remote sensing and model approach for impact assessment of future climate change on the carbon budget of global forest ecosystems. J. G. & CHANGE, P. 203, 103542.
[32] Scher, C., Steiner, N.C., Mcdonald, K.C. 2021. Mapping seasonal glacier melt across the Hindu Kush Himalaya with time series synthetic aperture radar (SAR). J. T. C. 15, 4465–4482.
[33] Grgić, M. and Bašić, T. (2021) "Radar Satellite Altimetry in Geodesy - Theory, Applications and Recent Developments," Geodetic Sciences - Theory, Applications and Recent Developments. IntechOpen. doi:10.5772/intechopen.97349.
[34] Abbas, S., Wong, M.S., Wu, J., Shahzad, N., Muhammad Irteza, S. 2020. Approaches of satellite remote sensing for the assessment of above-ground biomass across tropical forests: Pan-tropical to national scales. J. R. S 12, 3351.
[35] Abbes, A.B., Jarray, N., Farah, I.R. 2024. Advances in remote sensing based soil moisture retrieval: Applications, techniques, scales and challenges for combining machine learning and physical models. J. A. I. R 57, 224.
[36] Zhang, L., Zhang, L. 2022. Artificial intelligence for remote sensing data analysis: A review of challenges and opportunities. J. I. G. & MAGAZINE, R. S. 10, 270–294.
[37] Haut, J.M., Paoletti, M.E., Moreno-álvarez, S., Plaza, J., Rico-gallego, J.-A., Plaza, A. 2021. Distributed deep learning for remote sensing data interpretation. J. P. O. T. I. 109, 1320–1349.
[38] Ahmad, M. (2023) "Spatially-Aware Artificial Intelligence for Sustainable Development Goals," Advances in Civil and Industrial Engineering. IGI Global. doi:10.4018/979-8-3693-0044-2.ch024.

[39] Jiang, J.C., Kantarci, B., Oktug, S., Soyata, T. 2020. Federated learning in smart city sensing: Challenges and opportunities. J. S. 20, 6230.
[40] Chaddad, F., Mello, F.A., Tayebi, M., Safanelli, J.L., Campos, L.R., Amorim, M.T.A., de Sousa, G.P.B., Ferreira, T.O., Ruiz, F., Perlatti, F. 2022. Impact of mining-induced deforestation on soil surface temperature and carbon stocks: A case study using remote sensing in the Amazon rainforest. J. J. O. S. A. E. S. 119, 103983.
[41] Kim, J., Kim, H., Jeon, H., Jeong, S.-H., Song, J., Vadivel, S.K.P., Kim, D.-J. 2021. Synergistic use of geospatial data for water body extraction from Sentinel-1 images for operational flood monitoring across southeast asia using deep neural networks. J. R. S. 13, 4759.
[42] Travassos, X.L., Avila, S.L., Ida, N. 2021. Artificial neural networks and machine learning techniques applied to ground penetrating radar: A review. J. A. C. & Informatics 17, 296–308.

Aditya Vardhan*, Amarjeet Singh Chauhan, Sanjay Saini,
Akshay Jhingran

Computational techniques in RADAR remote sensing from a machine and deep learning perspective

Abstract: This research explores how advanced machine learning and deep learning techniques are revolutionizing RADAR remote sensing by enhancing its capabilities and applications. Scientists can process signals by applying sophisticated computational techniques that make them more effective in extracting critical features from imagery. The article highlights significant advancements in environmental monitoring, disaster management, and surveillance, demonstrating how modern computational methods and algorithms enhance established RADAR technologies by integrating them with recently developed technological approaches. The research underscores the significant role of computational techniques in improving data understanding and analysis, addressing current challenges, and exploring future opportunities.

Keywords: Remote sensing, advanced machine learning algorithms, deep learning techniques, signal processing optimization, remote sensing data analysis, computational models in RADAR

1 Introduction

Remote sensing is a powerful technology that allows for collecting information about Earth's surface and atmosphere from a distance, typically using satellites, aircraft, or drones. Capturing data through various sensors that detect electromagnetic radiation, remote sensing provides critical insights into environmental changes, land use, climate patterns, and geographic features without direct physical contact. This technology has revolutionized fields like meteorology, agriculture, urban planning, and environmental monitoring by offering comprehensive, real-time global perspectives

***Corresponding author: Aditya Vardhan**, Department of Physics and Computer Science, Dayalbagh Educational Institute, Agra, India, e-mail: vardhana3098@gmail.com, ORCID: 0009-0008-7038-988X
Amarjeet Singh Chauhan, Department of Physics and Computer Science, Dayalbagh Educational Institute, Agra, Uttar Pradesh, India, e-mail: amarjeetsinghchauhan@gmail.com
Sanjay Saini, Department of Physics and Computer Science, Dayalbagh Educational Institute, Agra, Uttar Pradesh, India, e-mail: sanjay.sani@dei.ac.in
Akshay Jhingran, School of Engineering, South East Technological University, Waterford, Ireland, e-mail: er.jhingranakshay0809@gmail.com

https://doi.org/10.1515/9783111572970-012

previously impossible to obtain. Satellites like the Seasat satellite, developed in the 1960s and 1970s, enable the observation of the conditions of oceans, land, and atmosphere, as shown in Figure 1. It was very useful in monitoring large-scale environmental changes, as sensors are not confined by cloud cover and daylight [1]. This led to advances in applications ranging from agriculture and forestry to disaster management, urban planning, and climate change monitoring; therefore, RADAR established itself as a core technology of modern remote sensing [2].

1.1 Computational techniques in remote sensing

Importantly, the basis for remote sensing systems relies heavily on computational techniques, particularly for handling large, complex datasets generated by technologies like RADAR. The implications of these techniques lie in the efficient processing, analysis, and interpretation of data. They automate various processes, including noise reduction, signal enhancement, and image classification, which facilitate the extraction of valuable information from the data [3]. Advanced algorithms, especially in machine learning and pattern recognition, can identify hidden patterns and subtle changes that are not readily visible with conventional methods. These techniques are also used to simulate the progression of natural phenomena through computational models that support climate monitoring, disaster management, and urban planning [4]. Earth observation is critical because it utilizes RADAR technology as part of remote sensing, enabling the capture of high-resolution images and terrain mapping for effective environmental monitoring. This has various applications in disaster management, agricultural assessment, and climate studies, using advanced signal processing and machine learning techniques for enhanced data interpretation [5].

1.2 Emergence of machine and deep learning

It revolutionized the process of remote sensing, which now employs more advanced tools, reviewing enormous and complex data efficiently and accurately compared to the traditional methods that involved manual interpretation and were, therefore, time-consuming and error-prone. According to it, automation of processes like land classification and object detection in RADAR and satellite images becomes possible through algorithms like support vector machines and random forest. Deep learning has pushed this further with neural networks, particularly convolutional neural networks (CNNs), which automatically learn features from raw data and, thus, have dramatically proven their effectiveness for real complex pattern recognition. Using these models has significantly improved tasks such as image classification, anomaly detection, and environmental monitoring. These capacities of deep learning concerning large, unstructured data have opened new avenues toward real-time monitoring and predictive modeling, making it an indispensable tool in climate studies, disaster management, and smart agriculture.

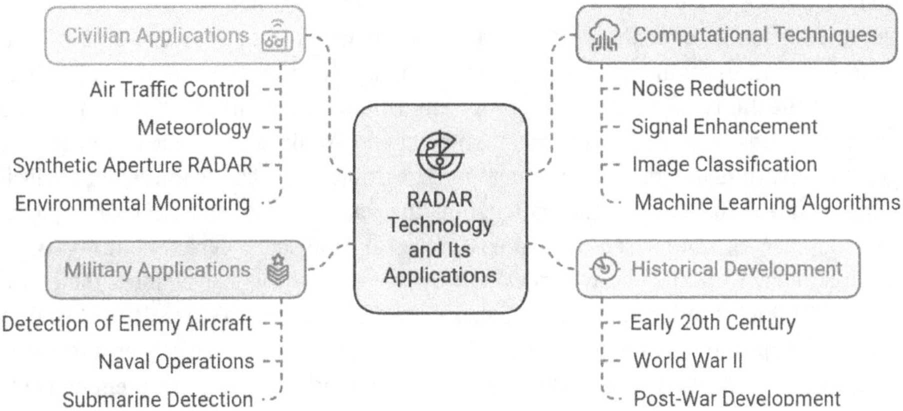

Figure 1: Overview of RADAR technology and its applications.

This set the course for developing applications in agriculture, forestry, disaster management, and urban planning, as well as observing climate change and consolidating RADAR as the basic component of modern remote sensing technology.

2 Fundamentals of remote sensing

2.1 The basic principle of RADAR

A RADAR system sends out electromagnetic waves and analyzes the return signals after these waves have interacted with objects. The radio wave emitted by the system travels through the atmosphere, and if it encounters an object, part of the signal gets reflected to the receiver in the RADAR. In this process, the system can measure the time delay of the returned signal along with its strength. The reflection, according to various factors, depends on the object's size, shape, material, surface texture, and the angle at which the waves hit. Through this, valuable information about the location and movement of the object is derived. Its ability to penetrate through clouds, fog, and even foliage makes RADAR highly effective in weather forecasting, air traffic control, and environmental monitoring, whereas traditional optical systems may be less effective [6].

2.2 Types of RADAR systems

Several forms of RADAR systems are designed for various applications and capabilities. The most widely applied type in remote sensing and Earth observation is synthetic aperture radar (SAR). This system achieves high-resolution imaging by moving the RADAR sensor over the target area, synthesizing a larger aperture through advanced signal processing rather than relying on a physically large antenna. SAR has wide applicability in terrain mapping, environmental monitoring, and imaging through clouds or at night. It sends high-frequency radio waves that penetrate the ground toward detect buried structures, utilities, and geological features; its applications include archaeological excavation, building construction, and geological exploration. Doppler RADAR is used in weather forecasting and speed detection; it measures the frequency shift of radio waves caused by movement. This has enabled the monitoring of Doppler radar velocities ranging from raindrops to vehicles. It is crucial in storm tracking and wind pattern analysis, enabling accurate weather forecasts. Though each RADAR may find its niche, the common principle in all of them depends on using electromagnetic waves to collect data on objects and their movement [7].

2.3 Applications of RADAR in remote sensing

Since several RADAR applications involve remote sensing, it plays an important role in many sectors. For example, in land monitoring, deforestation, agricultural methods, and variations in land use can be tracked using RADAR systems. Due to its penetration capability through cloud cover, it allows continuous monitoring. In oceanography, sea surface mapping, tracing ocean currents, and locating oil spills are accomplished using RADAR systems. For instance, these services are important in both maritime navigation and climate modeling, as well as the protection of the environment. There is also an aspect of urban planning, for example, in RADAR: detailed data from the infrastructure, detection of urban expansion, and monitoring subsidence or the integrity of buildings. Climate studies utilize RADAR to monitor significant atmospheric functions, such as storms, wind, and precipitation trends, thus generating better weather forecasts and climate models [8].

3 Computational techniques in RADAR in remote sensing

Advanced noise filtering, enhancement of signal quality, and automation of tasks such as object detection and classification through computations require complex data processing. Machine learning and deep learning techniques further enhance the accuracy of analyzing complex RADAR imagery, which is crucial for applications like environmental monitoring, urban planning, and disaster management [9].

3.1 Traditional image processing algorithms for RADAR data

Traditional image processing algorithms play a crucial role in RADAR data analysis, particularly in enhancing image quality, correcting distortions, and extracting relevant features. These include techniques commonly known as thresholding, edge detection, and segmentation. Thresholding is typically applied using a specific value for pixel intensity, which enables certain objects to be separated from their background, making it highly useful for detecting anomalies or changes in RADAR images. Similarly, edge detection algorithms, such as Sobel and Canny operators, are applied to identify boundaries by detecting sharp changes in intensity; as a result, objects are better defined, and their features can be projected more clearly. Techniques such as region-growing or clustering divide the RADAR image into meaningful sections, isolating areas of interest for further analysis. These foundational techniques facilitate basic preprocessing for interpreting the data obtained from RADAR and lay the groundwork for more advanced machine learning and deep learning applications [10].

3.2 Signal processing for RADAR systems

Signal processing is highly important for improving RADAR performance; several important techniques include Fourier transforms, wavelet-based methods, and time-frequency analysis. Time-frequency analysis allows one to carry out signal processing in both time and frequency domains to determine the dynamic behavior of moving targets. Another aspect of the time-domain signal is that Fourier transforms can transfer it into the frequency domain, making it easier to analyze wave patterns and even detect objects based on frequency shifts. In contrast, wavelet-based techniques break down the signal into different scales. They are quite precise in detecting transient signals with a good amount of localizing ability, making them suitable for identifying fine details in the highly complex data analysis of RADAR systems. In so doing, these methodologies increase the resolution and confidence of signals while making the whole RADAR application system more effective in whatever application is used in surveillance, environmental observation, etc. [11].

4 Machine learning approaches in RADAR remote sensing

Machine learning approaches in RADAR remote sensing automatically analyze data by learning patterns from large datasets, enhancing the performance of critical tasks such as object detection, classification, and anomaly detection. Additionally, accuracy and efficiency are improved with more complex applications in monitoring environmental changes, urban mapping, and predicting disasters [12].

4.1 Introduction to machine learning in remote sensing

Machine learning in remote sensing implements different techniques, which include supervised, unsupervised, and reinforcement learning for analyzing complex data sets. Supervised learning procedures use labeled data when training the models to perform either classification or prediction; it finds abundant uses in land cover classification and object detection. Unsupervised learning uses unlabeled data, helping in clustering and pattern identification, especially in anomaly detection and image segmentation. The salient advantages of these techniques are efficiency and accuracy in analyzing data, which transform how processed and interpreted remote sensing data appears [13].

4.2 Feature extraction and selection in RADAR data

These techniques include principal component analysis (PCA) analysis of the data, k-means clustering of the data, and decision trees. PCA reduces the dimensionality by projecting data onto principal components that preserve important features while maximizing, or nearly so, their mutual information, thereby reducing redundancy. K-means clustering helps cluster data with similar patterns for improved recognition. Decision trees aid in classification and feature selection or relevance for sound detection and classification in radar systems, as shown in Table 1 [14].

4.3 Application of machine learning

- **Support vector machines (SVMs) for terrain classification:** SVMs are highly efficient in classifying various types of terrain in radar signals using the optimal hyperplane constructed between the distinct terrain classes [15].
- **Random forests for object detection in RADAR imagery:** Random forests improve object detection in radar imagery by using an ensemble of decision trees to provide accurate and robust identification of different objects [16].

- **K-nearest neighbors (K-NN) for land use classification**: In this technique, K-NN classifies land usage patterns using radar data, considering the proximity of the data points to their nearest neighbors, thereby achieving accurate classification based on similarity [1].

Table 1: Technical overview of machine learning approaches in RADAR.

Task	Machine learning technique	Use case in RADAR remote sensing
Feature extraction and selection [17]	Principal component analysis (PCA), k-means clustering, decision trees	Reducing the dimensionality of RADAR data, grouping similar features, and selecting important data attributes for better model performance.
Terrain classification [18]	Support vector machines (SVMs)	Using SVMs to classify terrain types from RADAR data, enhancing land cover and landscape mapping.
Object detection [19]	Random forest	Applying random forest to detect objects such as vehicles and buildings in RADAR imagery.
Land use classification [2]	K-nearest neighbors (K-NN)	Utilizing K-NN for land use classification, distinguishing among agricultural, urban, and natural landscapes.

5 Deep learning for advanced RADAR remote sensing

Deep learning techniques, such as CNNs, enhance radar data analysis by automatically extracting features for object detection, classification, and terrain mapping. As shown in Table 2, these methods improve accuracy and efficiency in complex remote sensing tasks.

5.1 Introduction to deep learning

Deep learning is the application of artificial neural networks to represent complex patterns in data through interconnected layers of nodes, mimicking the brain's functions. CNNs are uniquely suited for processing spatial data, such as images, particularly in feature extraction and radar imagery applications. Generative models, such as deep belief networks, learn hierarchical representations, improving unsupervised learning, and pattern recognition [21].

Table 2: Use cases of deep learning techniques in advanced RADAR remote sensing.

Deep learning technique	Description	Use case in RADAR remote sensing	Impact on RADAR data processing
Neural networks (NNs) [15]	Introduction to deep learning: general-purpose neural networks	Used for basic radar data pattern recognition and initial classification.	Lays the foundation for more advanced deep learning models, such as CNNs and RNNs.
CNNs [19]	Architecture and layers specialized for RADAR imagery	CNNs are employed for classifying objects and land types in RADAR imagery (e.g., identifying buildings, vehicles, etc.).	Achieves higher accuracy in object detection and land-cover classification by leveraging spatial hierarchies in data.
Recurrent neural networks (RNNs) [8]	Analyzing time-series RADAR data	RNNs track temporal patterns in RADAR data, such as changes in weather patterns (e.g., rainfall prediction and wave analysis).	Enhances the analysis of dynamic RADAR data for real-time environmental monitoring.
Generative adversarial networks (GANs) [20]	Data augmentation via synthetic data generation	GANs generate additional RADAR data to train models on rare events or small datasets (e.g., extreme weather or rare objects).	Expands the dataset for better training and improves the robustness of machine-learning models.
Autoencoders [11]	Reducing noise in RADAR signals	Autoencoders denoise radar signals, improving data quality for better model training and analysis.	Reduces artifacts in data, leading to clearer and more accurate radar images.

5.2 Architecture and layers of CNNs specialized for RADAR image data

The CNN architectures for radar image classification include convolutional, pooling, and fully connected layers. Convolutional layers capture spatial features, and pooling reduces dimensionality. The architecture is effective for detecting patterns in radar data, especially object shapes and terrain textures [22].

5.3 Case studies of CNNs for object detection and land classification

In particular, different works have proven the efficiency and effectiveness of CNNs for object detection in radar imagery, including vehicles and buildings, as well as in land classification, such as forests, urban areas, and water bodies, with very high accuracy in remote sensing applications [23].

5.4 Application of RNNs for analyzing time-series RADAR data

RNNs have excellent abilities when sequential radar data are concerned, as previous inputs are remembered. Therefore, these types of data fit very well in time-series analysis. For instance, RNNs can determine the pattern and wave movement concerning rainfall and other temporal radar data [24]. They can predict weather conditions or track environmental changes over time, thereby enhancing forecasting and pattern recognition in dynamic radar sensing applications [25].

5.5 Generative adversarial networks (GANs) in RADAR data augmentation

Existing datasets generated through GANs provide synthetic radar data, which can positively impact models with limited data [26]. Creating realistic synthetic radar images using GANs helps augment the training data toward object detection, classification, and terrain analysis tasks, ultimately enhancing the accuracy and generalization ability of machine learning models applied to radar-based applications [27].

6 Advanced techniques for big data in RADAR remote sensing

6.1 Handling big data in RADAR remote sensing

Big data in RADAR remote sensing poses significant computational challenges, such as data processing and storage, but also offers opportunities for advanced techniques to improve data analysis, enhance image resolution, and support informed decision-making [28]. Modern machine learning algorithms enable efficient processing of massive datasets, allowing researchers to extract meaningful insights from complex signal information. By leveraging deep learning methods, scientists can manage, analyze, and interpret large-scale RADAR data more effectively, transforming how we understand and utilize remote sensing technologies across environmental, surveillance, and disaster management domains.

6.2 Cloud computing and edge computing for RADAR data processing

6.2.1 Cloud platforms for distributed processing and storage

Cloud platforms, such as AWS and Google Cloud, enable infrastructure scalability, as shown in Table 3. Flexible storage accommodates the large volume of data generated by continuous radar sensing. Cloud services' support for real-time data access and analytics makes them ideal for addressing big data challenges in remote sensing [29, 17].

Table 3: Use cases and advantages of CC and EC.

Computing paradigm	Description	Use case	Advantages
Cloud computing [30]	Cloud platforms, such as AWS and Google Cloud, provide scalable infrastructure for distributed processing and storage.	Enables parallel computation of vast RADAR datasets, accommodating the high volume from continuous sensing and supporting real-time analytics.	Scalable infrastructure, flexible storage solutions, and real-time data access for large datasets.
Edge computing [8]	Edge computing processes data closer to RADAR sensors, allowing for real-time analysis and faster decision-making.	Essential for time-sensitive applications like autonomous vehicles and disaster monitoring, it ensures immediate insights and responses.	Reduces latency and bandwidth usage, improving efficiency in dynamic environments.

6.3 High-performance computing (HPC) in RADAE remote sensing

Using parallel computing and GPUs, HPC significantly expedites machine and deep learning algorithms to analyze radar data. Because computations are equally distributed over multiple processors, HPC aids in the efficiency of exhaustive operations such as image classification, object detection, and time-domain analysis [13]. GPUs further accelerate processing with an edge to address large radar datasets in real-time, which is crucial for environmental monitoring and autonomous systems [31] applications.

7 AI-Enhanced subsurface RADAR imaging

7.1 Enhancing ground-penetrating RADAR (GPR) with deep learning

Integrating GPR with deep learning enhances subsurface imaging capabilities in infrastructure health monitoring, archeology, and geophysics [32]. The artificial intelligence (AI) algorithms, specifically CNNs, can then analyze the GPR data to recognize and classify subsurface features with high precision, thereby detecting structural anomalies in civil engineering, locating archeological artifacts, and mapping geological formations. This advanced analysis improves the reliability of GPR systems and can better inform decisions in different fields with more definitive and detailed subsurface insights [19].

7.2 Object detection and classification in subsurface imaging

The primary strength of neural networks lies in extracting and classifying buried objects in subsurface imaging; these models help accurately identify different structures and materials. These models can process complex GPR data using deep learning methods to differentiate between several types of buried objects for even better detection capabilities [33]. Deep learning is also used in geotechnical studies to identify tunnels and voids. Since it essentially interprets subsurface images, this application has helped identify anomalies possibly caused by voids or tunnels. It addresses the shortcomings of safety assessments by informing infrastructure planning and maintenance based on subsurface conditions [23].

7.3 AI in geological and environmental applications

Resource exploration is being revolutionized by AI in subsurface radar systems, which enhance the detection of minerals, oil, and gas within the Earth, allowing for more accurate and efficient resource identification. Advanced machine learning techniques enable these systems to process complicated radar data that would otherwise reveal resource-rich areas [34]. Beyond this, deep learning facilitates remote environmental monitoring of subsurface structures, helping determine degrees of soil health, groundwater levels, and contamination. It integrates AI, improves resource management and discovery, and supports sustainable practices in geological and environmental studies, as shown in Figure 2 [24].

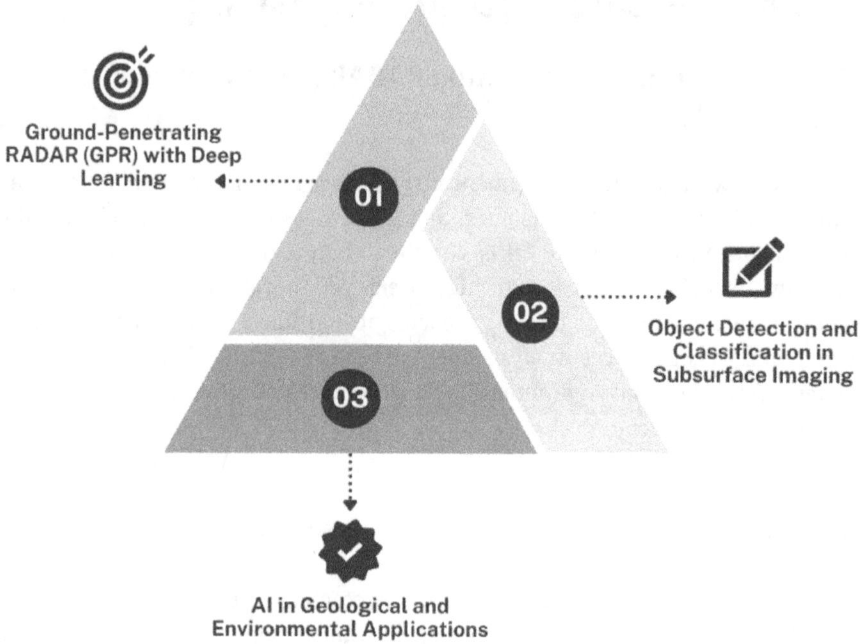

Figure 2: Subsurface RADAR imaging fields in AI.

8 Challenges and future directions

8.1 Ethical and environmental considerations

RADAR systems raise grave moral and environmental concerns regarding privacy and potential ecosystem interruptions. On the one hand, there is the privacy issue: radar technology can collect detailed information about people and environments, so comprehensive regulation must protect personal data [35]. Additionally, the environmental impacts of radar systems must be assessed, including their effects on wildlife and natural habitats in sensitive regions. Ethical AI usage in radar applications is equally important as algorithms must be designed to avoid bias and ensure fairness in decision-making [36].

8.2 Future trends in RADAR remote sensing using AI

AI integration in radar remote sensing is expected to drive significant advancements, especially in relation to autonomous systems and real-time analysis. Emerging technologies enable radar systems to operate independently and without human intervention; thus, continuous monitoring of tasks and data will be achieved [37]. Integrating radar systems with the Internet of Things (IoT) will also facilitate smart applications. This integration will create smart networks by interconnecting sectors through shared data across entities, thereby promoting cooperation. This trend will mold and shape radar remote sensing into more efficient and responsive systems capable of addressing complex challenges in diverse environments [9].

9 Conclusion

This revolution in the field of radar remote sensing has advanced the analysis of data, feature extraction, and detection of objects through machine and deep learning. These AI-driven technologies have improved the interpretation of complex signals with precision, detailing their application in environmental monitoring, disaster management, and autonomous navigation. AI enables real-time processing capabilities, allowing rapid analysis of large datasets and improving decision-making in dynamic environments. Radar remote sensing holds a promising future with advancing machine learning and AI technologies. With advancements in the research avenues mentioned previously, more autonomous and sophisticated systems will emerge, leading toward more accurate data, faster processing, and better environmental analysis. Further and worthwhile radar applications will emerge with the integration of IoT and cloud computing technologies.

Reference

[1] VinilaKumari, S., Bhargavi, P., Jyothi, S. 2020. Identification of neighbourhood cities based on landuse bigdata Using K-Means and K-NN algorithm. In: Jyothi, S., Mamatha, D.M., Satapathy, S.C., Raju, K.S., Favorskaya, M.N. (Eds.) Advances in Computational and Bio-Engineering, Learning and Analytics in Intelligent Systems, Cham: Springer International Publishing, 111–125. https://doi.org/10.1007/978-3-030-46939-9_10

[2] Hao, C., Orlando, D., Liu, J., Yin, C. 2022. Introduction to Radar systems. In: Advances in Adaptive Radar Detection and Range Estimation, Singapore: Springer Singapore, 1–22. https://doi.org/10.1007/978-981-16-6399-4_1

[3] Varghese, J., Joseph, N., Jantunen, H., Behera, S.K., Kim, H.T., Sebastian, M.T. 2020. Microwave materials for Defense and Aerospace applications. In: Mahajan, Y.R., Johnson, R. (Eds.) Handbook of Advanced Ceramics and Composites, Cham: Springer International Publishing, 165–213. https://doi.org/10.1007/978-3-030-16347-1_9

[4] Wu, Y., Liu, J.-W., Zhu, C.-Z., Bai, Z.-F., Miao, Q.-G., Ma, W.-P., Gong, M.-G. 2021. Computational Intelligence in Remote Sensing Image Registration: A survey. International Journal of Automation and Computing, 18, 1–17. https://doi.org/10.1007/s11633-020-1248-x

[5] Nemati, M., Kim, Y.H., Choi, J. 2022. Toward joint radar, communication, computation, localization, and sensing in IoT. IEEE Access, 10, 11772–11788. https://doi.org/10.1109/ACCESS.2022.3146830

[6] Liu, F., Masouros, C. 2021. A tutorial on joint radar and communication transmission for vehicular networks – Part I: Background and fundamentals. IEEE Communications Letters, 25, 322–326. https://doi.org/10.1109/LCOMM.2020.3025310

[7] Geng, Z. 2020. Evolution of Netted Radar Systems. IEEE Access, 8, 124961–124977. https://doi.org/10.1109/ACCESS.2020.3007774

[8] Ottinger, M., Kuenzer, C. 2020. Spaceborne L-band synthetic aperture radar data for geoscientific analyses in coastal land applications: A review. Remote Sensing, 12, 2228. https://doi.org/10.3390/rs12142228

[9] Chen, G., Jiang, Z., Kamruzzaman, M.M. 2020. Radar remote sensing image retrieval algorithm based on improved Sobel operator. Journal of Visual Communication and Image Representation, 71, 102720. https://doi.org/10.1016/j.jvcir.2019.102720

[10] Cruz, H., Véstias, M., Monteiro, J., Neto, H., Duarte, R.P. 2022. A review of synthetic-aperture radar image formation algorithms and implementations: A computational perspective. Remote Sensing, 14, 1258. https://doi.org/10.3390/rs14051258

[11] Zhang, J.A., Liu, F., Masouros, C., Heath, R.W., Feng, Z., Zheng, L., Petropulu, A. 2021. An overview of signal processing techniques for joint communication and Radar sensing. IEEE Journal of Selected Topics in Signal Processing, 15, 1295–1315. https://doi.org/10.1109/JSTSP.2021.3113120

[12] Chen, N., Yu, L., Zhang, X., Shen, Y., Zeng, L., Hu, Q., Niyogi, D. 2020. Mapping paddy rice fields by combining multi-temporal vegetation index and synthetic aperture radar remote sensing data using Google Earth engine machine learning platform. Remote Sensing, 12, 2992. https://doi.org/10.3390/rs12182992

[13] El Bouchefry, K., De Souza, R.S. 2020. Learning in big data: Introduction to machine learning. In: Knowledge Discovery in Big Data from Astronomy and Earth Observation, Elsevier, 225–249. https://doi.org/10.1016/B978-0-12-819154-5.00023-0

[14] Li, P. 2020. Research on radar signal recognition based on automatic machine learning. Neural Computing and Applications, 32, 1959–1969. https://doi.org/10.1007/s00521-019-04494-1

[15] Vulpi, F., Milella, A., Marani, R., Reina, G. 2021. Recurrent and convolutional neural networks for deep terrain classification by autonomous robots. Journal of Terramechanics, 96, 119–131. https://doi.org/10.1016/j.jterra.2020.12.002

[16] Conceição, M.R.A., De Mendonça, L.F.F., Lentini, C.A.D., Da Cunha Lima, A.T., Lopes, J.M., De Vasconcelos, R.N., Gouveia, M.B., Porsani, M.J. 2021. SAR oil spill detection system through random forest classifiers. Remote Sensing, 13, 2044. https://doi.org/10.3390/rs13112044

[17] Yadav, M., Vardhan, A., Chauhan, A.S., Saini, S. 2023. A study on creation of Industry 5.0: New Innovations using big data through artificial intelligence, Internet of Things and next-origination technology policy. In: 2023 IEEE International Students' Conference on Electrical, Electronics and Computer Science (SCEECS). Presented at the 2023 IEEE International Students' Conference on Electrical, Electronics and Computer Science (SCEECS), Bhopal, India: IEEE, 1–12. https://doi.org/10.1109/SCEECS57921.2023.10063069

[18] Hong, H., Zhao, J., Hong, T., Tang, T. 2022. Radar–Communication Integration for 6G Massive IoT Services. IEEE Internet Things Journal, 9, 14511–14520. https://doi.org/10.1109/JIOT.2021.3064072

[19] Tong, Z., Gao, J., Yuan, D. 2020. Advances of deep learning applications in ground-penetrating radar: A survey. Const and Buil Mater, 258, 120371. https://doi.org/10.1016/j.conbuildmat.2020.120371

[20] Sharma, A., Sharma, V., Jaiswal, M., Wang, H.-C., Jayakody, D.N.K., Basnayaka, C.M.W., Muthanna, A. 2022. Recent Trends in AI-Based intelligent sensing. Electronics, 11, 1661. https://doi.org/10.3390/electronics11101661

[21] Bacciu, D., Errica, F., Micheli, A., Podda, M. 2020. A gentle introduction to deep learning for graphs. Neural Network, 129, 203–221. https://doi.org/10.1016/j.neunet.2020.06.006

[22] Oveis, A.H., Giusti, E., Ghio, S., Martorella, M. 2022. A survey on the applications of convolutional neural networks for synthetic aperture radar: Recent advances. IEEE Aerospace and Electronic Systems Magazine, 37, 18–42. https://doi.org/10.1109/MAES.2021.3117369
[23] Zhang, X., Han, L., Han, L., Zhu, L. 2020. How well do deep learning-based methods for land cover classification and object detection perform on high resolution remote sensing imagery?. Remote Sensing, 12, 417. https://doi.org/10.3390/rs12030417
[24] Himeur, Y., Rimal, B., Tiwary, A., Amira, A. 2022. Using artificial intelligence and data fusion for environmental monitoring: A review and future perspectives. Inf Fusion, 86–87, 44–75. https://doi.org/10.1016/j.inffus.2022.06.003
[25] Zhang, M., Xie, C., Tian, B., Yang, Y., Guo, Y., Zhu, Y., Bian, S. 2023. Application of gated recurrent unit neural network for flood extraction from synthetic aperture Radar time series. Water, 15, 3779. https://doi.org/10.3390/w15213779
[26] Taye, M.M. 2023. Understanding of machine learning with deep learning: architectures, workflow, applications and future directions. Computers, 12, 91. https://doi.org/10.3390/computers12050091
[27] Lee, H., Kim, J., Kim, E.K., Kim, S. 2020. Wasserstein generative adversarial networks based data augmentation for Radar Data Analysis. Applied Sciences, 10, 1449. https://doi.org/10.3390/app10041449
[28] Freire, W.P., Melo, W.S., Do Nascimento, V.D., Nascimento, P.R.M., De Sá, A.O. 2022. Towards a secure and scalable maritime monitoring system using blockchain and Low-Cost IoT technology. Sensors, 22, 4895. https://doi.org/10.3390/s22134895
[29] Sandhu, A.K. 2022. Big data with cloud computing: Discussions and challenges. Big Data Mining and Analytics, 5, 32–40. https://doi.org/10.26599/BDMA.2021.9020016
[30] Sun, S., Petropulu, A.P., Poor, H.V. 2020. MIMO radar for advanced driver-assistance systems and autonomous driving: Advantages and challenges. IEEE Signal Process Magazine, 37, 98–117. https://doi.org/10.1109/MSP.2020.2978507
[31] Zhang, S., Xue, Y., Zhou, X., Zhang, X., Liu, W., Li, K., Liu, R. 2022. State of the art: High-performance and high-throughput computing for remote sensing big data. IEEE Geoscience and Remote Sensing Magazine, 10, 125–149. https://doi.org/10.1109/MGRS.2022.3204590
[32] Abedi, H., Ansariyan, A., Morita, P.P., Wong, A., Boger, J., Shaker, G. 2023. AI-powered noncontact in-home gait monitoring and activity recognition system based on mm-Wave FMCW radar and cloud computing. IEEE Internet Things Journal, 10, 9465–9481. https://doi.org/10.1109/JIOT.2023.3235268
[33] Gini, F. 2021. Grand challenges in Radar Signal Processing. Frontiers in Signal Processing, 1, 664232. https://doi.org/10.3389/frsip.2021.664232
[34] Gupta, D.K., Prashar, S., Singh, S., Srivastava, P.K., Prasad, R. 2022. Introduction to RADAR remote sensing. In: Radar Remote Sensing, Elsevier, 3–27. https://doi.org/10.1016/B978-0-12-823457-0.00018-5
[35] Morozov, O.G., Nureev, I.I., Sakhabutdinov, A.Z., Kuznetsov, A.A., Gabdulkhakov, I.M. 2020. Integrated microwave quantum sensing for Radar type problems decisions. In: 2020 Systems of Signal Synchronization, Generating and Processing in Telecommunications (SYNCHROINFO). Presented at the 2020 Systems of Signal Synchronization, Generating and Processing in Telecommunications (SYNCHROINFO), Russia: IEEE, Svetlogorsk, 1–6. https://doi.org/10.1109/SYNCHROINFO49631.2020.9166102
[36] Butts-Wilmsmeyer, C.J., Rapp, S., Guthrie, B. 2020. The technological advancements that enabled the age of big data in the environmental sciences: A history and future directions. Current Opinion in Environmental Science & Health, 18, 63–69. https://doi.org/10.1016/j.coesh.2020.07.006
[37] Lanzagorta, M., Uhlmann, J. 2020. Opportunities and challenges of Quantum radar. IEEE Aerospace and Electronic Systems Magazine, 35, 38–56. https://doi.org/10.1109/MAES.2020.3004053

Suresh Devaraj*, Kalel Ahamed A., Dileep Kumar Gupta, and Kaliraj S.

Deep learning-based water body segmentation in SAR imagery: enhancing accuracy with CNN-U-Net and EfficientNet

Abstract: Accurate water body segmentation in synthetic aperture radar (SAR) imagery is crucial for hydrological analysis, flood monitoring, and environmental management. This study investigates the effectiveness of deep learning (DL) techniques, particularly the convolutional neural network-based U-Net model with EfficientNet as the encoder, to enhance water body classification in Sentinel-1 SAR images. The proposed model demonstrates significant improvements over traditional methods, such as KMeans clustering, achieving an accuracy of 97.78%. Integrating contrast-stretched SAR imagery and speckle simulation augmentation enhances model robustness, addressing common issues such as speckle noise and boundary misclassification. The model reduces segmentation errors, thus improving the precision of water body delineation and providing a reliable method for SAR-based water mapping. Despite these improvements, challenges persist, including backscatter intensity variations, seasonal changes, and complex land-water interfaces. The research demonstrated that DL methods significantly improve SAR image classification of water bodies, serving as powerful tools for environmental monitoring and resource management.

Keywords: Image classification, SAR, machine learning, U-Net model, Sentinel-1

1 Introduction

Waterbody mapping is widely used in hydrological analysis, climate change studies, urban development, and disaster management [1, 2]. Due to speckle noise, complex land-water boundaries, and non-uniform backscatter intensities, segmentation of water bodies in remote sensing images is a challenging process, mainly in synthetic

*Corresponding author: Suresh Devaraj, Center for Remote Sensing and Geoinformatics, Sathyabama Institute of Science and Technology, Chennai 600119, Tamil Nadu, India, e-mail: devaraj.suresh1991@gmail.com
Kalel Ahamed A., Central Water Commission, New Delhi 110066, India
Dileep Kumar Gupta, Department of Electronics, School of Engineering, Galgotias University, Greater Noida 203201, Uttar Pradesh, India; Galgotias Multi Disciplinary Research and Development Cell (G-MRDC), Galgotias University, Greater Noida, Noida 203201, Uttar Pradesh, India
Kaliraj S., National Centre for Earth Science Studies (NCESS), Ministry of Earth Sciences (MoES), Thiruvananthapuram 695011, India

https://doi.org/10.1515/9783111572970-013

aperture radar (SAR) imagery [1]. The traditional approaches for classifying water bodies based on thresholding, clustering, and machine learning (ML)-based classifiers fail to account for the spatial and contextual variations in SAR images [3].

The techniques to map water bodies have evolved over the past few decades, transitioning from visual, manual, and digitizing of aerial and satellite images [4]. Statistical and ML methods used to classify water bodies in SAR images [5]. Thresholding is the most common method, where an adaptation or fixed threshold is used to break the SAR intensity values between water and non-water regions [6]. This technique is highly sensitive to local variations in backscatter intensity and cannot generalize to diverse landscapes. Otsu's thresholding, an enhancement to global thresholding, attempts to optimize segmentation by maximizing inter-class variance but is susceptible to speckle noise [7].

Another technique used extensively is KMeans clustering, an unsupervised learning process that clusters pixels into groups based on intensity values [8]. Although computationally efficient, KMeans struggles with poor performance at mixed land-water boundaries, resulting in misclassification in urban, agricultural, and vegetative areas [9]. Supervised ML techniques, such as support vector machines and random forest, have been employed to segment SAR water bodies with better accuracy [10, 11, 12]. However, these techniques rely on extensive feature engineering (e.g., texture, backscatter intensity, and statistical descriptors), limiting their adaptability to other SAR datasets. Recently, model-based classification techniques, including Markov random fields [13], active contour models [13], and region-growing algorithms [14], have been explored. While these techniques address spatial dependency and neighborhood relations, they are parameter-intensive and cannot handle large-sized datasets.

Deep learning (DL) development has advanced remote sensing image classification to a new stage, promising a solution to traditional ML methods. For example, convolutional neural network (CNN)-based DL methods have been largely applied in semantic segmentation and have surpassed traditional classifiers by learning multi-scale spatial and spectral features [15–17]. The U-Net, one of the most used architectures due to its encoder-decoder form and skip connections for fine-grained pixel-wise classification, has been utilized by many state-of-the-art medical image segmentation methods [18].

Transformed image segmentation involves replacing convolutional layers with fully connected layers to provide dense pixel-wise predictions, which are known as fully convolutional networks (FCNs) [19]. However, multiple pooling result in a loss of spatial resolution by FCNs. To improve upon FCNs [20], DeepLabV3 + was introduced, incorporating atrous spatial pyramid pooling (ASPP) to supply multi-scale contextual information. Despite the computational cost required, DeepLabV3 + is still not computationally affordable enough for large-scale SAR segmentation.

Several studies have experimented with ResNet-based models using natural image-trained pre-trained architectures [15, 21, 22]. These models offer better generalizability but struggle to capture SAR-specific backscatter behavior due to domain differences. As skip connections allow the retention of an image's spatial context, the U-Net architecture was initially proposed for biomedical image segmentation [23]. It has been widely applied in remote sensing. In several studies, U-Net has been successfully applied to SAR water body segmentation, incorporating improvements such as attention mechanisms, multi-scale feature fusion, and hybrid loss functions [24–26].

The present study attempts to develop a CNN-based U-Net model using EfficientNet as the main feature extractor to create better results while maintaining computational efficiency. The model differs from basic U-Net designs because it uses stretched contrast images, which help improve feature representation. Additionally, the model receives random speckle distortion enhancement to develop better resistance against SAR signal disturbances. The method uses dice loss and binary cross-entropy Loss to address water body delineation problems when class imbalance occurs. Analysis reveals that the developed model outperforms traditional KMeans clustering in precision and allows the calculation of better *F*1 and recall values. The proposed system generates masks and attaches their correct spatial positions through georeferencing, ensuring that classified outputs can be utilized in location-based projects.

2 Materials and methods

The research begins by processing SAR satellite data, followed by preparing it for DL and developing a CNN for automated water detection. The data collection was sourced from the Copernicus Open Access Hub using Sentinel-1 ground range detected (GRD) product forms. The dataset contains unique image-mask pairs that mark water regions with a value of 1 and other territories with a value of 0. The datasets underwent several preprocessing steps to improve model training, reduce noise, and normalize input size. The initial processing steps changed the Sentinel-1 SAR data type from raw backscatter measurements to sigma-naught values to normalize reflectance changes. The Lee adaptive filter was applied to reduce speckle noise, enabling the model to detect water areas more accurately. SAR side-looking geometry requires range Doppler terrain correction using SRTM DEM to generate spatially correct and georeferenced images. The model input size for all images was standardized to 256 × 256 pixels through cropping and resampling steps.

In this study, a U-Net architecture with EfficientNet as the encoder was used for the segmentation model due to its hierarchical feature extraction capabilities, leveraging such information to improve segmentation accuracy. U-Net consisted of an encoder and decoder structure that could effectively capture high-resolution spatial features while maintaining context inside skip connections. The decoder used transpose convolutions to upsample feature maps and reconstruct pixel-level classifications with fine detail. The final layer was a 1 × 1 convolution with sigmoid activation to produce binary segmentation masks. All the datasets are split into 1,600 training, 400 validation, and 400 testing images to have a balanced representation of each water body's features. In model training, different variants of cross-entropy and dice loss were used to tackle class imbalance. A learning rate of $1e^{-4}$ was used to achieve good convergence with the Adam optimizer. Data augmentation techniques such as random horizontal flipping, rotation, scaling, and speckle simulation were used to improve the model's generalizability and robustness. The model was trained for 50 epochs, with early stopping implemented to prevent overfitting. Segmentation performance was assessed using multiple metrics, including accuracy, precision, recall, and *F*1-score, emphasizing intersection-over-union (IoU) to evaluate the overlap between predicted and ground truth masks. The framework implemented in the present study is represented in Figure 1.

3 Results and discussion

CNN-based U-Net model demonstrated enhanced segmentation accuracy in extracting water bodies from non-water areas in Sentinel-1 datasets. Visual comparisons between CNN-U-Net segmentation and KMeans clustering (Figure 2) showed a significant improvement in the DL approach. The U-Net model achieved an average accuracy of 97.78%, outperforming KMeans, which exhibited a highly-variable accuracy range due to its sensitivity to noise and intensity variations in SAR imagery. This trend is further illustrated in the scatter plot of accuracy across 200 images (Figure 3), where the CNN-U-Net model consistently maintains high accuracy with minimal fluctuations.

The CNN-U-Net model attained a precision of 98.3%, a recall of 97.5%, and an *F*1-score of 97.9%, demonstrating its efficiency in accurately identifying water bodies with minimal misclassification. In contrast to previous studies, where high precision reflected reduced false positives, high precision here ensures that most water bodies are correctly identified, while strong recall confirms that most are captured. The DL approach achieves a higher *F*1-score than KMeans, resulting in a more balanced performance.

The CNN-U-Net model performs better in terms of the visual aspect than KMeans segmentation, as the CNN-U-Net model gives better, smoother, and more continuous water body delineations. Thus, it performs extremely well concerning spatial features, preserving fine boundaries in water and non-water regions while maintaining their boundaries as they are. Hence, it resists speckle noise, producing clearer water body contours. KMeans often produces fragmented classifications, particularly in regions with ambiguous water boundaries and mixed pixels. This is especially true in more complex water systems such as wetlands or river deltas, where KMeans cannot accurately characterize the continuous water regions. While the results demonstrated strong performance, uncertainty remains a challenge in delineatingcontours with

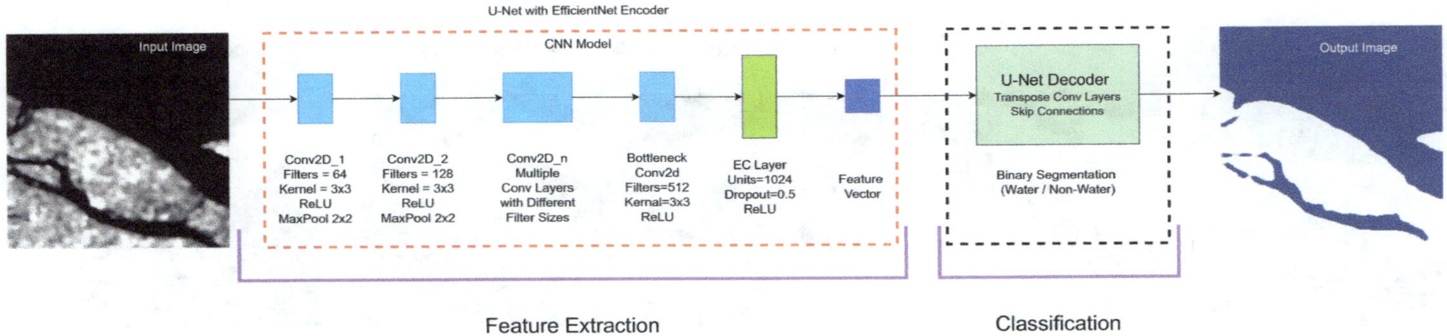

Figure 1: The methodology implemented for the extraction of water bodies.

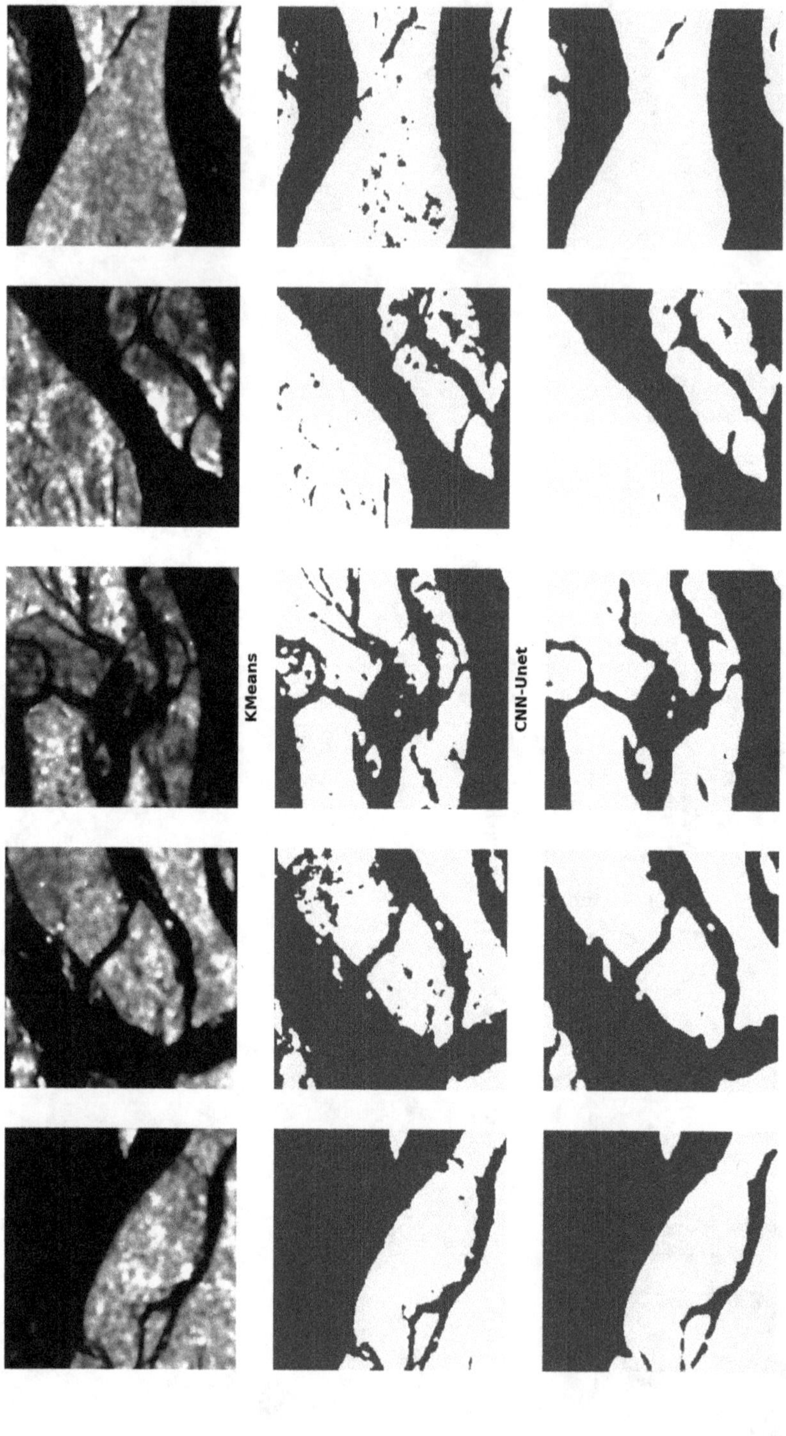

Figure 2: Water bodies extracted from SAR images using kmeans and CNN-U-Net.

SAR-based water segmentation. Misclassification is influenced by speckle noise, seasonal water fluctuations, and ambiguities due to border areas being flooded or marshy. Such uncertainties in identifying land and water are minimized but not entirely removed with the CNN-U-Net model, which relies on deep hierarchical feature extraction; false positives and false negatives occur near the boundaries where the SAR backscatter properties of land and water overlap. Further improvements could enhance the stability of classification by integrating multi-temporal Sentinel-1 images and improve validation and correction by combining Sentinel-2 optical data [27].

Future work could explore self-supervised learning and domain adaptation techniques to further improve segmentation accuracy. Incorporating attention mechanisms within the U-Net architecture could help the model focus on key regions while minimizing errors. Additionally, hybrid DL approaches that integrate SAR, optical, and LiDAR data could enhance performance in complex terrains.

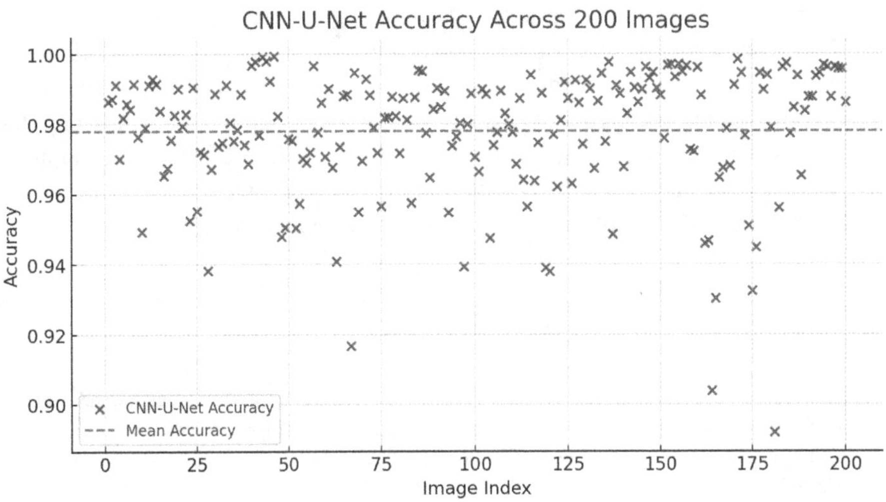

Figure 3: Accuracy of the CNN-U-Net-based water bodies extracted from SAR images.

4 Conclusion

The present study highlights the effectiveness of DL techniques, particularly the CNN-based U-Net model with EfficientNet as the encoder, in automating water body segmentation in Sentinel-1 SAR imagery. The findings confirm that DL significantly outperforms traditional methods like KMeans clustering, which is prone to errors due to speckle noise and boundary misclassification. The proposed CNN-U-Net model achieved 97.78% accuracy, which efficiently delineates water bodies. Using contrast-stretched SAR imagery and speckle simulation augmentation in training data improved the model's robustness and overall segmentation performance. Nonetheless, differences in backscatter intensity, seasonal changes in the water surface, and the uncertainty between land and water areas require improvements in segmentation methods. Method improvement, data integration improvements, and the expansion of the scope of applications of the model are some directions for future research. Self-supervised learning methods could decrease reliance on labeled datasets, while attention mechanisms (e.g., Transformer-based architectures) could sharpen the model's focus on relevant areas.

Using hybrid DL approaches that combine U-Net and GANs can provide greater stability in segmentation, which is especially useful in areas with complex microterrain. Domain adaptation techniques could help bridge differences between SAR and optical imagery, enhancing model generalization. Combining multi-temporal analysis of Sentinel-1 images may enhance segmentation stability and reduce seasonal misclassification errors. Combining SAR with Sentinel-2 optical imagery and LiDAR elevation data is expected to improve classification performance, especially in wetland and floodplain areas. This approach also has the potential for real-time flood monitoring, hydrological modeling, and disaster response applications. Better segmentation can help climate change studies by identifying variations in water bodies over time. Continued improvements in areas such as DL architectures, data fusion, and computational efficiency will still provide more accurate and scalable surface water mapping from SAR-based water mapping, making them more applicable in several fields, including environmental monitoring and resource management.

References

[1] Sundaram, S., Devaraj, S., Yarrakula, K. 2023. Mapping and assessing spatial extent of floods from multitemporal synthetic aperture radar images: A case study over Adyar watershed, India. Environmental Science and Pollution Research, 30, 63006–63021. https://doi.org/10.1007/s11356-023-26467-7

[2] Sundaram, S., Devaraj, S., Yarrakula, K. 2021. Modeling, mapping and analysis of urban floods in India – A review on geospatial methodologies. Environmental Science and Pollution Research, 28, 67940–67956. https://doi.org/10.1007/s11356-021-16747-5

[3] Irukumati, S., Vittal, A.R., Gurunarayan, S.L. 2025. Deciphering flood inundation zones using multitemporal SAR datasets for central brahmaputra river Basin. Remote sens. Earth System Science, https://doi.org/10.1007/s41976-025-00206-7

[4] McFeeters, S.K. 1996. The use of the normalized difference water index (NDWI) in the delineation of open water features. International Journal of Remote Sensing, 17, 1425–1432. https://doi.org/10.1080/01431169608948714

[5] Kubendiran, I., Ramaiah, M. 2024. Modeling, mapping and analysis of floods using optical, lidar and SAR datasets – A review. Water Resource, 51, 438–448. https://doi.org/10.1134/S0097807823600614

[6] Surampudi, S., Yarrakula, K. 2020. Mapping and assessing spatial extent of floods from multitemporal synthetic aperture radar images: A case study on Brahmaputra River in Assam State, India. Environmental Science and Pollution Research, 27, 1521–1532. https://doi.org/10.1007/s11356-019-06849-6

[7] Jacinth Jennifer, J., Saravanan, S., Abijith, D. 2022. Integration of SAR and multi-spectral imagery in flood inundation mapping – A case study on Kerala floods 2018. ISH Journal of Hydraulic Engineering, 28, 480–490. https://doi.org/10.1080/09715010.2020.1791265
[8] Xu, H., Ma, C., Lian, J., Xu, K., Chaima, E. 2018. Urban flooding risk assessment based on an integrated k-means cluster algorithm and improved entropy weight method in the region of Haikou, China. Journal of Hydrology, 563, 975–986. https://doi.org/10.1016/j.jhydrol.2018.06.060
[9] Celebi, M.E., Kingravi, H.A., Vela, P.A. 2013. A comparative study of efficient initialization methods for the k-means clustering algorithm. Expert Systems with Applications, 40, 200–210. https://doi.org/10.1016/j.eswa.2012.07.021
[10] Avcı, C., Budak, M., Yağmur, N., Balçık, F. 2023. Comparison between random forest and support vector machine algorithms for LULC classification. International Journal of Engineering Geology, 8, 1–10. https://doi.org/10.26833/ijeg.987605
[11] Sheykhmousa, M., Mahdianpari, M., Ghanbari, H., Mohammadimanesh, F., Ghamisi, P., Homayouni, S. 2020. Support vector machine versus random forest for remote sensing image classification: A meta-analysis and systematic review. IEEE Journal of Selected Topics in Applied Earth Observations and Remote Sensing, 13, 6308–6325. https://doi.org/10.1109/JSTARS.2020.3026724
[12] Siemers, F.M., Bajorath, J. 2023. Differences in learning characteristics between support vector machine and random forest models for compound classification revealed by Shapley value analysis. Scientific Reports, 13, 5983. https://doi.org/10.1038/s41598-023-33215-x
[13] Xu, Y., Han, Y. 2022. Deep learning application-water region extraction in SAR image based on Markov random field. In: 2022 7th International Conference on Intelligent Computing and Signal Processing (ICSP), 121–124. https://doi.org/10.1109/ICSP54964.2022.9778482
[14] Zheng, X., Chen, J., Zhang, S., Chen, J. 2017. Water extraction of SAR image based on region merging algorithm. In: 2017 International Applied Computational Electromagnetics Society Symposium (ACES), 1–2.
[15] Farooq, B., Manocha, A. 2025. Small water body extraction in remote sensing with enhanced CNN architecture. Applied Soft Computing, 169, 112544. https://doi.org/10.1016/j.asoc.2024.112544
[16] Gharbia, R. 2023. Deep learning for automatic extraction of water bodies using satellite imagery. Journal of the Indian Society of Remote Sensing, 51, 1511–1521. https://doi.org/10.1007/s12524-023-01705-0
[17] Wang, J., Wang, S., Wang, F., Zhou, Y., Wang, Z., Ji, J., Xiong, Y., Zhao, Q. 2022. FWENet: A deep convolutional neural network for flood water body extraction based on SAR images. International Journal of Digital Earth, 15, 345–361. https://doi.org/10.1080/17538947.2021.1995513
[18] Radha, K., Yepuganti, K., Saritha, S., Kamireddy, C., Bavirisetti, D.P. 2023. Unfolded deep kernel estimation-attention UNet-based retinal image segmentation. Scientific Reports, 13, 20712. https://doi.org/10.1038/s41598-023-48039-y
[19] Long, J., Shelhamer, E., Darrell, T. 2014. Fully Convolutional Networks for Semantic Segmentation, CoRR, abs/1411 4.
[20] Chen, L.-C., Zhu, Y., Papandreou, G., Schroff, F., Adam, H. 2018. Encoder-decoder with atrous separable convolution for semantic image segmentation bt – computer vision – ECCV 2018. In: Ferrari, V., Hebert, M., Sminchisescu, C., Weiss, Y. (Eds.) Proceedings of the European conference on computer vision (ECCV), Cham: Springer International Publishing, 833–851.
[21] Cao, H., Tian, Y., Liu, Y., Wang, R. 2024. Water body extraction from high spatial resolution remote sensing images based on enhanced U-Net and multi-scale information fusion. Scientific Reports, 14, 16132. https://doi.org/10.1038/s41598-024-67113-7
[22] Liu, X., Li, N. 2024. Water area extraction method based on res2net-unet. in: proceedings of the international conference on image processing, machine learning and pattern recognition, IPMLP '24. Association for Computing Machinery, New York, NY, USA, 99–105. https://doi.org/10.1145/3700906.3700922

[23] Ronneberger, O., Fischer, P., Brox, T. 2015. U-net: convolutional networks for biomedical image segmentation, CoRR, abs/1505.0.
[24] Jonnala, N.S., Gupta, N. 2024. SAR U-Net: Spatial attention residual U-Net structure for water body segmentation from remote sensing satellite images Multimed.. Multimedia Tools and Applications, 83, 44425–44454. https://doi.org/10.1007/s11042-023-16965-8
[25] Li, W., Dong, Y., Wang, Y., Xu, T., Liu, Z., Yu, K., Xiao, C. 2024. SE-UNet: channel attention based unet for water body segmentation from SAR image. In: You, P., Liu, S., Wang, J. (Eds.) Proceedings of International Conference on Image, Vision and Intelligent Systems 2023 (ICIVIS 2023), Singapore: Springer Nature Singapore, 100–107.
[26] Li, Z., Demir, I. 2023. U-net-based semantic classification for flood extent extraction using SAR imagery and GEE platform: A case study for 2019 central US flooding. Science of the Total Environment, 869, 161757. https://doi.org/10.1016/j.scitotenv.2023.161757
[27] Vyas, N., Singh, S., Sethi, G.K. 2024. A novel image fusion-based post classification framework for agricultural variations detection using Sentinel-1 and Sentinel-2 data. Earth Science Informatics, 18, 40. https://doi.org/10.1007/s12145-024-01506-0

Dankan Gowda V.*, P. Arockia Mary, Christian Rafael Quevedo Lezama, Madan Mohanrao Jagtap, and Sampathirao Suneetha

Artificial intelligence in RADAR remote sensing: advances, challenges, and future prospects

Abstract: The integration of artificial intelligence (AI) in RADAR remote sensing is revolutionizing data analysis, feature extraction, and object identification. Machine learning and deep learning models, including convolutional neural networks and recurrent neural networks, significantly enhance RADAR imagery interpretation by improving object detection, terrain classification, and noise reduction. Synthetic aperture radar (SAR), interferometric SAR (InSAR), and polarimetric RADAR benefit from AI-driven solutions that enable real-time processing, improving environmental monitoring, defense applications, and disaster response. Advanced AI techniques, such as explainable AI and generative adversarial networks, optimize feature extraction while addressing challenges like data noise, high computational costs, and low-resolution imagery. AI-driven RADAR systems are crucial for automation in self-driving vehicles, precision agriculture, and military surveillance. This chapter explores these advancements, discussing future prospects in AI-driven RADAR sensing, including cloud computing integration and enhanced computational efficiency for real-time, large-scale applications.

Keywords: Artificial intelligence, RADAR remote sensing, machine learning, deep learning, data processing, object detection, synthetic aperture radar (SAR), explainable AI, real-time data analysis, environmental monitoring, defense applications

*__Corresponding author: Dankan Gowda V.__, Department of Electronics and Communication Engineering, BMS Institute of Technology and Management, Bangalore, Karnataka, India, e-mail: dankan.v@bmsit.in

P. Arockia Mary, Department of Information Technology, V.S.B. Engineering College, Karur, Tamil Nadu, India, e-mail: mary.vsbec@gmail.com

Christian Rafael Quevedo Lezama, Electrical and Electronics Engineer, Universidad Nacional Mayor de San Marcos, Cercado de Lima, Peru, e-mail: christian.quevedo1@unmsm.edu.pe

Madan Mohanrao Jagtap, Department of Operations Management, Symbiosis Institute of Operations Management, Nashik Campus, Constituent of Symbiosis International (Deemed University), Pune, Maharashtra, India, e-mail: madan.jagtap@siom.in

Sampathirao Suneetha, Department of Computer Science and Engineering, Koneru Lakshmaiah Education Foundation, Vaddeswaram, Andhra Pradesh, India, e-mail: sampath.suneetha@gmail.com

https://doi.org/10.1515/9783111572970-014

1 Introduction

Radio detection and ranging (RADAR) is an all-purpose, non-contact remote sensing technique that uses electromagnetic waves, particularly radio waves, to identify objects and their characteristics. As with all radar technologies, the general concept of RADAR involves the creation of electromagnetic waves and the capture of reflected signals from surfaces, followed by further data analysis to determine the object's location, size, and/or velocity [1]. With synthetic aperture radar (SAR), RADAR systems have greatly benefited from high-resolution scanning that is independent of weather or lighting conditions [2]. Interferometric SAR (InSAR) has further enhanced RADAR's versatility by extending its capability to observe surface displacement as small as 1 mm; this technique has important applications in geology, land-use planning, and risk management related to geological hazards [3].

On the other hand, polarimetric RADAR is useful for discriminating different types of surfaces by using information on the polarization state of the transmitted and received waves [4]. One of the main problems with traditional RADAR systems is that they generate a large amount of data. Recently, machine learning (ML) and deep learning (DL) approaches have revolutionized the way RADAR data is preprocessed, analyzed, and utilized. Convolutional neural networks (CNNs) have been instrumental in enhancing object detection, tracking targets, and analyzing terrains in RADAR images. Using models like CNNs, object detection can be performed more precisely, even in noisy regions and when objects are partially occluded. AI also improves the functionality of RADAR systems in real-time operations, where the timeliness of data processing is valuable. Recent advances in AI include using neural networks with RADAR systems in real time for practical applications such as directional navigation for automobiles, disaster response, and defense [5]. Moreover, explainable AI or explainable AI is now a significant factor in RADAR remote sensing since it helps make AI model decision-making more understandable and accurate. It extends the functionality of RADAR systems to new fields such as climate surveillance, city construction, public safety, and more [6].

2 Principles of RADAR systems

With signals received over time, SAR systems produce high-density images useful in remote sensing [7]. In contrast to other optical systems, SAR has no restrictions for imaging at any time of the day or night and in every kind of weather, offering reliable imaging [8]. Another notable innovation in RADAR technology is polarimetric RADAR, which deals with the polarization of both the transmitted and the received waves. This approach enables one to distinguish between different surfaces and improve the categorization of natural and anthropogenic objects on the Earth's surface. Polarimetric RADAR, in particular, is useful in agricultural, forestry, and environmental applications. The final technique, InSAR, is vital and applies phase differences between two or more SAR images collected at different times. InSAR is very useful for measuring smaller changes in the surface; therefore, it is invaluable for tracking tectonic activity, landslides, and structural stability. These next-generation RADAR systems, including the use of polarimetry and interferometry, greatly improve the versatility of remote sensing by offering precise, accurate, and multi-layered measurements that have applications in various fields of engineering and sciences, as well as environmental, defense, and urban planning sectors.

Another problem is the low resolution of RADAR imagery especially in the vertical plane. Even though SAR can offer very high ground resolution, the resolution in elevation dimension is typically lower, leading to confusion between approximate height and terrain type. Furthermore, the enormous volume of data provided by today's RADAR systems [9], especially in SAR, polarimetry, and InSAR, is technically demanding in terms of storage, processing, and analysis [10]. The requirement for real-time or near-real-time processing in some applications, such as disaster response or self-driving vehicles, imposes another challenge [11]. Data compression, cloud computing, AI, and big data processing techniques have been used to overcome these challenges. However, these solutions introduce their own problems, including the need for algorithms capable of processing a wide variety of data types, with their complexity being high and frequently varying, as well as a requirement for reduced-computational time that does not compromise accuracy.

3 AI techniques in RADAR remote sensing

Modern RADAR remote sensing relies heavily on ML as one of the methods to analyze and interpret the significant and often complex datasets received. Examples that include random forests, support vector machine (SVM), and K-nearest neighbors (K-NN) are among the most successful classification algorithms for land cover, object identification, and differentiation of natural and man-made objects in SAR and other RADAR imagery. Furthermore, techniques like k-means clustering and Gaussian mixture models (GMMs) have been used when the number of labeled data sets is small. These models can find implicit structures and trends in the data, which makes them beneficial for proper anomaly detection, terrain surveillance, and the assessment of disasters, where fast identification of changes in the surface is required. Another area of RADAR remote sensing research that has recently received a boost from ML is feature extraction, which pertains to the ability of the system to detect and separate features that may be obfuscated by noise or interfering objects. For instance, principal component analysis (PCA) and independent component analysis (ICA) are extensively utilized to decrease the size of large amounts of data in RADAR while retaining vital in-

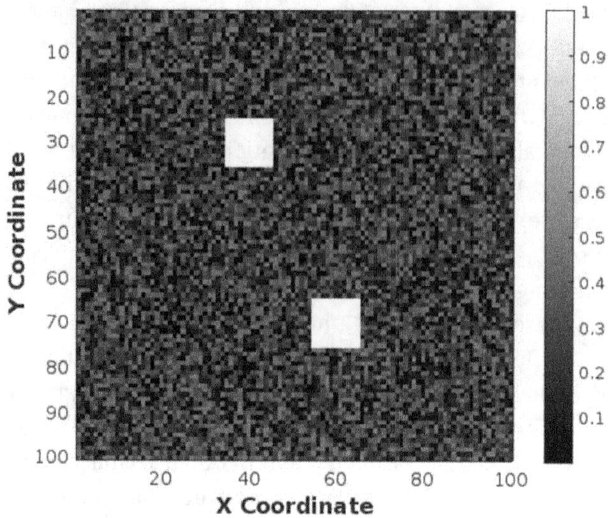

Figure 1: AI-based object detection in RADAR imagery.

formation [12]. These ML techniques increase the accuracy of object detection and the classification of images, making them crucial in environmental monitoring, defense, and automated systems.

The AI used to identify objects situated in RADAR data is illustrated in Figure 1. It represents a 2D grid in which background noise indicates typical RADAR interference, and two other distinct objects appear as bright spots to signify detection. This illustrates the object detection provided by AI that enhances RADAR imagery analysis for various uses, including security and ecological surveillance. ML has taken RADAR remote sensing to a new level with deeper learning, especially through CNN and RNN (recurrent neural network). CNNs, in particular, have attracted wide interest in enhancing image processing tasks, including object detection and classification in RADAR data. The capability of CNNs is robust because they automatically detect spatial differences in the given data with multiple convolutional layers. These layers allow CNNs to capture fine details of features, including textures, shapes, and edges, a characteristic relevant to RADAR imagery feature detection.

4 Literature survey

AI was introduced in the early stages of RADAR in the 1970s, and the initial approach to AI in RADAR was to use rule-based expert systems to automate the decision-making process. However, these early methods had major limitations, such as not being able to formalize rules for specific applications. Moving to the 1980s and 1990s, the key breakthrough was the introduction of ML, which broadened the use of AI for RADAR. SVM and K-NN are some algorithms that emerged to enhance the identification and recognition of intended objectives, mainly in SAR spectral band images. These models eliminated the need to manually interpret features, which had previously been performed manually [5].

The models provided better accuracy in noisy conditions and complex terrains. From the late 1990s and into the early 2000s, the growth in available computing power and storage, along with the reduction in the cost of these technologies, led to the introduction of AI techniques, including neural networks, to RADAR systems [13]. Major research contributions made during this period focused on object detection and image classification using neural networks and large-scale RADAR datasets for anomaly detection. Additionally, with the introduction of InSAR and PolSAR, which are based on more advanced forms of remote sensing, the information generated required data analysis techniques based on AI.

New developments in RADAR remote sensing based on AI have been tailored toward utilizing DL to analyze and interpret sensing metrics, including CNNs and RNNs. The applications of these techniques have been found particularly useful in high-precision and real-time decision-making problems, including self-driving cars and disaster relief management [14]. A recent development has been the application of CNNs for object detection and identification with SAR images, where the property of CNNs to identify intricate spatial patterns, termed feature learning, automatically has boosted the accuracy of the results relative to previous procedures [15]. The synthesis of DL techniques in vehicle detection, urban area classification, and land cover mapping shows that RADAR image analysis can be fully automated with little to no human interaction. The second trend is the development and utilization of AI with a view toward noise reduction in existing RADAR systems, particularly in the case of polarimetric RADAR and InSAR information [16]. To improve the quality of noisy images used in RADAR, methods like generative adversarial networks (GANs) and denoising autoencoders have been employed to clean and maintain important features for analysis. Furthermore, this has served as the basis for real-time RADAR data processing, which is highly important for applications such as air traffic control and autonomous drones [17].

5 AI-driven solutions for RADAR data processing

Data preprocessing in RADAR remote sensing is a crucial step, as decisions made during this stage may affect the effectiveness of subsequent processes like object detection, classification, and analysis of the territory [18]. Through AI, several approaches to preprocessing for RADAR data have been enhanced in terms of noise removal, high resolution, and efficient filtration of large amounts of data. Many filtering techniques, including median and Gaussian filters, are used to reduce noise, although they may inadvertently erase valuable image characteristics. However, AI-based techniques have introduced more refined solutions to this problem. Methods such as CNNs and denoising autoencoders are now capable of effectively reducing noise [19].

These models can also learn the patterns of the images and decide what kinds of noise they may eliminate and what image details they have to retain. GANs have also been used, where the generative model allows clean input images to be generated from noisy input images while improving image quality [20]. Another important challenge in data processing in the context of RADAR is resolution. In subsequent years, several preprocessing techniques have been applied to RADAR images to enhance their spatial resolution using super-resolution algorithms. Super-resolution networks are DL models capable of increasing the resolution of images, thus improving object detection and classification. Accuracy (A) is calculated as the ratio of correctly predicted outcomes to the total number of predictions:

$$A = \frac{\mathrm{TP} + \mathrm{TN}}{\mathrm{TP} + \mathrm{TN} + \mathrm{FP} + \mathrm{FN}}$$

where TP is true positives, TN is true negatives, FP is false positives, and FP is false negatives.

This metric helps to measure the performance of classification models in RADAR systems. It shows the model's accuracy in identifying the correct objects, such as vehicles, buildings, or terrains, from the RADAR data. One of the widely used techniques is bicubic interpolation, which approximates pixels based on other pixels by applying a weighted average method. The bicubic interpolation formula is given by:

$$I(x,y) = \sum_{i=1}^{4} \sum_{j=1}^{4} w(i,j) \cdot I(x+i, y+j)$$

where $I(x,y)$ is the intensity of the pixel at position $(x,y)(x,\ y)(x,y)$ and $w(i,j)$ is the weight associated with the neighboring pixels.

Estimating the position and velocity of moving objects in RADAR data is usually done by forecasting the next position of the object using state-space models, including the Kalman filter. The Kalman filter uses raw RADAR measurements to estimate the state of an object, such as its position and velocity. The update equation for the Kalman filter is

$$xk = Axk - 1 + Buk + wk$$

where xk is the state vector (position, velocity) at time k, A is the state transition matrix, B is the control input matrix, uk is the control input at time k, *and* wk is the process noise.

This equation helps the AI model sort targets, such as vehicles or aircraft, in the real-time RADAR data stream. The most popular technique for noise removal from the RADAR data is the Gaussian filter. The Gaussian filter smooths the image by averaging nearby pixel values weighted by a Gaussian distribution:

$$G(x,y) = \frac{1}{2\pi\sigma^2}\exp\left(-\frac{x^2+y^2}{2\sigma^2}\right)$$

where $G(x,y)$ is the Gaussian filter value at position (x,y) and, σ is the standard deviation of the Gaussian distribution.

This filter can be applied in AI algorithms that use the RADAR data to clean up speckle noise from images, as has been seen in noise reduction applications.

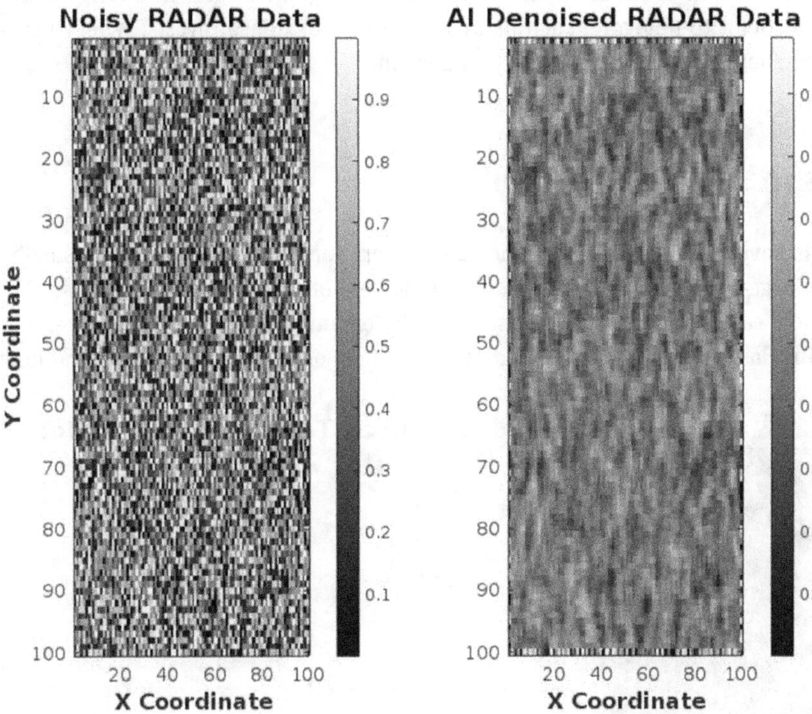

Figure 2: Noise reduction using AI in RADAR data.

Figure 2 presents the use of AI to minimize noise affecting RADAR imagery. The left side of Figure 2 shows typical noisy RADAR data, which has random signal variations superimposed on the signal envelope. In particular, object detection and classification tasks in RADAR remote sensing have benefited from AI, which has automated processes that were previously exceedingly time-consuming and prone to errors. Thanks to the application of CNNs and other forms of DL, RADAR systems can now detect and recognize objects within constantly evolving environments. In conventional RADAR data analysis, object detection typically requires additional interpretation to distinguish targets, clutter, and noise based on the operator's experience. These models are semiautomated, and layout features from the data are necessary to classify objects, such as edges, texture, and shapes. For example, in urban monitoring, AI object detection tools are incorporated to identify and categorize buildings, roads, and other structures [21]. In military applications, AI-based RADAR systems can identify and recognize military vehicles, ships, and planes in real time, thus providing vital situational information. Another area in which AI performs exceptionally well is tracking multiple targets simultaneously, where the presence and characteristics of each target must be identified. In these cases, common RNNs and their modifications, such as long short-term memory (LSTM), are particularly useful as they can track objects over time [22]. AI models have also been employed to recognize targets in environments that are difficult to navigate, such as urban settings or dense forests, where using other technologies would be extremely challenging.

6 Results and discussion

AI models have been crucial in advancing the operation of RADAR remote sensing by enabling large-scale, accurate analysis. With the help of modern developments in ML and DL, it is easier to detect targets and identify terrain and features. Figure 3 shows the terrain classification in RADAR data with the help of AI to better understand how

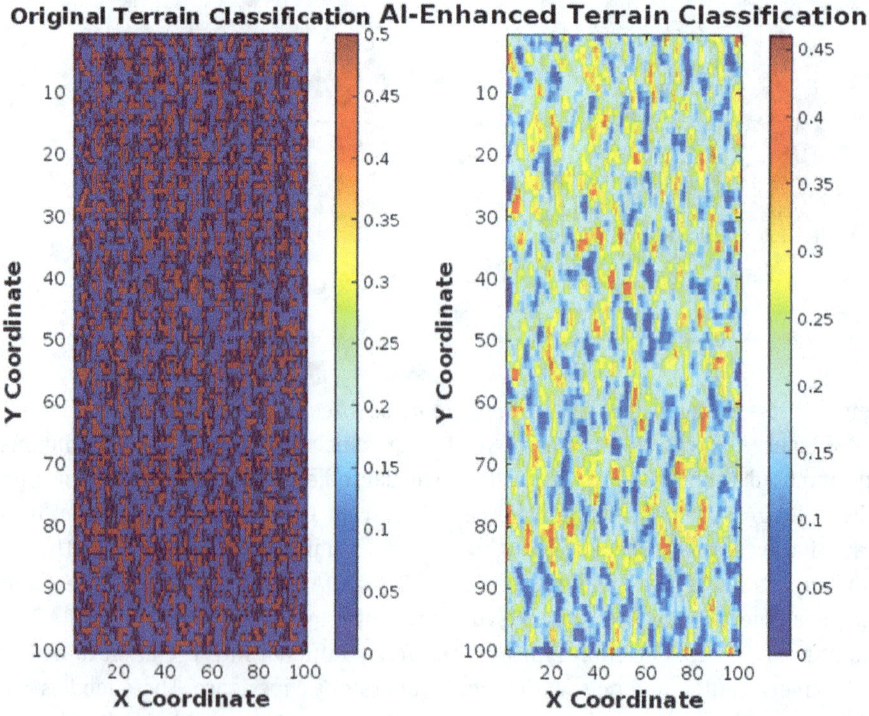

Figure 3: AI-enhanced terrain classification in RADAR data.

AI can help identify boundaries that are not visible on paper. Such an expansion in classification makes it easier to differentiate terrain types using this approach compared to more traditional methods. This improvement makes identifying specific terrain types more precise, particularly in RADAR imagery, which has many applications, such as in environmental studies and urban planning.

It has been illustrated in the previous sections that there is some level of success in applying different AI processing techniques to the received RADAR data to achieve the intended outcomes. For instance, Figure 4 demonstrates how AI improves the spatial resolution of RADAR imagery. This enhancement is particularly useful in high-resolution imagery applications, including disaster management and precision farming.

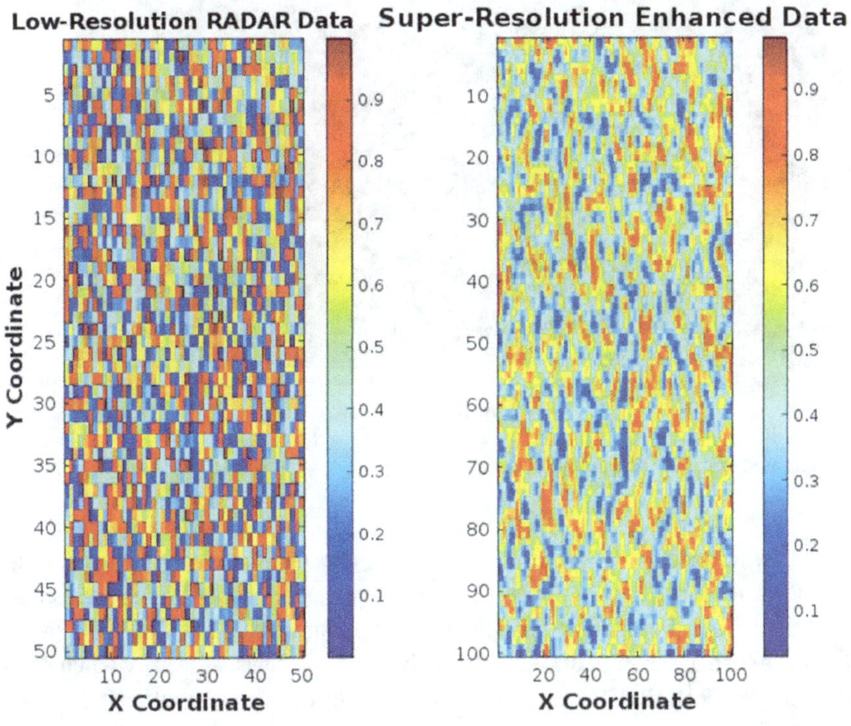

Figure 4: Resolution enhancement using AI.

Besides, AI has demonstrated effectiveness in analyzing large-scale RADAR data, for example, by applying CNNs to learn features more efficiently than previous approaches in terms of both time and accuracy. These methods are sensitive to the size of the data, with larger datasets posing challenges, and, as stated in Figure 7, the costs of training AI models increase as a function of dataset size during the model's training. CNNs and RNNs have been found to be particularly efficient for large-scale RADAR applications. Specifically, Figure 5 shows how AI can track objects in motion in real time. However, the real-time processing of a large amount of data from RADAR systems may exceed the computational capacity of existing resources.

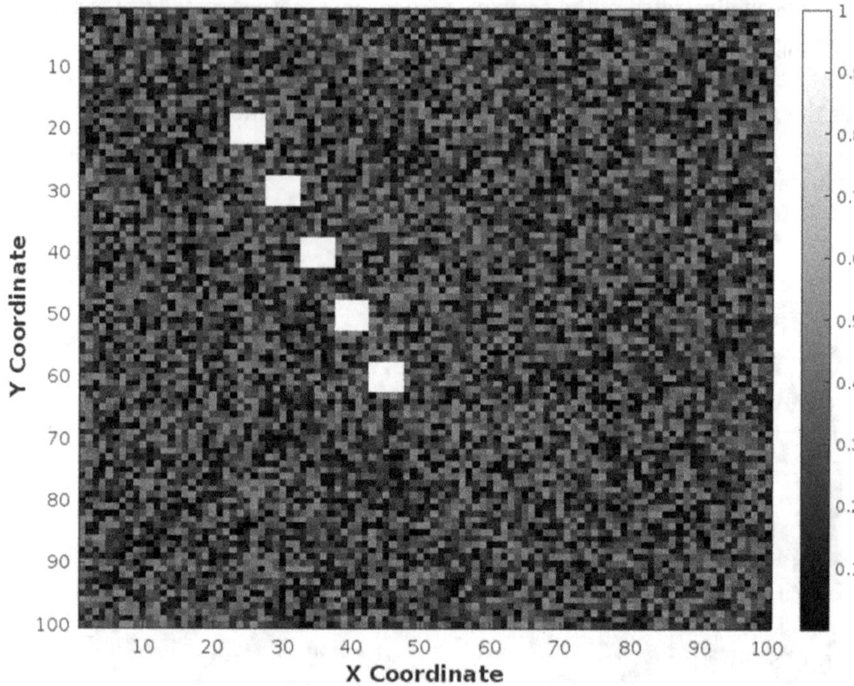

Figure 5: AI-based target tracking in RADAR data.

In Figure 6, which is a comparison of the precision and recall of classification models, the SVM, CNN, RF, and RNN are shown as some of the models involved in the classification, and they are compared based on their precision and recall. The CNNs are recognized to have higher accuracy and sensitivity than other models, especially when dealing with complex RADAR data sets, which makes pattern recognition difficult. Further, the impact of data size on model training time is shown in Figure 7, while Figure 8 reveals the comparison of feature extraction techniques and their effect on classification accuracy, where we can deduce that Gabor filters offer a higher classification accuracy in the RADAR data. This shows that the feature extraction technique depends on the kind of input data applied to it, underlining that, in the RADAR application under consideration, one has to properly select the kind of feature extraction technique to be used. However, there are still limitations to the proposed AI framework for remote sensing RADAR, such as computational problems and data acquisition. Here, the major concern is the elevated computation costs of AI models, especially with DL models.

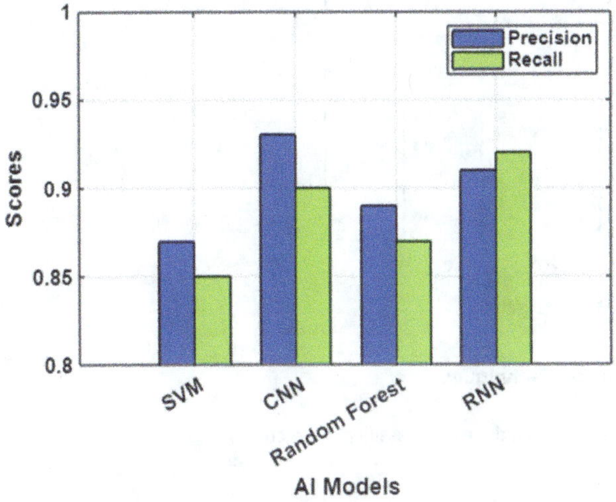

Figure 6: Precision and recall comparison of classification models.

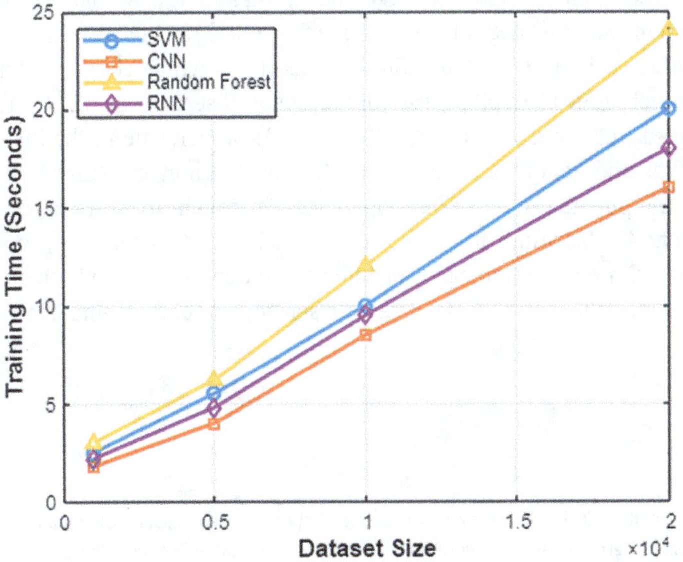

Figure 7: Impact of dataset size on model training time.

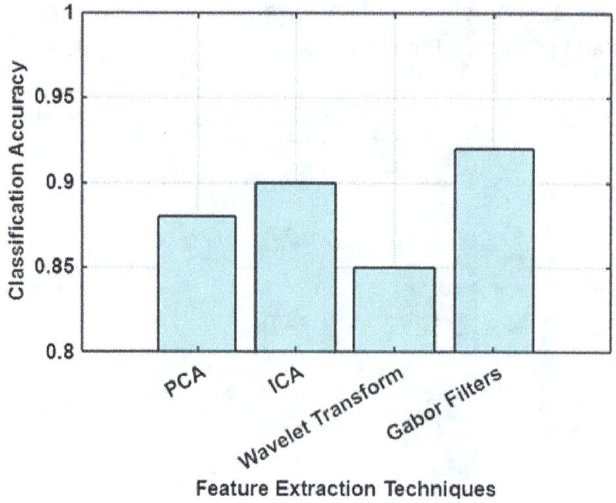

Figure 8: Comparison of feature extraction techniques on classification accuracy.

7 Conclusion

AI models are also used to track the intended target with high accuracy. We have seen that AI in super-resolution has boosted image quality, making RADAR data more useful in disaster response and ecological surveys. Furthermore, the contrast of feature extraction techniques shows that Gabor filters generally enhance classification accuracy over other techniques. Despite these foundational observations, CNNs, as well as RNNs, displayed high accuracy and recall quality. However, due to the high computational demands and data availability issues that persist in every RADAR application, AI still has the potential to push development forward. Future work is suggested to refine current AI algorithms to reduce computational costs. Real-time processing and interaction with new technologies, including cloud computing and others, will only strengthen the application of RADAR remote sensing in complex and evolving scenarios.

References

[1] Abduljawad, M., Alsalmani, A. 2022. Towards creating exotic remote sensing datasets using image generating AI. In: 2022 International Conference on Electrical and Computing Technologies and Applications (ICECTA), Presented at the 2022 International Conference on Electrical and Computing Technologies and Applications (ICECTA), 84–88. https://doi.org/10.1109/ICECTA57148.2022.9990245

[2] Bhavanasi, G., Werthen-Brabants, L., Dhaene, T., Couckuyt, I. 2023. Open-set patient activity recognition with radar sensors and deep learning. IEEE Geoscience and Remote Sensing Letters, 20, 1–5. https://doi.org/10.1109/LGRS.2023.3235243

[3] De Albuquerque, A.O., De Carvalho, O.L.F., Silva, C.R.E., Luiz, A.S., De Bem, P.P., Gomes, R.A.T., Guimarães, R.F., Júnior, O.A.D.C. 2021. Dealing with clouds and seasonal changes for center pivot irrigation systems detection using instance segmentation in Sentinel-2 time series. IEEE Journal of Selected Topics in Applied Earth Observations and Remote Sensing, 14, 8447–8457. https://doi.org/10.1109/JSTARS.2021.3104726

[4] Dräger, N., Xu, Y., Ghamisi, P. 2023. Backdoor attacks for remote sensing data with wavelet transform. IEEE Transactions on Geoscience and Remote Sensing, 61, 1–15. https://doi.org/10.1109/TGRS.2023.3289307

[5] Feng, W., Hu, X., He, X. 2024. Artificial Intelligence (AI)-based radar signal processing and radar imaging. Electronics, 13, 4251. https://doi.org/10.3390/electronics13214251

[6] Liu, J., Wang, Y., Lu, Y., Zhao, P., Wang, S., Sun, Y., Luo, Y. 2024. Application of remote sensing and Explainable Artificial Intelligence (XAI) for wildfire occurrence mapping in the mountainous region of Southwest China. Remote Sensing, 16, 3602. https://doi.org/10.3390/rs16193602

[7] Kim, K.-H., Shin, Y., Lee, S., Jeong, D. 2019. Use of seasonal climate forecasts in agricultural decision-making for crop disease management. In: Iizumi, T., Hirata, R., Matsuda, R. (Eds.) Adaptation to Climate Change in Agriculture: Research and Practices, Singapore: Springer, 173–191. https://doi.org/10.1007/978-981-13-9235-1_12

[8] Li, H. 2021. An overview on remote sensing image classification methods with a focus on support vector machine. In: 2021 International Conference on Signal Processing and Machine Learning (CONF-SPML), Presented at the 2021 International Conference on Signal Processing and Machine Learning (CONF-SPML), 50–56. https://doi.org/10.1109/CONF-SPML54095.2021.00019

[9] Liu, S., Bai, Y., Han, X., Yuille, A. 2023. Understanding pan-sharpening via generalized inverse. https://doi.org/10.48550/arXiv.2310.02718

[10] Ogut, M., Bosch-Lluis, X., Kangaslahti, P., Ramos-Perez, I., Munoz-Martin, J.F., Cooperrider, J., Yue, Q., Swope, J., Tavallali, P., Chien, S., Pradhan, O., Deal, W., Cooke, C. 2022. Autonomous capabilities and command and data handling design for the smart remote sensing of cloud ice. In: IGARSS 2022 – 2022 IEEE International Geoscience and Remote Sensing Symposium, Presented at the IGARSS 2022 – 2022 IEEE International Geoscience and Remote Sensing Symposium, 7119–7122. https://doi.org/10.1109/IGARSS46834.2022.9883491

[11] Patil, S., Kumar, S., Almusawi, M., Malathy, V., Sundaram, S.M. 2024. Multiscale convolution fusion filters with heterogenous remote sensing images for land cover change detection. In: 2024 International Conference on Integrated Circuits and Communication Systems (ICICACS), Presented at the 2024 International Conference on Integrated Circuits and Communication Systems (ICICACS), 1–5. https://doi.org/10.1109/ICICACS60521.2024.10498917

[12] Wang, X. 2022. Managing land carrying capacity: Key to achieving sustainable production systems for food security. Land, 11, 484. https://doi.org/10.3390/land11040484

[13] Zhao, T., Wang, S., Ouyang, C., Chen, M., Liu, C., Zhang, J., Yu, L., Wang, F., Xie, Y., Li, J., Wang, F., Grunwald, S., Wong, B.M., Zhang, F., Qian, Z., Xu, Y., Yu, C., Han, W., Sun, T., Shao, Z., Qian, T., Chen, Z., Zeng, J., Zhang, H., Letu, H., Zhang, B., Wang, L., Luo, L., Shi, C., Su, H., Zhang, H., Yin, S., Huang, N., Zhao, W., Li, N., Zheng, C., Zhou, Y., Huang, C., Feng, D., Xu, Q., Wu, Y., Hong, D., Wang, Z., Lin, Y., Zhang, T., Kumar, P., Plaza, A., Chanussot, J., Zhang, J., Shi, J., Wang, L. 2024. Artificial intelligence for geoscience: Progress, challenges, and perspectives. The Innovation, 5, 100691. https://doi.org/10.1016/j.xinn.2024.100691

[14] Janga, B., Asamani, G.P., Sun, Z., Cristea, N. 2023. A review of practical ai for remote sensing in earth sciences. Remote Sensing, 15, 4112. https://doi.org/10.3390/rs15164112

[15] Zhang, Y., Hao, Y. 2022. A survey of SAR image target detection based on convolutional neural networks. Remote Sensing, 14, 6240. https://doi.org/10.3390/rs14246240

[16] Li, Z., Chen, B., Wu, S., Su, M., Chen, J.M., Xu, B. 2024. Deep learning for urban land use category classification: A review and experimental assessment. Remote Sensing of Environment, 311, 114290. https://doi.org/10.1016/j.rse.2024.114290

[17] Ilesanmi, A.E., Ilesanmi, T.O. 2021. Methods for image denoising using convolutional neural network: A review. Complex and Intelligent Systems, 7, 2179–2198. https://doi.org/10.1007/s40747-021-00428-4

[18] Bai, C., Bai, X., Wu, K. 2023. A review: Remote sensing image object detection algorithm based on deep learning. Electronics, 12, 4902. https://doi.org/10.3390/electronics12244902

[19] Mohan, E., Rajesh, A., Sunitha, G., Konduru, R.M., Avanija, J., Ganesh Babu, L. 2021. A deep neural network learning-based speckle noise removal technique for enhancing the quality of synthetic-aperture radar images. Concurrency and Computation: Practice and Experience, 33, e6239. https://doi.org/10.1002/cpe.6239

[20] Porkodi, S.P., Sarada, V., Maik, V., Gurushankar, K. 2023. Generic image application using GANs (Generative Adversarial Networks): A review. Evolving Systems, 14, 903–917. https://doi.org/10.1007/s12530-022-09464-y

[21] Al-Obaidi, K.M., Wang, J., Hossain, M. 2025. Data-driven urbanism: Image processing techniques for urban analytics. In: He, B.-J., Prasad, D., Yan, L., Cheshmehzangi, A., Pignatta, G. (Eds.) International Conference on Urban Climate, Sustainability and Urban Design, Singapore: Springer Nature, 709–720. https://doi.org/10.1007/978-981-97-8401-1_51

[22] Bistron, M., Piotrowski, Z. 2021. Artificial intelligence applications in military systems and their influence on sense of security of citizens. Electronics, 10, 871. https://doi.org/10.3390/electronics10070871

Neha Bhati*, Narayan Vyas, Rajesh Yadav, Rakesh Sharma,
Koushik Sundar

Revolutionizing agricultural and environmental analytics with synthetic aperture radar (SAR): innovations, challenges, and future directions

Abstract: Synthetic aperture radar (SAR) has made significant advances in exploring different scattering mechanisms and target geometries, as its evolution has opened numerous opportunities to enhance agricultural classification and environmental monitoring. SAR is independent of weather conditions and natural light, guaranteeing high-quality images at any time and playing a crucial role in effective monitoring. This chapter explains important methods such as Polarimetric SAR (PolSAR), Interferometric SAR (InSAR), and multi-temporal SAR techniques, used to improve crop classification, soil-moisture estimation, and crop-disease detection. Moreover, the synergistic role of SAR with machine learning (ML) and artificial intelligence (AI) is discussed highlighting how it enables multi-dimensional data fusion, predictive analysis, and improved decision-making outcomes. It also explores the application of SAR in land-use change, urbanization, and environmental degradation. The chapter proposes future research directions, such as combining SAR data with optical and thermal imagery and downsizing SAR systems to enable their operation on a larger scale at a reasonable cost.

Keywords: Synthetic aperture radar (SAR), agriculture, environment, classification, monitoring, remote sensing

***Corresponding author: Neha Bhati**, Department of Research and Development, Flexxited, Bengaluru, Karnataka, India, e-mail: nehabhati184@gmail.com, ORCID: 0009-0008-0171-2786
Narayan Vyas, Department of Computer Science and Application, Vivekananda Global University, Jaipur, Rajasthan, India, e-mail: narayanvyas87@gmail.com, ORCID: 0000-0003-4225-0764
Rajesh Yadav, Department of Zoology, JECRC University, Jaipur, Rajasthan, India, e-mail: ryadav70@yahoo.co.in
Rakesh Sharma, Department of Computer Science and Application, Vivekananda Global University, Jaipur, Rajasthan, India, e-mail: srak.911@gmail.com
Koushik Sundar, Citibank NA, Jersey City, NJ, USA, e-mail: koushiksundar@gmail.com, ORCID: 0009-0003-7119-456X

https://doi.org/10.1515/9783111572970-015

1 Introduction

Synthetic aperture radar (SAR) is a significant remote sensing technological advancement, widely recognized for its applications in agriculture and environmental monitoring. This chapter will demonstrate ways in which SAR can be used to improve agricultural classification and environmental change detection. In agriculture, SAR is primarly used to enhance crop classification and crop yield assessment [1]. These improvements are essential for optimizing agricultural output and assisting in efforts to implement better resource management plans. Similarly, SAR is used to monitor environmental changes associated with landscape alterations. Change detection can identify and analyze land surface changes caused by natural processes or human activities, providing crucial information that enables near real-time decision-making [2].

SAR technology offers qualitative image data that is difficult, if not impossible, to obtain from traditional optical remote sensing systems under most environmental conditions, due to its intrinsic capabilities. Most optical sensors cannot operate at night and struggle under cloudy conditions. However, SAR is independent of natural light, and its ability to penetrate most cloud cover makes it more reliability in providing consistent data at all hours of the day and in all weather conditions [3]. This is particularly important in areas where people often face adverse weather conditions and in locations that require constant monitoring. The high-resolution imaging capability, both night and day, enhances the versatility and application of SAR for large-scale landscape monitoring and agricultural management [4].

SAR technology has evolved over time, continuously improving and enhancing current operations for society's benefit while opening new pathways for scientific exploration. Modern SAR systems demonstrate the potential to overcome limitations and improve aspects such as spatial and temporal resolution, as well as the ability to resolve land cover and better represent the Earth's surface for various applications, including monitoring agricultural lands and environmental change [5]. This technology has also paved the way for advanced data analytics, which are essential for understanding complex environmental relationships and improving management practices in agriculture [6]. Figure 1 illustrates SAR's diverse roles in land use, agriculture, forestry, wetlands, and environmental monitoring.

This chapter will explore some game-changing advancements in SAR technology specifically applied to these fields. It will also discuss how SAR data is integrated with other types of data, the new algorithms developed for processing it, and the practical implications of these technologies in practice through relevant case studies. By providing an overview of capabilities and developments, this introduction lays the groundwork for further discussion on the applications of SAR technology in facilitating and advancing agricultural classification and change detection processes – critical components of achieving global sustainability in this arena [7].

Figure 1: Applications of SAR in earth observation.

2 Principles of SAR technology

SAR operates based on to the principles of radar technology but is specifically designed to achieve high-resolution imagery of the Earth's surface under any weather conditions and at any time. SAR systems emit microwave signals toward the Earth's surface from a moving aircraft or satellite. When these signals interact with surface elements, they are reflected toward the radar antenna. The strength and time delay of these signals help SAR to create detailed two-dimensional images and three-dimensional reconstructions of landscapes. An key feature of SAR is its ability to synthesizes an antenna much larger than is physically possible by moving along a flight path and combining signals obtained at separate points. This process, known as synthetic aperture, is the foundation behind the radar's name [8]. It allows the radar to extend its effective antenna through these signals, thereby capturing high-resolution data. By applying advanced algorithms to these signals, SAR systems can achieve resolution not limited by the actual antenna size, but by the length of the synthetic aperture. This technique enables the observation of fine details at various operational distances, making it invaluable for both research and practical applications [9].

SAR technology is essential in several applications due to its all-weather imaging capabilities. Optical and mid-IR sensors rely on sunlight, and their performance can be affected by cloud cover or the total absence of light at night. In contrast, SAR operates consistently under all light conditions and can penetrate through clouds, rain, fog, and smoke. This feature is a significant advantage in monitoring farmlands, as weather conditions can change rapidly. In fact, the technology enables the radar to gather reliable data consistently over time, performing well across different seasons and climate variations [10]. In practical terms, SAR can detect significant variations in surface reflections or emissions. Additionally, its ability to observe environmental changes is invaluable across several sectors. For example, with the increase in carbon emissions, SAR can proves to be a valuable tool in identifying the source of emissions. An observer can determine the source of the carbon emissions. By analyzing the amount of carbon emitted into the air, the radar can calculate and express the result in metric units, helping to gauge the environmental impact of these emissions [11].

3 SAR techniques for agricultural classification

SAR is an essential tool for agricultural management and monitoring due to its unique physical properties, making it significant in classifying various agricultural components. Such techniques utilize SAR's high-resolution imaging and all-weather capabilities to differentiate, monitor, and predict agricultural phenomena, providing vital data that can facilitate sustainable farming practices and effective resource management [12]. Figure 2 illustrates SAR's role in cropland mapping, vegetation classification, and environmental degradation monitoring.

3.1 Overview of SAR techniques in agriculture

In agriculture, various types of SAR techniques are suitable for specific applications, depending on the landscape, crop types, and the information to be obtained [13]. Table 1 presents advanced classification algorithms applied to SAR data, detailing their types, applications, and effectiveness in agricultural settings.

3.2 Applications of SAR in agricultural classification

SAR techniques have wide applications in agriculture. The ability of SAR to acquire data under all weather conditions, independently of cloud cover and illumination, makes it particularly useful for consistent monitoring of extensive agricultural areas [14]. Some key applications include:

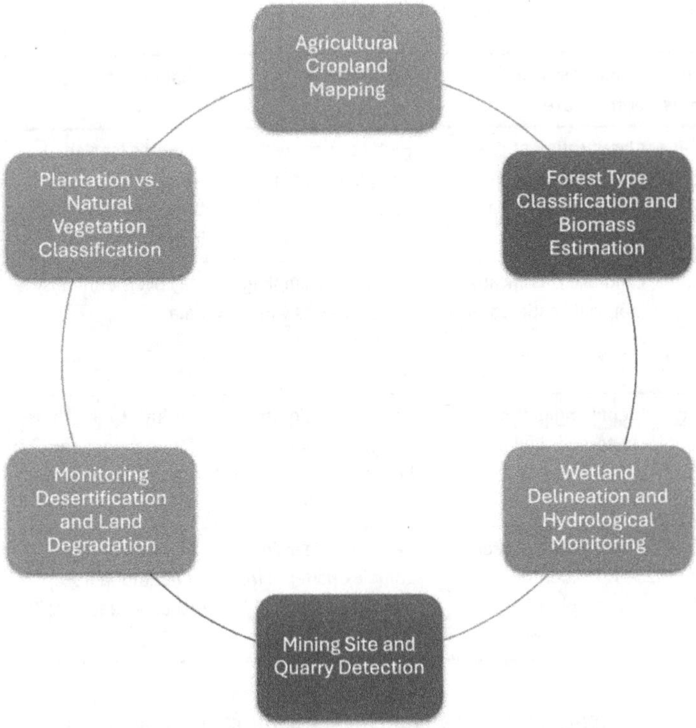

Figure 2: SAR applications in agricultural mapping.

- **Crop type classification**: Classifying crop types across large tracts of land can aid in mapping agricultural land, which is important for crop rotation planning and subsidy allocation.
- **Soil moisture estimation**: SAR's ability to penetrate the surface allows for accurate and timely assessing soil moisture, which is essential for irrigation practices and water resource management.
- **Monitoring crop health**: The reflectance and structural information captured from SAR images help assess plant health and facilitate the early detection of stress caused by drought, nutrient deficiencies, or disease.

The combination of SAR techniques with other remote sensing datasets and ground-truth measurements provides comprehensive information for researchers and farmers, enabling efficient management in challenging landscapes. When integrated with other data sources, SAR enhances decision-making, leadingto higher productivity, improved sustainability, and reduced environmental impacts [15]. With ongoing technological advancements, the accuracy and application range of SAR for agricultural clas-

Table 1: Classification algorithms for SAR data in agricultural applications.

Algorithm type	Common algorithms	Applications in agriculture	Advantages	Challenges
Supervised Learning	SVM	Classification of crop types, disease detection, and land cover mapping	High accuracy with adequate training data	Requires labeled training data and can be computationally intensive
	Random Forests	Land use classification, crop yield estimation	Effective at handling large datasets with multiple input features	May overfit on noisy data
Unsupervised Learning	Clustering Techniques (e.g., K-means)	Identifying natural clusters of similar crops or land uses	Useful in exploratory analysis without labeled data	Sensitive to the choice of parameters and initial conditions
Deep Learning	CNNs	High-resolution crop classification, phenotyping	Capable of learning complex patterns from large-scale data	Requires extensive computational resources and data for training

sification will continue to expand, further advancing agricultural remote sensing and management [16]. Table 2 represents the discussed techniques, datasets, characteristics, limitations, and applications.

Table 2: SAR for land-use and land-cover classification.

Technique	Dataset	Characteristics	Limitations	Applications	Source
CTGAN[1]	PolSAR[2]	Fusion of SAR and optical datasets generates synthetic data to address class imbalance by increasing minority class samples, leading to improved classifier performance (e.g., XGBoost, KNN)	Synthetic data might not fully capture all real-world variability and can be computationally expensive	Crop classification: addressing imbalanced datasets in agricultural remote sensing	[17]

Table 2 (continued)

Technique	Dataset	Characteristics	Limitations	Applications	Source
MCANet [3]	WHU-OPT-SAR Dataset	Development of a semantic segmentation framework for the generation of multimodal images, named MCANet	Requires large, annotated datasets for training; computationally intensive	Land-use classification, agriculture monitoring, and environmental management	[18]
FCN[4]	Polarimetric RADARSAT-2 Imagery[5]	Encoder-decoder architecture uses inception modules and skip connections with residual units; it is end-to-end trainable	Requires labeled SAR data for training, complex feature engineering, and is computationally intensive	Wetland mapping, complex land cover ecosystem classification	[19]
Feature-level fusion and SVM	Landsat OLI[6] and ALOS-2[7]	Combines spectral, texture, and spatial features (NDVI[8], elevation, slope), and uses object-oriented segmentation and SVM for classification	No statistical analysis of terrain-corrected images was performed for ALOS-2 data due to the large temporal difference between the Landsat and ALOS-2 datasets	Land Use and Land Cover (LULC) classification in mountainous and cloudy regions, including vegetation, forest, and water extraction	[20]
WOFOST[9] and 4-DEnSRF	HJ-1A/B, GF-1 and RADARSAT-2	Development of a crop yield simulation scheme using WOFOST and the 4-DEnSRF assimilation algorithm, incorporating time series of LAI retrieved from optical and SAR data	Lower accuracy in winter wheat estimation using SAR images, and high-dependence on optical images	Winter Wheat Yield Simulation	[21]

Table 2 (continued)

Technique	Dataset	Characteristics	Limitations	Applications	Source
Random Forests Classifier	Landsat and L-band SAR data (JERS-1, ALOS-2/PALSAR-2), 1995–2015, Tanintharyi Region	Combination of optical and radar data; use of SAR textures; 20 year data span	Lower accuracy with SAR-only; sensitivity issues	Land cover change detection; sustainable land management, and the study of agricultural expansion	[22]
1DCNN-MRF[10] Model	HH-HV model data from Gaofen-3, Dongting Lake area	Utilizes improved dual-pol radar vegetation index (DpRVIm[11]), incorporates terrain factors, and is designed to enhance land cover type separability	Limited polarization information and speckle noise affect accuracy	Land cover classification under adverse weather; dynamic environment monitoring	[23]
SVM[12], ML[13], RF[14], MD, CART[15] (ArcGIS Pro & Google Earth Engine)	Satellite data from Landsat, Sentinel, and Planet (2017–2021), Charlottetown, Canada	Evaluation of multiple classifiers and satellite datasets; systematic performance assessment; utilization of ArcGIS Pro and Google Earth Engine for classification	Not specified, but typically includes computational demands and varying accuracies across classifiers and data types	Developing accurate LULC maps, conducting change detection for urbanization studies, and promoting sustainable resource management	[24]

CTGAN[1]: Conditional Tabular Generative Adversarial Network; PolSAR[2]: Polarimetric Synthetic Aperture Radar; MCANet[3]: Multimodal-Cross Attention Network; FCN[4]: Fully Convolutional Network; RADARSAT-2[5]: Radar Satellite-2; OLI[6]: Operational Land Imager; ALOS-2[7]: Advanced Land Observing Satellite-2; NDVI[8]: Normalized Difference Vegetation Index; WOFOST[9]: World Food Studies; 1DCNN-MRF[10]: One-Dimensional Convolutional Neural Network with Markov Random Field; DpRVIm[11]: Dual-Polarization Radar Vegetation Index; SVM[12]: Support Vector Machine; ML[13]: Machine Learning; RF[14]: Random Forest; CART[15]: Classification and Regression Trees

4 SAR techniques for change detection

SAR is one of the emerging and useful techniques in environmental change detection, as it provides both high spatial resolution and efficiency. This unique capability of high-resolution imaging in all weather conditions and through darkness can be utilized to perform change detection in various types of terrain and under multiple conditions. This section has reviewed some of the existing SAR-based methods for environmental change detection, as well as their operational principles and application domains [25].

4.1 Overview of change detection techniques

SAR technology provides a wide range of techniques for detecting environmental changes across various landscapes and at different resolution levels, which are determined by the size of the radar cell.

- **Differential Interferometric SAR (DInSAR):** Identification and measurement of temporal physical changes. Interferograms, or phase-difference maps, are created using two or more SAR images acquired from the same position at different times. Such variations may indicate ground motion (displacement, subsidence, landslides, or earthquake deformations) [26]. DInSAR is an application of the Interferometric Synthetic Aperture Radar (InSAR) model that can achieve precise measurements based on the common practice of closely monitoring infrastructure with unreliable instrumentation to detect very small displacements, where active interference techniques are necessary, making it an active sensor of choice in much of the infrastructure monitoring region, particularly in areas that are highly geologically active.
- **Multi-temporal SAR analysis:** The methods that use the temporal dimension of SAR data are based on multi-temporal SAR images for change detection. Changes in land use, vegetation cover, or damage post-disaster can be identified by observing differences in returns from radar signals. Multi-temporal analysis is key to the continuous monitoring of environmental status and has found important applications in agriculture (tracking crop growth), forestry (detecting reforested/deforested areas), and urban regions (monitoring construction and development).
- **PolSAR change detection:** Polarimetric Synthetic Aperture Radar (PolSAR) explores the polarization characteristics of the radar beam and targets to improve material and surface detection. By comparing the polarimetric signatures of SAR images acquired over time, this analysis allows the detection of changes in surface properties, vegetation structure, or even water content. This process works especially well for ecological surveys, such as tracking wetland shifts or forest loss.
- **Classification-based change detection:** This approach first classifies SAR images at two different times into categories (e.g., water, vegetation, urban) and then compares the classified images for change detection. These data are then submitted to supervised models (like Random Forests) or unsupervised models (like clustering) to improve accuracy. This method is particularly advantageous for large-area land cover and land-use change research.
- **Time-series analysis:** SAR time-series analysis is a series of images over time that has been introduced to observe changes or trends. This can highlight sea-

sonal alterations, yearly resurgences of plants, or incremental urban spread [27]. Statistical models are used in time-series analysis to derive changes and predict trends based on historical data.

4.2 Applications of SAR for change detection

SAR has been utilized in several change detection applications. The ability of this technology to provide fast and accurate information has made it an essential disaster and environmental management tool. Some of the applications of SAR for change detection include:

- **Environmental monitoring:** SAR is important for accurate reporting of environmental changes; for example, it encompasses the dynamics of deforestation, processes of desertification, and coastal zone changes due to sea level rise or erosion.
- **Disaster management:** A rapid evaluation is necessary following a flood, wildfire, or perhaps an earthquake. SAR is a powerful tool that can quickly provide damage maps and assist with effective response coordination.
- **Urban planning and monitoring:** During the rapid urbanization of many regions, SAR helps monitor city expansion, land use changes, and infrastructure development, which provides very useful data for urban planning and future developments.
- **Agricultural monitoring:** Monitoring changes in agricultural practices, crop types, and irrigation practices helps maximize agricultural productivity and conserve resources.

With continuous improvements in radar sensors and computational algorithms, this technology will play an increasingly important role in environmental monitoring and change detection [28]. The integration of SAR data with other geographic and observational data has the potential to provide more comprehensive insights, ultimately facilitating more informed decision-making and improved management of natural resources and hazards. Table 3 in this section effectively showcases the discussed techniques and their applications in change detection.

5 Implications and future directions

ML and AI for SAR data processing represent some of the most important trends. They enhance the resolution and analysis of images, enabling advanced pattern recognition and predictive analytics. This integration facilitates multi-sensor analysis for change detection and predictive modeling of crop yields using both historical time series data and real-time SAR inputs. Miniaturization and price reductions in SAR sys-

Table 3: SAR for change detection.

Technique	Dataset	Characteristics	Limitations	Applications	Source
Unsupervised DL[1] and Transfer Learning	Bi-temporal or multi-temporal SAR images	Utilizes unsupervised DL models to extract feature maps; incorporates transfer learning from pre-trained models; effectively handles speckle noise	Challenges in gathering labeled multi-temporal data include dependency on the similarity between pre-trained model data and target SAR images	Earthquake damage assessment; general change detection in any weather and lighting conditions	[29]
Non-parametric detection with recursive median filtering	Time series of RADARSAT, ERS[2], and ENVISAT[3] images	Utilizes recursive median filtering for sparse representation and change detection; focusing on reliable pixel values as change indicators	Speckle noise challenges sparsity and requires pre-processing for accurate data representation	Environmental monitoring and operational change detection in radar image series	[30]
High-resolution CCD[4] with GIS[5] post-processing	Sentinel-1 SAR images and optical images of Manchester	Utilizes CCD to identify minute structural changes, enhanced with GIS to reduce false positives	Sensitivity to minor changes can trigger unwanted detections in urban environments	Urban change detection, damage assessment, cadastral mapping, and monitoring illegal activities	[31]
Interferometric coherence and intensity correlation	Multi-temporal SAR data	Reviews multi-temporal SAR methods, such as interferometric coherence and intensity correlation, for damage assessment; includes combined methods for improved accuracy	Limitations of current SAR missions are affecting global applicability	Rapid damage mapping post-disasters is essential for rescue and reconstruction operations	[32]

Table 3 (continued)

Technique	Dataset	Characteristics	Limitations	Applications	Source
Pixel, Feature, and Decision Level Integration using SVM[6] RF[7]	SAR data from TerraSAR-X and ENVISAT ASAR in WSM and IMP modes, combined with optical data	Compares integration levels of SAR and optical data using ML methods and examines feature distributions and texture analysis	Effectiveness depends on data distribution and resolution; not all methods are suitable at every integration level	Urban land cover classification in the Pearl River Delta	[33]
Conditional RF Model	TerraSAR-X and RADARSAT-2 images, Mont-Saint-Michel Bay, France (632 ha)	Utilizes X-/C-band frequencies, dual-/ quad-polarization, and multi-temporal acquisitions; employs 25 SAR features, including Shannon entropy for correlation analysis; ANOVA[8] for impact assessment	High variability in wetland ecosystems; polarization mode is less influential	Wetland ecosystem analysis: discrimination of vegetation types for conservation efforts	[34]
RoF[9] with Coarse-to-Fine Uncertainty Analyses	High-resolution remote sensing images, multi-temporal datasets	Utilizes vector-raster integration, multi-scale fine segmentation; employs neighborhood correlation for pre-classification; and uses RoF for final object classification with majority voting	Scale sensitivity in object-based change detection	Urban area change detection; improving change detection accuracy in complex environments	[35]

[1]DL: Deep Learning; [2]ERS: European Remote Sensing; [3]ENVISAT: Environmental Satellite; [4]CCD: Coherent Change Detection; [5]GIS: Geographic Information System; [6]SVM: Support Vector Machine; [7]RF: Random Forest; [8]ANOVA: Analysis of Variance; [2]DInSAR: Differential Interferometric Synthetic Aperture Radar; [9]RoF: Rotation Forest

tems are also making the technology more affordable. Additionally, the advent of small satellite constellations with SAR sensors offers frequent and affordable Earth observations. This democratization enables global monitoring of agricultural and environmental conditions, increasing the scalability of SAR applications. Improvements in SAR's multi-frequency and multi-polarization capabilities aid in investigating surface textures and characteristics. These improvements assist in detailed land cover classification and subtle environmental change detection, essential for precision agriculture and in-depth environmental monitoring [36].

5.1 SAR technology's research opportunities

One of the major research opportunities lies in combining SAR data with other remote sensing data sources (e.g., optical and thermal). This approach allows for the fusion of different types of information as well as more complex and distinct detection of environmental or agricultural phenomena, which may be difficult to detect using a single sensing method. Considering the upcoming satellite launches, as well as the increased volume of SAR imagery to process, the automatic development of stable and reproducible processing codes for SAR images will constitute another key research line in the near future [37]. Distributed cloud-based processing platforms, such as Google Earth Engine (GEE), can provide efficient and scalable processing of SAR data [38]. The characteristics of the SAR signal are influenced by changes in soil moisture and vegetation due to environmental conditions, which is beneficial for interpreting the data, such as in soil moisture estimation and vegetation health monitoring. An improved understanding of these interactions would increase the validity and transferability of SAR systems. Such research directions will enhance the technical performance of SAR systems and their applications for assessing and monitoring the natural environment.

6 Conclusion

This chapter has illustrated how the evolution of SAR technology has transformed agricultural classification and vegetation assessment into critical research fields, as will be discussed in further detail. SAR can offer high-resolution images regardless of the weather conditions, which helps improve the accuracy and efficiency of monitoring agricultural lands. By employing ML and AI technologies, SAR can develop cutting-edge capabilities in the areas of pattern recognition, predictive analytics, and multi-sensor analysis with advanced sophistication. With the development of these technologies, data acquisition and analysis through SAR have become integral tools for sustainable agriculture and resource management. Additionally, due to the decreasing size and cost of SAR systems, small satellite constellations can be launched, enabling regular and economical monitoring of the Earth from space. This data availability has made it easier for researchers to source data while ensuring continuous, reliable, and timely-quality monitoring, thereby facilitating decision-making in agriculture and environmental sustainability.

References

[1] Gao, G. 2010a. Statistical modeling of SAR Images: A survey. Sensors, 10, 775–795, https://doi.org/10.3390/s100100775

[2] Shang, J., Liu, J., Chen, Z., McNairn, H., Davidson, A. 2022. Recent advancement of synthetic aperture radar (sar) systems and their applications to crop growth monitoring, https://doi.org/10.5772/intechopen.102917

[3] Liu, C., Chen, Z., Shao, Y., Chen, J., Hasi, T., Pan, H. 2019. Research advances of SAR remote sensing for agriculture applications: A review. Journal of Integrative Agriculture, 18, 506–525, https://doi.org/10.1016/S2095-3119(18)62016-7

[4] Ajadi, O., McAlpin, D. (Eds.) 2023. Recent Advances and Contribution of Synthetic Aperture Radar (SAR) Applications for Agricultural Monitoring, MDPI – Multidisciplinary Digital Publishing Institute. https://doi.org/10.3390/books978-3-0365-7359-5

[5] Freeman, A. 1992. SAR calibration: An overview. IEEE transactions on geoscience and remote sensing, 30, 1107–1121, https://doi.org/10.1109/36.193786

[6] Gao, G. 2010b. Statistical modeling of SAR images: A survey. Sensors, 10, 775–795, https://doi.org/10.3390/s100100775

[7] Hein, A. 2004. Processing of SAR data, signals and communication technology, Berlin, Heidelberg: Springer, https://doi.org/10.1007/978-3-662-09457-0

[8] Alibakhshikenari, M., Babaeian, F., Virdee, B.S., Aïssa, S., Azpilicueta, L., See, C.H., Althuwayb, A.A., Huynen, I., Abd-Alhameed, R.A., Falcone, F., Limiti, E. 2020. A comprehensive survey on "Various decoupling mechanisms with focus on metamaterial and metasurface principles applicable to SAR and MIMO antenna systems. IEEE Access, 8, 192965–193004, https://doi.org/10.1109/ACCESS.2020.3032826

[9] Singh, P., Diwakar, M., Shankar, A., Shree, R., Kumar, M. 2021. A review on SAR image and its despeckling. Archives of Computational Methods in Engineering, 28, 4633–4653, https://doi.org/10.1007/s11831-021-09548-z

[10] Tsokas, A., Rysz, M., Pardalos, P.M., Dipple, K. 2022a. SAR data applications in earth observation: An overview. Expert Systems with Applications, 205, 117342, https://doi.org/10.1016/j.eswa.2022.117342

[11] Wang, Y., Hong, W., Zhang, Y., Lin, Y., Li, Y., Bai, Z., Zhang, Q., Lv, S., Liu, H., Song, Y. 2020. Ground-based differential interferometry SAR: A review. IEEE Geoscience and Remote Sensing Magazine, 8, 43–70, https://doi.org/10.1109/MGRS.2019.2963169

[12] Cui, J., Zhang, X., Wang, W., Wang, L. 2020. Integration of optical and SAR remote sensing images for crop-type mapping based on a novel object-oriented feature selection method. International Journal of Agricultural and Biological Engineering, 13, 178–190, https://doi.org/10.25165/ijabe.v13i1.5285

[13] Tsokas, A., Rysz, M., Pardalos, P.M., Dipple, K. 2022b. SAR data applications in earth observation: An overview. Expert Systems with Applications, 205, 117342, https://doi.org/10.1016/j.eswa.2022.117342

[14] Li, H., Zhang, C., Zhang, S., Atkinson, P.M. 2020. Crop classification from full-year fully-polarimetric L-band UAVSAR time-series using the random forest algorithm. International Journal of Applied Earth Observation and Geoinformation, 87, 102032, https://doi.org/10.1016/j.jag.2019.102032

[15] Silva-Perez, C., Marino, A., Lopez-Sanchez, J.M., Cameron, I. 2021. Multitemporal polarimetric SAR change detection for crop monitoring and crop type classification. IEEE Journal of Selected Topics in Applied Earth Observations and Remote Sensing, 14, 12361–12374, https://doi.org/10.1109/JSTARS.2021.3130186

[16] Parikh, H., Patel, S., Patel, V. 2020. Classification of SAR and PolSAR images using deep learning: A review. International Journal of Image and Data Fusion, 11, 1–32, https://doi.org/10.1080/19479832.2019.1655489

[17] Mirzaei, A., Bagheri, H., Khosravi, I. 2023. Enhancing crop classification accuracy through synthetic SAR-optical data generation using deep learning. ISPRS International Journal of Geo-Information, 12, 450, https://doi.org/10.3390/ijgi12110450
[18] Li, X., Zhang, G., Cui, H., Hou, S., Wang, S., Xin, L., Chen, Y., Li, Z., Zhang, L. 2022. MCANet: A joint semantic segmentation framework of optical and SAR images for land use classification. International Journal of Applied Earth Observation and Geoinformation, 106, 102638, https://doi.org/10.1016/j.jag.2021.102638
[19] Mohammadimanesh, F., Salehi, B., Mahdianpari, M., Gill, E., Molinier, M. 2019. A new fully convolutional neural network for semantic segmentation of polarimetric SAR imagery in complex land cover ecosystem. ISPRS Journal of Photogrammetry and Remote Sensing, 151, 223–236, https://doi.org/10.1016/j.isprsjprs.2019.03.015
[20] Gupta, P., Shukla, D.P. 2023. Combined optical and SAR remote sensing for LULC mapping of Imphal valley using machine learning algorithm. In: 2023 International Conference on Machine Intelligence for GeoAnalytics and Remote Sensing (MIGARS). Presented at the 2023 International Conference on Machine Intelligence for GeoAnalytics and Remote Sensing (MIGARS), 1–4. https://doi.org/10.1109/MIGARS57353.2023.10064582
[21] Wu, S., Ren, J., Chen, Z., Yang, P., Li, H., Liu, J. 2021. Evaluation of winter wheat yield simulation based on assimilating LAI retrieved from networked optical and SAR remotely sensed images into the WOFOST model. IEEE Transactions on Geoscience and Remote Sensing, 59, 9071–9085, https://doi.org/10.1109/TGRS.2020.3038205
[22] De Alban, J.D.T., Connette, G.M., Oswald, P., Webb, E.L. 2018. Combined landsat and L-Band SAR data improves land cover classification and change detection in dynamic tropical landscapes. Remote Sensing, 10, 306, https://doi.org/10.3390/rs10020306
[23] Huang, Y., Meng, M., Hou, Z., Wu, L., Guo, Z., Shen, X., Zheng, W., Li, N. 2023. Land cover classification of SAR based on 1DCNN-MRF Model using improved dual-polarization radar vegetation index. Remote Sensing, 15, 3221, https://doi.org/10.3390/rs15133221
[24] Basheer, S., Wang, X., Farooque, A.A., Nawaz, R.A., Liu, K., Adekanmbi, T., Liu, S. 2022. Comparison of land use land cover classifiers using different satellite imagery and machine learning techniques. Remote Sensing, 14, 4978, https://doi.org/10.3390/rs14194978
[25] Wan, L., Xiang, Y., You, H. 2019. A post-classification comparison method for SAR and optical images change detection. IEEE Geoscience and Remote Sensing Letters, 16, 1026–1030, https://doi.org/10.1109/LGRS.2019.2892432
[26] Cheng, G., Huang, Y., Li, X., Lyu, S., Xu, Z., Zhao, H., Zhao, Q., Xiang, S. 2024. Change detection methods for remote sensing in the last decade: A comprehensive review. Remote Sensing, 16, 2355, https://doi.org/10.3390/rs16132355
[27] Liu, S., Marinelli, D., Bruzzone, L., Bovolo, F. 2019. A review of change detection in multitemporal hyperspectral images: Current techniques, applications, and challenges. IEEE Geoscience and Remote Sensing Magazine, 7, 140–158, https://doi.org/10.1109/MGRS.2019.2898520
[28] Saha, S., Bovolo, F., Bruzzone, L. 2021. Building Change Detection in VHR SAR Images via Unsupervised Deep Transcoding. IEEE Transactions on Geoscience and Remote Sensing, 59, 1917–1929, https://doi.org/10.1109/TGRS.2020.3000296
[29] Bergamasco, L., Bovolo, F. 2022. Change detection in SAR images using deep learning methods. In: Rysz, M., Tsokas, A., Dipple, K.M., Fair, K.L., Pardalos, P.M. (Eds.) Synthetic Aperture Radar (SAR) Data Applications, Cham: Springer International Publishing, 25–62. https://doi.org/10.1007/978-3-031-21225-3_2
[30] Mercier, G. 2010. Progressive change detection in time series of SAR images. In: 2010 IEEE International Geoscience and Remote Sensing Symposium. Presented at the 2010 IEEE International Geoscience and Remote Sensing Symposium, 3086–3089. https://doi.org/10.1109/IGARSS.2010.5652452

[31] Manzoni, M., Monti-Guarnieri, A., Molinari, M.E. 2020. High-resolution sar coherent change detection in Urban environment. International Archives of the Photogrammetry, Remote Sensing and Spatial Information Sciences, XLIII-B3- 2020, 1569–1575. https://doi.org/10.5194/isprs-archives-XLIII-B3-2020-1569-2020

[32] Plank, S. 2014. Rapid damage assessment by means of multi-temporal SAR – A comprehensive review and outlook to Sentinel-1. Remote Sensing, 6, 4870–4906, https://doi.org/10.3390/rs6064870

[33] Zhang, H., Xu, R. 2018. Exploring the optimal integration levels between SAR and optical data for better urban land cover mapping in the Pearl River Delta. International Journal of Applied Earth Observation and Geoinformation, 64, 87–95, https://doi.org/10.1016/j.jag.2017.08.013

[34] Rapinel, S., Betbeder, J., Denize, J., Fabre, E., Pottier, É., Hubert-Moy, L. 2020. SAR analysis of wetland ecosystems: Effects of band frequency, polarization mode and acquisition dates. ISPRS Journal of Photogrammetry and Remote Sensing, 170, 103–113, https://doi.org/10.1016/j.isprsjprs.2020.10.007

[35] Feng, W., Sui, H., Tu, J., Huang, W., Xu, C., Sun, K. 2018. A novel change detection approach for multi-temporal high-resolution remote sensing images based on rotation forest and coarse-to-fine uncertainty analyses. Remote Sensing, 10, 1015, https://doi.org/10.3390/rs10071015

[36] Thangi, D.S. 2024. Artificial intelligence models for remote sensing applications. In: Artificial Intelligence Techniques for Sustainable Development, CRC Press.

[37] García, L.P., Furano, G., Ghiglione, M., Zancan, V., Imbembo, E., Ilioudis, C., Clemente, C., Trucco, P. 2024. Advancements in onboard processing of Synthetic Aperture Radar (SAR) Data: enhancing efficiency and real-time capabilities. IEEE Journal of Selected Topics in Applied Earth Observations and Remote Sensing, 17, 16625–16645, https://doi.org/10.1109/JSTARS.2024.3406155

[38] Adrian, J., Sagan, V., Maimaitijiang, M. 2021. Sentinel SAR-optical fusion for crop type mapping using deep learning and Google Earth Engine. ISPRS Journal of Photogrammetry and Remote Sensing, 175, 215–235, https://doi.org/10.1016/j.isprsjprs.2021.02.018

Editors' biographies

Dr. Alessandro Vinciarelli is a full professor at the University of Glasgow, affiliated with both the School of Computing Science and the Institute of Neuroscience and Psychology. As a member of the Social AI group, he collaborates with Tanaya Guha, Mary Ellen Foster, Mathieu Chollet, and Marwa Mahmoud. His primary research interest lies in social signal processing (SSP), focusing on the analysis and synthesis of nonverbal behaviors, such as facial expressions, gestures, and vocalizations in human-human and human-machine interactions. His work aims to infer psychological constructs such as personality, conflict, and social roles from these cues. He currently leads significant projects, including the UKRI Centre for Doctoral Training in Socially Intelligent Artificial Agents (SOCIAL) and the SONICOM project that explores nonverbal communication in augmented reality/virtual reality environments. Previously, he coordinated the SSP network and has served as the principal investigator for over 10 national projects in Switzerland and the UK. Additionally, he is a cofounder of Klewel, a knowledge management company, and acts as a scientific advisor for Substrata.

Dr. Sartajvir Singh is working as associate director and professor (University Institute of Engineering) at Chandigarh University, Punjab, India. He is also practicing as Regd. Indian Patent Agent (IN/PA 5806). He has more than 10 years of experience in academics, research, and administration. Previously, he worked as the head of Department of Electronics and Communication Engineering and assistant director of Intellectual Property Rights and Consultancy Cell at Chitkara University, Himachal Pradesh, India. He has been awarded the Teacher Associateship for Research Excellence (TARE) Fellowship and International Travel Support (ITS) by the Science and Engineering Research Board (SERB), Government of India, in 2019 and 2021, respectively. His research interests include satellite sensors, remote sensing, and digital image processing. He authored many SCI-indexed articles and indexed book chapters and holds inventions. He is IEEE Senior Member and active member of various international/national societies such as IEEE Young Professional, IEEE Geosciences and Remote Sensing Society (GRSS), IEEE Sensors Council, European Union of Geosciences (EGU), International Society of Photogrammetry and Remote Sensing (ISPRS), Indian Society of Remote Sensing (ISRS), Indian Society of Technical Education (ISTE), and Himalayan Geology.

Narayan Vyas is an assistant professor in the Department of Computer Science and Application at Vivekananda Global University, Jaipur, India, where he is actively involved in research and development in computer science. He qualified for the NTA UGC NET and JRF on his first attempt, showcasing his academic excellence. He has extensive knowledge of the Internet of things and mobile application development and has provided training to students worldwide. He has published numerous articles in reputed, peer-reviewed national and international Scopus-indexed conferences and journals. Additionally, he has served as a keynote speaker and resource person for several workshops and webinars conducted in India. His research areas include remote sensing, the Internet of things, machine learning, deep learning, and computer vision. He is an IEEE member and an active member of various international and national societies, such as IEEE Young Professionals, the Indian Society of Remote Sensing (ISRS), the IEEE Geosciences and Remote Sensing Society (GRSS), the IEEE Sensors Council, ACM, and the International Society of Photogrammetry and Remote Sensing (ISPRS). He also received the International Distinguished Young Researcher Award from the *ASET Journal of Management Science*. He has edited over 12 books with various reputable publishers, including Wiley, De Gruyter, Apple Academic Press, and IGI Global.

https://doi.org/10.1515/9783111572970-016

Dr. Mona Abdelbaset Sadek Ali is an associate professor with a rich background in computer science, focusing on the intersections of deep learning, medical diagnosis, and pattern recognition. Throughout her academic career, she has authored over 17 publications in SCI journals and several papers in Scopus-indexed journals, demonstrating her prolific contribution to research. Her work spans a range of applications, from image and video processing technologies, including systems for iris recognition, landmine detection, and video shot segmentation, to innovative projects in mobile computing and social network analysis. Utilizing Bluetooth technology, she has explored indoor mobility tracking and analyzed opportunistic networks among users. Dr. Mona completed her PhD in computer science at Cardiff University's School of Computer Science & Informatics, where her research delved into the use of pervasive computing to extract social networks within organizational settings. She earned her BSc and MSc from Cairo University, excelling in projects from video processing to advanced pattern recognition.

Index

https://doi.org/10.1515/9783111572970-017

www.ingramcontent.com/pod-product-compliance
Lightning Source LLC
Jackson TN
JSHW061925070926
107856JS00005B/154